From the Hornets' Nest

to

Custer's Last Stand

The Immigrant Story of Norwegian

Sergeant Olaus Hansen

Ozzie Sollien

Front cover

No picture has been found of Olaus Hansen. The front cover shows him in his parade uniform in 1879, depicted by Norwegian artist **Kjell Strømsmoen**. He is wearing sergeant's stripes and the number 7 on his collar indicates the 7th U.S. Cavalry. The blue and red stripes on his arm signify two three-year enlistments in the infantry during the Civil War (war time is indicated by the red edges). The yellow stripes signify two five-year enlistments in the General Mounted Service and the 7th Cavalry in peace time. In 1879 he was on his fifth enlistment.

ISBN: 1484054571
ISBN-13: 9781484054574

To my wife, Deborah –

for enduring my single minded obsession with Olaus Hansen's story for more than twenty years.

In memoriam –

Kjell Hallbing as Louis Masterson, Norway's most successful author of historical western books with his series about U.S. Marshal Morgan Kane's adventures in the old American West and the 1976 "The sun stood still over Little Bighorn" – a great inspiration!

Vidar Hanssen, my history teacher at Kongsvinger Upper Secondary School 1970 – 1973, who taught me that history is not about kings, queens and global politics, but about common people, their everyday life and the decisions they made.

Table of Content

Introduction

Like most Norwegian boys born in the 1950s Asbjørn "Ozzie" Sollien grew up reading fictionalized stories about cowboys and Indians of the Old West. The books fueled a growing interest in American history, an interest enhanced by the knowledge that Norway and Norwegians had a special place in the development of the states in the Midwest, such as Illinois, Wisconsin, Iowa, Minnesota and the Dakotas. In 1990 he moved to the United States, delving into the vast and rapidly evolving literature about the West and the Civil War. At the same time he visited a long line of battlefields – more than sixty visits to Gettysburg alone - and got a profound feeling for the carnage of the battles.

A special interest in George Armstrong Custer and the 7th U.S. Cavalry led him to realize that two Norwegians fought at the battle of the Little Bighorn – Custer's Last Stand – in Montana in 1876. They were Sergeant Olans H. Northeg and Private John Sivertsen. Eager to find out more about the two soldiers he started to dig into their history. Northeg was apparently one of the few – if not the only - professional Norwegian soldier in the post-Civil War army before John Sivertsen enlisted in 1873, with a name about as un-Norwegian as imaginable. Many misinterpretations of his name made him the more difficult of the two to track. It was 2012 before the last piece of the puzzle fell into place, when living relatives were found in Arizona, Texas and Colorado.

Six years prior Norwegian relatives had been located in Nannestad, and it came as no surprise that Northeg had changed his name before he enlisted in the 7th Cavalry. He was Olaus Hansen, a cotter's son who emigrated to the United States in 1861, just in time to enlist in the 12th Iowa Volunteer Infantry Regiment recruiting for Civil War service in the autumn of that year.

This is Olaus' story, and it is also probably the most comprehensive recent history of the 12th Iowa. Olaus was never detached from the regiment and saw all the action throughout the entire war, except at Pleasant Hill and White River, which were both fought by detachments.

Acknowledgements

My deepest thanks to Åse Wethal Holen who - in one single day - brought me up to speed on who Olaus was, all of his family history in Nannestad and his emigration to America – incredible!!

I also had a lot of help from Tom O. Halvorsen and Villy Ruud, chairmen of the local historical chapter, who launched my investigation in Nannestad and supplied areal pictures of the Nordeeg and Lower Nannestad farms.

In the United States I particularly enjoyed all the late night e-mails from Tom O'Neil of Arrow and Trooper, Brooklyn, New York, who gave me a penetrating insight into the ocean of literature published about Custer's Last Stand at the Little Bighorn and how to interpret it.

Supervisory Collections Manager Patricia L. Nietfeld at the Smithsonian Institution, National Museum of the American Indian in Washington, DC deserves special mention. Not only did she set aside time to see me and present 1st Sergeant Botzer's roster book (High Bull's Victory Roster) – she held open every single page in the book for me to inspect, to see if there was anything I wanted to record! Thank you, Patricia!!

My sincere thanks to forensic scientist Katie Coppenhaver, who undertook the comparison of Olaus Hansen's hand writing on the documents from the 12th Iowa Volunteer Infantry and the 7th U.S. Cavalry.

For interpretation of military lingo in old handwriting I had help from retired colonel French McLean, author of "Custer's Best, Company M at the little Bighorn". I sincerely appreciated his e-mail replies to a novice in Civil War Army language.

For information about St. Louis Arsenal, Olaus' post for many years, I had help from Marc E. Kollbaum, curator at Jefferson Barracks Historic Park.

At the National Archives and Records Administration I. Juliette Arai and Arthur B. House Jr. gave me incredibly detailed information about how I could find and extract information from Olaus' service files.

Kjell Strømsmoen deserves special mention for enduring my instructions as to how to draw Olaus' parade uniform. Thanks, Kjell!

I am **GREATLY** indebted to John Murray and Richard Hanson - great grandson and great-great grandson of Hans Hansen, respectively - and Bobbie Hoy, great-great granddaughter of Ole Hansen, who finally gave me the key elements I needed to be able to fuse the beginning of the story together. Thank you very, very much!

Historical accuracy

Olaus Hansen's adventures during eighteen years as a soldier in the United States, is a true story. In spite of good command of the English language he apparently did not leave any diaries or memoirs behind.

His thoughts and actions are my own inventions, based on historical facts. What he experienced during the journey from Norway to Iowa in 1861 we can only surmise, but what immigrants generally experienced, we know quite a lot about. To be able to describe this to the reader, I have let Olaus encounter such events, and we see them through his eyes. However - the skirmishes and battles of the Civil War and Indian Wars are extremely well documented in firsthand accounts, virtually down to the minute. Scholars with intimate knowledge about the specific skirmishes and battles handled in this book will find the timelines and events to be accurate. We can pinpoint where Olaus was and what he did based on the movements and actions of his units and firsthand accounts by soldiers close to him.

Olaus lived a dramatic life during military campaigns which have become defining moments in American history. He came early enough from Norway to take part in the Civil War and lived long enough to see most of the Indian Wars. He was a product of his time and the life on the Frontier, and lived the way many Norwegian boys would have liked to live, when reading about it a hundred years later. What we youngsters did not understand, of course, was all the dangers involved – disease, accidents, injuries and possible torture and mutilation by the enemy in addition to the ignorance and malpractices of the medical profession of the era. It has been a learning experience to walk in Olaus' footsteps and attempt to see events the way he saw them, and to understand the decisions he made.

Bel Air, Maryland,
U.S.A.
March of 2013.

Ozzie Sollien

THE LETTER

Anne Marie Hansen Wiig stared out of the window into the cold Norwegian December night. The moon was full and bright, illuminating the undulating landscape surrounding the Nordeeg farm. A red fox trotted confidently across the fields, letting out a howling bark. Anne Marie should have been elated thinking about the impending Christmas of 1882. This was an old and celebrated custom in Lutheran Norway, and December was the month of Advent – waiting and preparing for the holiday to come. But her eyes were sad as they moved back to the letter she held in her hand – the letter the mail man brought today with news about her baby brother. She moved closer to the flickering candle and read it again, still not quite believing what she saw. There it was, in black and white, the message from her brother Hans in Lake Park, Becker County, Minnesota. Olaus was dead. Apparently he had taken his own life, Hans said. He did not know if this was true, or how it had happened. The coroner's report just stated that it was suicide.

Anne Marie let her thoughts wander as she kept looking out the window. He was still so alive in her mind, her little brother who went to America in April of 1861 to become a farmer in Iowa, just like his oldest brother, Ole. But within a few months developing events changed his plans, quickly laying them to waste. He was sent into the turmoil of the American Civil War, as were 6000 Norwegians with him. By November he was a soldier in the 12th Iowa Volunteer Infantry Regiment, going to war against the Confederate States of America.

He was so much younger than her – seventeen years – and had almost been more like a son to her than a brother. When he was born, June 26th of 1841, it was three days past Midsummer, another event celebrated in Norway, with bonfires and social gatherings. It was almost a surprise when he came – it was five years since the previous Hansen child was born, and his mother was forty three years old, his father fifty. Olaus had been lucky, born into a time when both the food and health situation in Norway was steadily improving. His chances for survival was vastly improved over children born just a few decades earlier, and at age five he had his mandatory smallpox vaccination.

Modern day Nannestadteiet. The log part of the shed/barn may be original, but the main house is probably not so. Photo: The author.

Memories of growing up in her childhood home, Nannestadteiet, came back to Anne Marie. "Tejet" was a cotter's house with a 1.25 acre parcel of land, belonging to the large farm Lower Nannestad. The six siblings had all been living in the small log cabin with their parents, Hans Henriksen and Kari Olesdaughter. Hans was a cotter – a sharecropper – and a cotter's life was all about making ends meet. Poverty was the order of the day, and cotters could work their own little share of the farm only when not required to work for the farmer himself. Often that meant at night, after a long day's work was already done.

Cotters' places crowded the countryside and all the arable land was taken. This made for sharp competition for the already existing places, giving the farmers the ability to keep the mutual agreements about compensation strict and to their own advantage. Cotters habitually needed additional income, and Hans was working as a blacksmith, something that had added a name to his home – Smedstua (The Blacksmith's Cabin).

Aerial picture of Nannestadteiet with two dwellings and the shed/barn indicated. The black line shows the circumference of the property. Photo: Morgan Andersen.

When the children were growing up, they had to help out as best they could, both on their own little parcel and at Nannestad. They planted and harvested potatoes and barley, helped drying and bringing in the hay, herded cattle in the summertime and hauled and chopped wood during the winter.

Anne Marie's thoughtful eyes still rested on the hillocks behind the large barn where the red fox disappeared, the same hillocks farmers here had rested their eyes on for a thousand years. Farming and forestry had comprised the bedrock of the community's economy all the way back to the Viking Age, and the name of the original farm, Nannestad, had now become both the name of the community and several of the current farms.

For as long as she knew, her ancestors had been cotters. Her great grandparents Pål Pettersen and Kari Larsdaughter, born in 1705 and 1719, had provided for their eight children at a time when the number of cotters rapidly grew, as did the population as a whole. Farmers became wealthier, but cotters remained poor and could not share in the wealth. She had even heard stories about people without means starving to death in the countryside just a hundred years ago.

Her grandmother Mari had been one of Pål and Kari's eight children, and her marriage to Henrik Brynhildsen in 1790 saw another union in the tradition of cotters. The following year her father Hans was born. What she had learned about her grandparents' life signified a time when both the food and health situation in Norway improved. The increasing production of potato and the booming herring fisheries made these two food items replace barley porridge as the food staple. Henrik and Mari enjoyed a better life than previous generations. But even if the cotters provided a substantial part of the production labor in Norway, and the farms could not be run successfully without them, they were still at the margins of society and at the mercy of the farmers' whims.

Hans was thirty three years old when he married her mother Kari, and yet another generation of cotters was about to emerge. However, for Anne Marie the future had something entirely different in store. In due time, she was about to move out

Olaus' father, Hans Henriksen, was a cotter at the farm Lower Nannestad.

of the cotters' class for good. In 1849, when she was twenty five years old, Ingel Pedersen at the farm Nordeeg asked for her hand in marriage. He was thirty nine years her senior, but the decision was easy to make. A major age difference between spouses was not uncommon in Norway, either sex could be younger or older. Farms could not be run by a widow or a widower alone, and a deceased spouse was quickly replaced. Accepting Ingel's proposal meant that she would be the lady of Nordeeg, one of the largest farms in Nannestad. It would elevate her status to the higher echelons of the local society, and put her in a position to help her family financially.

Olaus was still a youngster then, only eight years old and attending school. Religion was heavily emphasized in the curriculum, but other subjects like arts and science also had their fair share. Nationalism was on the rise in all parts of society, pointing to a future with Norway independent from its union with Sweden, and increasing social influence by Norwegian authors, artists, scientists and politicians. But these prospects were not a big part of Olaus' everyday life. In school, more

The Nordeeg farm.

important than anything else was still the intimate knowledge of people and places in the Bible. At fifteen years of age he was expected to pass a public, verbal test at the local church. This was the official termination of the attendance of public school, and passing the test proved that he would be able to assume his place as a valuable member of society. On October 12th, 1856 Olaus and his fellow class mates showed up at a crowded church in Nannestad parish, and were thoroughly tested in the Lutheran scriptures.

This was also the defining moment after which Olaus was considered an adult, and was expected to leave home to make a living. There were few opportunities for the son of a cotter if he stayed at home on the farm helping his father. If he was to take over the farm – and that was by no means certain – he had to be the oldest son. Even then, the farmer could decide that he wanted his land back, and the Henriksen family would have to move off the property.

His oldest brother, Ole, had early seen the untenable in this situation. At the age of twenty one, he set out for America. To leave for America was a life changing event. The distance was almost unfathomable, the journey with sail ship took ten weeks or more and the cost was prohibitive for as possible return. Still, the situation in Norway and other countries in Europe had changed so radically over the last century that it spurred a mass migration of fifteen million people from European shores.

Many different factors contributed to such a migration. One of the chief causes in Norway was simply an almost explosive increase in population, especially from the 17th century. From a mere 200 000 survivors after the devastating Bubonic Plague called the Black Death hitting Norway at the middle of the 14th century, the population at Olaus birth was soaring past 1.2 million due to increased food production, an improved national health system and the lowest infant mortality rate in Europe. Since Norway was late getting involved in the Industrial Revolution, and not being able to disburse the work force into the multitude of entrepreneurial opportunities this would have offered – almost everybody was still a farmer. With about 3 % arable land in all of Norway and the large farms already established, the situation also created a clear class difference between farmers and cotters.

Ole did not have to review the dismal economical predictions before making his decision - it was a foregone conclusion. His great grandparents had been poor, his grandparents had been poor, his parents were poor, he was poor, most likely his children were going to be poor. There was no future for a cotter's son, and neither for his children. He could have migrated cross country. In northern Norway land was still for the taking, although he would have had to fight long, cold winters and short growing seasons. However, northern Norway was a long, long way away – as far as the southern parts of Spain or Italy. He knew there was excellent land to be had in America, in a much better climate. Wisconsin and Iowa - unending tracts of fertile land to plow, timber to fell and vast streams full of fish and plenty of water for the animals. The country was free from land owner dependency, as he knew it in Norway. Ole wanted some of this land to create a better future for himself and his children, and all of his family to come.

The still restrictive emigration laws required him to have a "certificate" from local authorities to be able to leave his home community, and he had to "sign out" of the church book at his local parish to make his departure official. On the first Monday in May of 1851, the parish priest opened the book and meticulously worked his way to page 230. As the very first entry on the page, in the top right corner under the heading "Emigrated", he wrote: "Bachelor Ole Hansen Tejet. 21 ½ years old. To North America with certificate of May 5th, 1851". Ole was now set to embark on the long journey across the Atlantic Ocean, to a much better life than he could ever have hoped for in Norway. In his wake he left his parents and all his siblings, including his youngest brother Olaus. Neither Ole, nor his ten year old brother, had any way of knowing that in another ten years, they would meet again under entirely different and tragic circumstances. Olaus' hope for a peaceful and prosperous future would be completely devastated, and his life would take on a very different direction.

At Nordeeg, Anne Marie sighed as she folded the letter and put it back in the envelope with the hand written address across it. How unexpected and unpredictable life had turned out for her youngest brother. A tragic death had come to him in the frozen Dakota winter, thousands of miles away, at the age of forty one. She picked up the candle and walked slowly up the stairs to the bedroom on the second floor where her husband Lars was waiting. As she lay down and pulled the quilted blanket all the way up to her chin, they both knew she would not be getting any sleep that night. Again she heard the howling bark of the red fox. It was like the cold sound carried a bad omen through the dark winter night. If it did, Anne Marie felt it had already been fulfilled........

IOWA

In the early spring of 1843 astonished Winnebago Indians at the agency by Turkey River in northeast Iowa saw two men approaching, gliding across the snow covered plains on skis. It was Ole Halvorsen Valle and Ole Tollefson Kittilsland from the valley of Numedal in Norway en route to Fort Atkinson in Winneshiek County. The Army hired civilian laborers at twelve dollars a month. The two skiers left tracks in the snow cross country when they initially explored the prairie during the winter. An American biologist thought the tracks could possibly be from an undiscovered specie of animal still living in obscurity on the vast stretches of land between the Great Lakes and the Rocky Mountains. Valle and Kittilsland were the first to arrive from whom permanent settlements would later be established. During the next sixty five years 16 000 Norwegian farms would dot the prairies of Iowa. The men had come to the Rock Prairie settlement in the Koshkonong region of south central Wisconsin in 1841.This state would during the same period accumulate 35 000 Norwegian farms.

Norwegian skiers of the 19th century used only one ski pole. From an old post card in the author's collection.

Fort Atkinson in 1842. Wikipedia.org.

The three principle needs of the pioneers were wood, water and hay land. When all the areas meeting these requirements were taken, the new settlers moved on elsewhere. As most of Illinois was without trees, the Norwegians moved into Wisconsin. From there the migration continued from woodland to woodland, across the Mississippi, through the northeast corner of Iowa and into Minnesota. The colony at Jefferson Prairie in Rock County, Wisconsin had followed on the heels of famous Norwegian pioneer Cleng Peerson's founding of the Fox River Colony in Northern Illinois in 1834. Peerson was an intrepid explorer who tried to find new land in the Midwest already in 1821. He was under the impression that he was the first Scandinavian on the prairie west of Chicago. However, a sign nailed to an aspen outside the budding town of half a dozen log cabins stated: "Sacred to the memory of the fallen soldiers of Fort Dearborn, 1812, the first martyrs of the West." Frederick Peterson, a Norwegian who enlisted in 1808, had fallen here in a fight between the small garrison and 500 Potawatomi Indians.

Fort Atkinson had been established in 1840 to force the Winnebago - or Ho-Chunk - Indians to move from Wisconsin into northeast Iowa, and to prevent their return. As a temporary measure before further eviction, the Indian agents intended to teach them how to settle down, become farmers and abandon their nomadic way of life. Valle and Kittilsland were employed to plow the ground for the Indians, and they recalled plowing many parcels through the rolling hills later to become parts of the city of Decorah. The first year they plowed 46 acres, 23 near the mouth of Trout Run for Kinnoskik, or Winneshiek (Coming Thunder), and 23 at the mouth of Trout River for Kara-mani-ga (Old Walking Turtle).

Kinnoskik, chief of the Ho-Chunk. The author's collection.

In July of 1848 the Government decided to move the Indians 300 miles north, to Todd County in Minnesota. Ole Tollefson, his wife and a newcomer by the name of Ingeborg Nilsen were hired as cooks for the Indians on the long trek. Ole Valle and his wife had already moved thirty five miles southwest into Clayton County, where they started farming, as the first Norwegians in Iowa.

The move on the part of the Ho-Chunk was not entirely voluntary, and when their escort arrived they were painted as ready for war – blood red color splattered all over their bodies and also in their hair, which was set straight up on top of their heads. The first night out of the reservation they camped on a farm in section seventeen in Highland Township. Several hundred Ho-Chunk Indians were doing camp fire ceremonies and gala events before moving on to Winona, Minnesota to be taken by steamer to Todd.

By 1850 all the good land in Wisconsin was mostly taken. A trickle of immigrants started to find its way into northeast Iowa. This growing tidal wave would soon change direction, from Clayton County north to Allamakee and Fayette counties, but the county destined to become the future home for the largest population of Norwegians, was Winneshiek. The first settlement was formed on Washington

Prairie during the latter part of June 1850 by several families moving in from the Koshkonong region. The leader of the group was Eirik Anderson Rude from the town of Voss. The development of the wilderness in Iowa had barely begun, but soon the population in Winneshiek passed 5 000. By 1851 immigrants were pouring across the Mississippi River into the county.

In the spring of that year Ole Hansen decided that time was ripe to set out for America. The established Wisconsin settlements were already well known among the common people in Norway. In America pamphlets highlighting the state's virtues were published in Norwegian, German, Dutch and English and distributed throughout eastern U.S. ports, and in Europe. Advertisements were running in 900 newspapers. Emigration was on everybody's lips – either for, or against. Ole had not seen any of the pamphlets, but he had read many "America letters" from across the Atlantic Ocean, in glowing terms describing the fertile land and the great possibilities of creating a bright and prosperous future for a hard working settler.

There were also other, more pressing reasons at home helping him to make up his mind. An economic crisis hit Norway in 1848, further deteriorating the already unfavorable conditions for cotters. Slowly but steadily Ole caught the contagious disease spreading like wildfire among the rural classes of Norwegian society. He had contracted a severe case of "America Fever".

By April he had made up his mind. Anything was better than staying in Nannestad. Even if his prospects were dismal in Norway, there was one thing he knew how to do. He could farm. He had done nothing but farm work for as long as he could remember. And that was all he needed in America. His sister Anne Marie was already a well-to-do lady at Nordeeg. She had promised to help him with the ticket, and he would repay her from future earnings. He might have to spend ten or twelve weeks at sea on a sailing vessel and another three weeks traveling across the American continent to reach Milwaukee. To build a homestead he would have to log heavy timber and break sod never touched by a plow. He would have to carry heavy loads over long stretches of wilderness on foot. Initially he would live under primitive conditions – may be in a dug-out in a hillside, or a sod hut – with a plank for a table and a wooden box for a chair. But he knew he could do those things, and it would be worth it for a prosperous future.

In Wisconsin, more than 4000 miles away, 8600 Norwegians had already settled in. From 1838, when the first eighty acres were staked on Jefferson Prairie, Rock

Milwaukee in 1854. The Library of Congress.

County, the colonies had grown and spread out along a corridor towards northwest all the way to Barron and Polk counties. Most famous and easily accessible from Milwaukee were the large settlements at Muskego, Jefferson Prairie, Rock Prairie and Koshkonong. By 1850 the latter extended across twelve townships with almost 3000 Norwegians.

In July of 1851, when Ole set foot upon American shores, it was far too late in the season to establish a homestead. He still had to travel all the way to Wisconsin, and harvesting would soon be in progress. The most sensible thing to do was to hire out as a farm hand during the harvest, and over the first winter. Arriving at Milwaukee, he proceeded to Muskego, the closest colony. He immediately knew he did not want to stop there. Although initially praised as a prosperous settlement when it was established more than ten years earlier, the area had been ravished by cholera both in 1849 and 1850. Hundreds of people had died.

He was a bit astonished that a settlement was even established there. The area had large, old oak forests that needed to be cleared and stumps removed before any farming could be done. In the middle of the settlement was a mosquito ridden swamp, many miles across. Many settlers had contracted malaria and nobody in the medical field had yet connected the vector and the disease. Practically all the homes around the swamp had one or more family members shivering from the symptoms, and epidemics were not uncommon. Poverty was apparent among most of the settlers. Ole quickly learned that some of this was rooted in the fact that America did not yet have any factories ready to compete with English imports, and prices of everyday necessities were high. Textiles, knives, forks, pocket knives, razors – even sewing needles were English. As the farms at Muskego were small and prices on farmed goods in Milwaukee exceedingly low, the conditions in the settlement were characterized by the Norwegian phrase "starve-to-death".

Ole could have continued all the way to Iowa, but from the middle of May heavy rains had drenched the state for two months, and the incessant storms had washed away much of the crops. The flood water came surging down the river basins and wiped away buildings and livestock. Little was left to harvest of the most important crops like wheat and corn. After the water receded, a severe draught set in which lasted for the rest of the summer. Cholera struck again in the towns up and down the Mississippi River, like it had done the year before. He decided to stay in Wisconsin, at least for now.

There was a territorial road between Milwaukee and Madison, continuing to Mineral Point and beyond. Following an immigrant train, Ole walked on foot the eighty miles to Lake Koshkonong in Dane County. He could not believe that he had finally arrived. Milwaukee, Muskego, Jefferson Prairie, Rock Prairie – in Norway, these places had just been words on a piece of paper. Words carrying promises of a bright future, but still just words describing something he had never seen. Now he was standing on Koshkonong soil, looking at the forests and farm land he previously had only imagined in his mind. As he passed Lake Koshkonong and entered the prairie, he became aware of an old Indian trail leading towards northwest. Here he left the immigrant train and started to look for work.

Within a few days, Ole was a farm hand. The work was the same as he was familiar with from Nannestad. He stayed with a family who had been at Koshkonong for several years. They had developed the homestead to a point where the husband could no longer manage everything on his own. To improve, they needed hired help. The work was hard and the days were long, but the farmer was a good employer, the food very much Norwegian, and for a pay of nine dollars a month Ole could put away some money every payday. He was happy he did not have to learn English right away. In the overwhelmingly Norwegian populated settlements people of Polish and German descent often abandoned their native tongue, ignored English and spoke one of the Norwegian mountain dialects. Every day except Sunday Ole was hard at work on the farm. He did not mind doing work he knew well how to do. He saw it as a stepping stone towards his ultimate goal – to establish a homestead of his own. Ole was on his way to have his dream fulfilled.

Three years passed.

Ole was still working as a farm hand, saving money and waiting for the right opportunity to claim his own homestead. There was no more good land to be had in Wisconsin - he would have to move west to purchase a parcel. He had been watching immigrant wagon trains come and go in an unending stream since he came to Koshkonong. They were all headed for the ferry crossings on the Mississippi River. The last three years had seen an unprecedented influx of immigrants to Iowa which had made Prairie Du Chien, Dubuque, MacGregor, Davenport, Burlington and Keokuk into boom towns. During the month of June, 1854 almost 1 750 wagons were counted as they passed Preoria, Illinois, all of them going to Iowa. In Koshkonong the trains would stop for a few days, or even weeks, before they moved on west – always west – further and further away. The ferries across the Mississippi lagged far behind their schedules, and immigrant trains jammed the streets in the river towns for up to three days waiting to cross. Outside the towns were large camps with bonfires that never seemed to burn out,

Prairie du Chien in 1870. The Library of Congress.

some groups of immigrants coming and others leaving. The population in Iowa had surpassed 300 000, growing by 100 000 a year. Ole had become friends with a very nice, young Norwegian woman arriving with an immigrant train in July of 1853. She was twenty six year old Maren Carine Amundsen Aarnes who had come with her husband Carl Ambrosius from Nittedal, a few miles from Ole's home in Nannestad. They had brought their one year old daughter Marie Christine and Maren was pregnant with a second child. As the summer was at its height when they arrived, they followed the pattern of most immigrants – Maren worked as a maid on a farm while Carl worked at one of the saw mills over the winter. The following summer Carl was killed in an accident at the saw mill. Maren was suddenly alone with two young daughters.

In the fall of 1854 Ole was ready to embark on the last of his planned treks. He was going to Minnesota. Through the treaties of Traverse des Sioux and Mendota in 1851, the bands of the Lower Sioux had ceded 24 million acres of their homeland. It was subsequently thrown open for settlers. Ole wanted to claim a parcel as his new home. He had heard exiting stories about Minnesota's beauty and fertility from settlers moving along the road from Milwaukee to Prairie du Chien. On one of his frequent trips to the farm where Maren worked, he had asked her to marry him and come to Minnesota – and she had said yes. Ole would have an instant family. The winter was spent preparing for the long journey, and by April 1855 they were ready to go. It was important to get an early start, to be able to get the first crop in the soil.

Joining a wagon train from Muskego they set out for the Mississippi River. It would take them almost three weeks to get there. They had brought everything they needed to settle on their new homestead in a six-team, ox-drawn prairie schooner. Ole had purchased the steers for the going rate of fifteen dollars apiece. The equipment included a wood stove with the pipe dismantled and strapped onto the side of the wagon box. Stoves were few and far between in the Wisconsin settlements. The most important item taken along, however, was a steel moldboard plow. That would be the essential tool to break the virgin soil of the prairie, and the key to their survival and success.

All the equipment was stowed tightly inside the wagon box, which was covered with white canvas. Maren and the two girls were riding on the wagon, while Ole was walking ahead, carrying his gun. He was tempted to take his heavy boots off in the warm spring weather and walk bare footed along the trail. A few years

An immigrant wagon train. The Library of Congress.

prior another Norwegian, Ole Paulsen from Grue in Solør, had fallen for the same temptation. He was bitten by a timber rattlesnake and barely survived. This was timber rattler country – the snake was commonly found in the forested river valleys extending out on the prairie, where rodents abounded. Ole kept his boots on for protection against the dangerous reptiles. Rattlesnake bites this far away from medical help was usually fatal.

The long train stretched out along the Wisconsin trail counting almost eighty people, a herd of about 150 cattle and a few hogs and sheep. The wagons were creaking, oxen stomping and the men cracking their whips, shouting to press the teams on. The Wisconsin River had to be crossed from the south bank to reach Prairie du Chien – the Prairie of the Dog – named after a Fox Indian chief greeting the first explorers. It was a small ferry only capable of taking one wagon at the time. A horse placed on a tread-power furnished the propelling power for the paddle wheels. The cattle herd had to swim the river.

The second ferry, from a point below Prairie du Chien across the Mississippi to MacGregor, was larger. A Norwegian, Ole Nilsen, was the owner and operator. In the beginning he had used a team of four mules to turn the paddle wheels. Now he had installed machinery run by steam. He would take the immigrants the mile across to Clayton County, from where they would continue northwest into Iowa and Minnesota. The wagon train reached the ferry on the Wisconsin River, and after crossing proceeded to Prairie du Chien where they were finally ferried over to MacGregor on the Iowa side.

From MacGregor the train continued slowly towards northwest into the Upper Iowa River basin. Ole was struck by the lush and beautiful appearance of the forest – cottonwood, willows, sycamore, black walnut, white hickory, elm, buckeye and sugar maple. The aspen had fresh foliage and the plum and cherry trees were in full bloom. Only the oaks were slow, still far from leaved out. An abundance of birds in unfamiliar, sparkling colors filled the forest - rose breasted grosbeaks, goldfinches, robins and Baltimore orioles could be seen everywhere. The little killdeers with their long legs ran along the riverbeds, pretending not to have nests. Ole was most impressed by the bright red northern cardinals and scarlet tanagers. Never had he seen more beautiful birds than here, out west. If the travelers needed food, turkeys were plentiful. One day a huge flock of passenger pigeons passed overhead, almost darkening the sky. Some of the men said it counted several million birds. The cacophony of contact sounds between them created a loud, shrill roar. Ole had never seen anything like it – a part of the flock landed in a grove of trees within eyesight, and even the thickest branches swayed under the weight of all the birds. Little could the settlers have imagined that within half a century, this incredibly prevalent bird would be extinct.

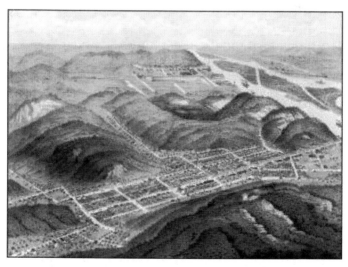

MacGregor in 1868. The Library of Congress.

The river basin was teeming with wildlife, and as in Wisconsin Ole marveled at the abundance of small mammals, something he was not used to from Norway. Raccoons, opossums, skunks, coyotes and cottontails, and more prevalent than any of the other animals – grey squirrels. None of them were endemic to the old country. The fox squirrels in the Iowa forests were enormous compared to the red squirrels he knew from home. He had noticed with interest, however, that the red fox looked exactly like the one in Europe. Fox hunts were popular along the Mississippi River, as was "barking" of squirrels. The fox hunts were often carried out by people who considered themselves somewhat of an "upper class", almost in the fashion of the old, English way. They commenced on a moonlight evening, went on all night and ended up with a bonfire and a cup of coffee in the morning, after a successful hunt. The "barking" was a scientific way of killing squirrels without ruining the fur. When the squirrel was lying on a branch resting, a shot was fired at the bark under its throat, the concussion killing the animal.

Fish of impressive size was seen both in the Upper Iowa River and its tributaries – small mouth bass, rock bass and trout. On the river banks Ole noticed many Indian graves. A ridge pole was extended between two forked sticks rammed into the ground, and thin planks were leaning on each side of the ridge pole, making the graves look like small houses. Underneath this roof, the body was buried in a sitting position, often with the head above the ground.

Moving through the river's water shed the wagon train entered section twelve in Winneshiek County, established in 1848. They were fast closing in on the Minnesota border. To the west they could see the continuous rolling tall grass prairie, almost giving the impression of an undulating ocean, stretching as far as the eye could see. The ocean was colored by the lead-gray turkey foot, Indian grass with its long, golden plume-like seed head, switch grass and rip gut with whip-like points on their leaves. The grass was stretching ten feet or more towards the prairie sky.

As they rolled through the hills along South Bear Creek, Ole and Maren had come to a decision about an issue they had been discussing since leaving McGregor. They were not going to Minnesota after all. The beauty and fertility of the country along the Upper Iowa River had won them over. Ole had gathered information about the parcels of section twelve, in the township known as Pleasant Prairie, but officially called Highland. The parcels – one mile square – had been open for sale from the Government since 1851, and he knew that some of the northernmost ones were still available. Wood, water and tillable land was abundant. During a midday break he left the wagon train to have a good look around. When he returned, he had found what he was looking for. The parcel he had selected was nearby, within close range of the river. It had timber for building a log cabin, tillable land, and – almost more important than anything else – a spring with drinking water within short walking distance. When the wagon train rumbled on towards Minnesota, Ole and Maren established a camp on the South Bear. They were not alone in their decision. Two more families joined in the venture, aiming to settle on neighboring plots.

While the beginning of May had been hot and dry, one of the first nights in June brought such a hard frost that potatoes and corn froze in many places. Towards the middle of the month the weather changed, and the heat became oppressive. By then, Ole and his two neighbors were on their way to Dubuque to buy and register their plots. They had already staked the corners of the parcels with their names on each stake, as the requirements demanded. Arriving in town they quickly became aware they were not the only ones claiming a homestead. Other settlers formed a long line outside the land office, sitting on the ground – or if lucky – on a wooden box they had obtained from some unknown source. If they were unable to get into the office the day they arrived, they simply had to wait in line until the next day.

The night was surprisingly chilly, and Ole sat huddled over cups of coffee together with his two neighbors. Others endured the wait with something stronger, and quite a few of them became loud and rowdy in the early morning hours, as they had been drinking since the night before. The three travelers from Highland wisely stayed away from the whiskey. They knew they had a long walk home in sweltering heat the next day. On Friday, June 15th they could finally enter the land office. Returning to the blistering hot street outside, they held the titles to forty acres of land each, bought for the Government price of fifty dollars pr. parcel. Soon they were on their way back to section twelve. On the way there they were taken by surprise by a sudden and violent rainstorm which produced hail stones the size of small walnuts. Returning to camp, the building of the homesteads could begin in earnest. Ole and Maren would stay at South Bear Creek for thirty four years, eking out a future for themselves, the two girls and eight more children to come. They were finally at home.

ACROSS THE OCEAN

On November 6th, 1860 Abraham Lincoln was elected President of the United States. Already before that fateful day there had been talk about secession in the South. After the election the movement to secede became even more intensified. By the time a constitutional convention to establish the Confederacy was held in February of 1861, six states had joined South Carolina, later to be the first to leave.

The majority of the Southern leaders anticipated a peaceful secession, not one which would lead to a bloody conflict. However, when Lincoln was inaugurated on March 4th, the nation seemed to be on an inescapable path to war. After the secession, South Carolina perceived herself as an independent state, but on a manmade island in Charleston Harbor Federal troops were still garrisoned at Fort Sumter, cannons pointing at the city. Running out of supplies the garrison was expecting a relief expedition, to include additional guns. In intercepting this intelligence the commander of the Confederate forces, General Pierre Gustave Toutant Beauregard, moved quickly to occupy the fort, and demanded its surrender. Major Robert Anderson refused to comply. At 4:30 am the next morning Confederate batteries opened fire on the fort, the first shots to be fired during the Civil War. It was Friday, April 12th.

On Monday, April 15th President Lincoln called for 75 000 volunteers to deal with the insurrection in the South. Less than twenty four hours later Olaus Hansen stepped into the office of the parish priest in Nannestad, cap in hand, to carry out some important business. He was signing out of the church book to go to America. Already when he left school at age fifteen he had been itching to go. Now emigration had become imperative. The harvest of 1859 had been very bad. In1860 it was disastrous. Fifteen heavy downpours hit during the first half of June washing away the seeds already in the ground. The autumn came early with more rain, cold weather and early frost which destroyed the crops. The hay was not dry and could not be salvaged for winter feed.

Olaus' brother Hans was coming along. He had been working in his father's blacksmith shop. Hans senior was already 70 years old and no longer able to

Hans Hansen. Courtesy of Richard Hanson.

swing the hammer in quite the same way as he did when he was younger. Strength was not in short supply with Hans junior, however. When he opened the first blacksmith shop in Lake Park, Becker, Minnesota in 1873 he earned the sobriquet "Horse Power Hanson". What precipitated Hans' decision to go was that his younger brother, Nils, could take over the blacksmith work. Nils had been working the anvil for several years, and Hans felt confident he could cover the necessary work while also running the cotter's place. Nils would later become very prosperous in his own right and purchase two farms, in 1881 and 1883. Anne Marie had promised to take care of the parents in due time – she could afford to provide a place for them at Nordeeg whenever they needed to move away from Smedstua.

During the day of Olaus' visit to church fifteen emigrants signed out, to include two of his travel companions, Ole Iver and Johanne Berg. A third acquaintance, Jens Kaxrud, was also coming along. Emigration laws changed in 1860 and none of them needed a certificate to be able to leave, as when Ole left ten years earlier. They were only required to notify the local authorities about the termination of their residency in the parish.

If April 16th had been a busy day, the priest saw an even longer line waiting to sign out on the 18th. In addition to Hans – having delayed his visit from Tuesday to Thursday – fifty three more emigrants gave their notice. The same day Georgia Governor Joseph E. Brown, in response to the Federal call for troops, called on all Georgia men to volunteer for military service. Virginia had already proclaimed her secession the previous day. Ignorant of the development in America, Olaus was consumed by the events involving the big move across the Atlantic Ocean. He was completely unaware that, even before he had left his native Norway, fate had already planned his future – and it was something entirely different to what he had in mind.

When preparing for the long journey the two brothers had agreed to travel as light as possible. Even so, they had to bring their own food for the sea voyage, which was anticipated to last between ten and twelve weeks. Recommended provisions for an adult person included seventy pounds of bread, eight pounds of butter, twenty four pounds of meat, twelve pounds of pork, one keg of herring, one cheese, coffee, tea, sugar, syrup, salt, pepper, vinegar and a sack of flour. Water would be provided on the ship – about three quarts a day. Once they came ashore on the American continent, the plan was to go straight to Ole's farm in Iowa. Hans had already been to Christiania and secured passage with one of the dozen emigrant vessels leaving in the spring. The bark Nordlyset - "The Northern Light"- was set to embark on April 27th. She was heading for the Canadian port of Quebec. The ticket price was thirteen Norwegian speciedaler a head (twelve U.S. dollars). They had only nine days to get ready and get their travel good to the capital.

Nannestad was a busy place in April of 1861. More than 150 emigrants were leaving for America, with all the hustle and bustle involved in the preparations. In a few short weeks many farms and cotters' cabins would be missing family members – or whole families – around the dinner table. The ones left behind would be wondering if they would see their sons, daughters and relatives ever again. Horse carriages had to be loaded with all necessities for a new start in a strange country, far, far away. A neighbor had volunteered to take Olaus, Hans, Jens Kaxruds and the Bergs to Christiania. They would have to travel in two carriages to be able to bring both the travelers and the baggage, and it would take the better part of a day to make the trip.

Finally the day of departure arrived, and a long line of carts set out for Christiania. Many of the emigrants were hopeful of a better life, and had great anticipations about their new home across the sea. Not all of them felt equally cheerful. Some of the travelers had ambiguous feelings about America. It was a dangerous and uninviting country filled with savage Indians and lawlessness, and a place where everybody could do as he pleased. As to underscore this feeling, a few men playing cards in a bar came out to have a look as the emigrants passed by.

"Where are you good people going?" one of them said with a speech slurred by drink.

"To America", Olaus answered.

"Ha-Haaaaaa!!" laughed the drunkard, slapping his thighs. "America! That is a place you will never see!"

Ominously, for many of the emigrants boarding the Northern Light the next day, his words would become true. But for the travelers in the column slowly winding its way down towards the docks in the setting sun, his offhand comment bore no premonition of impending disaster. It was just the rambling of a drunken bum.

Christiania in 1861 was a city in rapid development. After the Napoleonic Wars ended in 1815 Denmark was forced to cede Norway to Sweden, but the Norwegians were left with considerable autonomy. The city was now a capital, and a new and different class of Governmental officials provided for the construction of a series of monumental buildings associated with a sovereign state, giving it a brand new look. Some of the buildings were the Royal Castle, the Norwegian Bank and the Parliament. Ground was broken for the latter the same year as Olaus and his fellow travelers arrived from Nannestad. With a population of little more than 35 000 inhabitants, Christiania was still described as a city with more animals than people, ship building comprising the bulk of the industry.

Upon arriving at their destination Hans led them to an old building close to the docks where they would spend the night. There were no beds, but it was the only available quarter Hans had been able to find. At least they could rest, and it was close to the ship. They had to sleep on the floor the best they could, and one of the men had to be awake at all times watching the baggage, making sure nothing was stolen. It was a long night. The next morning Olaus looked out across a forest of masts on Christiania harbor. He had never seen so many sail ships in his life, let alone boarded one. The five travelers made their way to the spot where the Northern Light was moored. It was a bark rigged ship built in 1853, belonging to C. I. Backe at Ildjernet, a small island outside Christiania. She had been crossing the oceans non-stop for the last eight years, and it started to show. Captain J. A.

Christiania in 1850.

No picture has been found of the Northern Light. This image shows a bark rigged ship about the same size – 800 tons. Wikipedia.org

Hansen was at the rail, offering a welcome to everybody coming up the landing. The crew were hanging in the rig or running around on deck, yelling to each other, hastening to get the ship ready to embark on time. Pulleys were squeaking, ropes whipping, sails flapping loudly and waves slapping against the side of the ship. It was organized chaos.

Olaus was stunned by the garments worn by some of his fellow travelers. He had never seen outfits like the ones worn by the farmers from the southern part of Telemark County – could never even have imagined that there were people in Norway dressed that way. The men were exactly alike – almost like soldiers – with black knee pants closed at the knee with silver buttons, white long stockings embroidered with roses at the ankles and low cut, embroidered shoes. The shirts were white with red and blue decorations, as were the life wests, which also were closed with silver buttons. On the head they wore a cap with a tassel hanging down across the right ear. The women wore skirts reaching all the way up under their arms, and long scarfs made of wool were wrapped several times around their waists. They had short blouses made of wool, and their stockings were embroidered with roses around the ankles. The shoes were low and embroidered, and they wore head scarfs. The dialect they spoke sounded almost like a foreign language to Olaus, and it would take time before he could actually understand what they said. They brought some strange and beautiful instruments – violins with eight strings, heavily inlaid with mother of pearl.

Olaus entered the between-deck through a small hatch, climbing down a steep ladder to find the spaces assigned for their journey. The hold was in a state of perpetual semi-darkness. Two hatches – one fore and one aft – provided the only access to the passenger quarters, and they were normally covered with canvas. The ceiling height was about seven feet, and two small skylights let in precious little daylight. One row of bunks made of rough boards was lined up on each side of the hold from stem to stern. Each bunk was a double-deck bed, positioned in the direction of the ship. The beds were made to take three passengers each, and had mattresses filled with straw. The emigrants had to bring pillows and blankets for their own personal use. A small space in front of each bunk was set aside for preparation of food. On each side of the deck a primitive restroom was available. They would show hopelessly inadequate when sea sickness set in.

The bunks were numbered, and as Olaus slowly made his way past other travelers while he was looking for number seventeen. He found it amidships, and was satisfied with the location. Closer to the stem and stern the rolling of the ship would be more imposing on the high seas. At the middle of the ship they would be least influenced by the waves. After hauling the baggage aboard, Olaus was hanging over the rail looking at the other travelers making their way through the crowd gathering to watch the ship embark. He found it incredible that a boat the size of the Northern Light could take on as many passengers as he saw moving up the landing. Although he did not know much about ships, his inquisitive mind had hit the nail squarely on the head. She could not. As the Northern Light weighed anchor and slowly drifted away from the mooring, she carried 5 cabin passengers and 297 passengers in steerage – between the decks.

In 1828 Great Britain passed a Passenger Act, outlining the regulation for transport of passengers between European ports in the British Empire and ports in Canada and the U.S. The United States passed a Passenger Act in 1855 to improve conditions for immigrants traveling to America. The regulations were linked to the interior volume of the ship to ensure adequate space for each passenger, expressed in tonnage. If the ship's Captain was found to violate the regulations, he would be fined. With her 330 register tons the Northern Light was carrying twice as many passengers as the regulations allowed. However, by leaving from a port outside the

British Empire, and go directly to a port which was not in the U.S., but in Canada, the regulations were easily circumvented. As a consequence, the suffering on the part of the passengers during the long trip – especially in bad weather – was infinitely multiplied. When the bark entered the open seas west of the British Isles, the overcrowded quarters would become a factor seriously affecting the health and safety of the passengers.

Southbound in the Christiania Fjord – the sixty seven miles long, narrow passage from the capital to the Sea of Skagerrak – the ship sailed quietly past the small town of Drøbak. Darkness had fallen, and Olaus could see the dim lights from houses along the shore, not knowing if they belonged to one town or the next. The twin towns of Moss and Horten came and went during the night, on opposite sides of the Northern Light. Next day, skirting on the leeward side of the islands of Nøtterø and Tjømø, the new cast iron light house at Ferder, built in 1857, seemed so close they could almost touch it. The ship stood down on a southwesterly course along the Norwegian coast, passing the towns of Kragerø, Arendal, Grimstad and Christianssand. Eventually she slipped out from the coast, heading towards the German Sea. The wind picked up, and the ship began to roll. Sea sickness immediately started to take serious effect. The between-deck resounded by moaning from passengers not being able to get to the restroom or up on deck before the inevitable vomiting, mixed with the crying of babies and young kids. The stench became overwhelming in the badly ventilated hold, and few of the passengers, if any, were in shape to do any kind of remedial cleaning. The crew made sure to stay as far away from the "tween-deck" as possible.

Olaus was upstairs on deck – he kept the sickness at bay by looking at the ocean and the birds still hanging above the masts. Down in the hold, feeling the rolling of the ship, he instantly became nauseous. Preventing sea sickness was not the only incentive to stay on deck – fleas and body lice abounded in the overcrowded hold, and it was a relief to get out in daylight where he could see some of the critters, and remove them. The second night was falling, and in the darkness flashes of light could be seen far out on the port side horizon.
"Hanstholm!" nodded a couple of the old men, pretending to know something about the lighthouses in Denmark. Most likely they were just regurgitating information recently acquired from the ship's crew. Much later another light appeared as a tiny, bright spot to the southeast.
"Sylt!" The old men also professed knowledge about the location of lighthouses in Germany.

Next morning, there was nothing to see but water. Every day was like the previous – waves as far as the eye could see, until sea met sky on the far horizon. Olaus knew there would be more sightings of land up ahead, before taking on the Atlantic Ocean. They were heading for the English Channel. One morning the Northern Light stood through the four mile wide strait between South Foreland at Dover in the County of Kent, England, and Cap Gris Nez in Pas des Calais in France. Doing good speed she passed north of the Channel Islands, Jersey and Guernsey. The isles of Scilly came and went on the starboard side before the bark turned northeast towards the southern tip of Ireland.

Beyond Ireland was the seemingly endless circle route to America – 3000 miles in a great arc across one of the most unpredictable and dangerous ocean stretches in the world. The only living creatures seen as fixtures around the ship for the duration of the journey to the New World were the small, black birds the sailors called Mother Cary's Chickens. Storm petrels – their appearance reminding the emigrants of barn swallows – were pelagic birds spending their entire life on the wing across the oceans of the world. Their habit of showing up ahead of storms and hiding in lee of ships had inspired their name. Veering southwards from 53 degrees to 40 degrees northern latitude the circle route crossed a vast area of the earth representing a battle ground between prevailing southwesterly winds and massive ocean currents. The collision of these opposing forces of nature created weather conditions completely unpredictable for sail ships depending on wind power. Any new voyage was a challenge different to the previous, as the variable winds fought westbound ships heading from Europe to America.

Bad weather and headwinds became every day conditions once in the Atlantic Ocean. The bark was lying still for days – sometimes even appearing to move backwards – while storm after storm mercilessly pounded deck and rigging. Adding to the already existing havoc inside the ship was the pouring rain, leaking from the decks above, soaking everything in the hold through and through. The passengers were kept in the badly ventilated between-deck days on end – sometimes a week – hatches battened down. The air became foul from the smell of vomit and diarrhea. Adding to the stench was herring, potatoes and biscuits rolling around in the standing water on the floor. As the crew tried to keep the ship up against the wind, it rolled and rolled without stop, throwing the passengers about. During a heavy roll people were sometimes completely dislodged from their bunks, ending up bruised on the floor.

The month of May came to an end, and soon Midsummer was approaching. Olaus had never thought he would celebrate his twentieth birthday aboard a tossing and

A funeral at sea. The Library of Congress.

turning ship, crossing one of the world's largest oceans. The severe conditions started to make an impact. He wanted to be on deck as much as possible, but the Captain's orders to stay below could not be ignored. The lack of hygiene and smell of vomit and diarrhea made him want to escape, but there was an even more compelling reason for him to stay away from the hold. He could not endure the never ending crying of babies and young children. Worst of all – death had started to take its toll, and Olaus had learned that when he ceased to hear a baby cry, a funeral at sea was imminent. Some of the passengers had apparently been infected with measles when they left Norway, and living in such close proximity made the disease quickly spread. Soon the little ones began to pass away.

He had witnessed the first funeral – a two year old girl had expired after days of crying and refusing to eat and drink. In the end the measles, dehydration and exhaustion caused her death. The ship's crew made a small coffin of pinewood. To make it sink faster they drilled holes through the top and bottom, and filled it with sand. The careful preparation did not have the desired effect. When the coffin slid off the plank extending over the side of the ship, Olaus could clearly see the light pine colored lid as it slowly – extremely slowly – sank through the dark blue water. He did not want to attend the next funeral. But there would indeed be another one.....and another one....and another one. Before the Northern Light reached Canada, twenty nine passengers had died. Unwittingly, the drunken card player had foretold the future. In spite of his apprehension, Olaus did attend the funerals – one after another - noticing a gradual change in the demeanor of the passengers as coffin after coffin slid over the railing into a wet grave. As the captain held a short service on the upper deck, the shocked and horrified faces he had seen at the first funeral had taken on an expression of fatalistic resignation as the ship approached the Canadian shores.

As they were closing in on the coast of Newfoundland, the bark drifted into the confluence of the cold Labrador Current and the North Atlantic Current, the latter being the northern branch of the warm Gulf Stream. From its equatorial origin outside the coast of South America, the Gulf Stream picked up speed as the Loop Current between Cuba and the Florida Keys and ran up the eastern seaboard of the United States as a thirty to fifty miles wide "river" in the ocean. Even if it gradually lost momentum, by the time it reached Nova Scotia it was still hauling about 200 million cubic yards of water every second at a speed of two knots – about 10 000 times the volume of the Mississippi River. Strange, exotic animals drifting from the subtropics with the winds and currents were seen on occasion – like the Portuguese man-of-war – a foot long jellyfish like creature with a large, purplish baggy "sail" extending above water, and several feet of poisonous tentacles trailing under the surface. Porpoises were dancing at the bow of the ship and dolphins were rolling alongside. Flying fishes darted up in the air, sailed on their wing-like fins and dropped back into the water. On moonless nights Olaus watched with awe the phosphorescent appearance of the sea, making it look like the Northern Light was gliding through liquid fire. At no time during his education had he been taught about the millions and millions of microscopic dinoflagellates illuminating the oceans.

As the two currents merged, it created the most extreme temperature differences in any ocean on earth, causing dramatic variations in both wind speed and direction, and water currents superficial and deep. Apart from unpredictable gales, churning waves and driving rain, the most noticeable characteristic was a dense fog, engulfing vast areas days and weeks on end. The blanket of fog could stretch down along the American coast all the way to Boston and New York. By midsummer, at the time the Northern Light made its way through the dangerous passage, the fog was constant. Condensed water was driving like ice cold rain from the ship's masts and superstructure. Olaus was keeping an eye on the odd looking banks of fog as the bark was moving in and out of them. Some had geometrical shapes, others looked like large slabs suddenly swallowing the ship, shrinking the visibility to twenty feet. Nothing could be seen except the waves immediately ahead of the stem. The fog horn was never quiet - sounds got muffled and distorted and were deceptive as to which direction they came from. To increase the perils even more dangerous, natural obstacles were lurking ahead.

One day while he was peering through the fog at the trail the ship left in the water, Olaus noticed an abrupt change in temperature. It was like opening the door to the outside on a Norwegian winter's day. There was even a different smell in the air as the ship entered the most hazardous sector of the circle route. More than 2000 miles off the Irish coast the Northern Light had entered the main Labrador Current, carrying icebergs south from Greenland. Every year the massive glaciers covering the arctic island calved thousands of icebergs into the Davis Strait, to see them slowly drift southwards. The iceberg season peaked from April to July – just as the Scandinavian immigrant ships approached the American continent. Most of the icebergs would slowly melt away, but some 400 of them made it into the shipping lanes. Weighing a 100 000 tons or more each they created dangerous conditions, and lookouts had to be on constant alert. The area was known as the graveyard of the Atlantic, and innumerable ships had gone down as a result of gale force winds and collisions with icebergs in the fog.

Disease continued to affect the weakest of the passengers. A little boy had been suffering with stomach pains for days. The captain finally dug deep into his medicine chest and pulled out a small bottle with skull and crossbones on the label, containing a reddish brown liquid. Olaus cold read the name next to the skull as the captain administered a few drops to the patient.

LAUDANUM

He had never seen the word before. Asking a member of the crew he learned that it was one of – if not the – most powerful painkillers available, also working well against most other ailments. What he did not learn was the decisive impact the potent tincture, containing 10 % opium in alcohol, would have on his life..........

In spite of the treatment the little boy never recovered, but eventually died from his illness. Olaus was about to attend the most harrowing funeral yet. The boy was encased in a bag of canvas, and as he slid down the plank and hit the water, a horrifying scene developed, leaving the passengers in shock and utter disbelief. Several sharks had been following the ship for days, and no sooner was the boy in the water before the sharks tore the canvas bag open and fought over the content. Olaus did not dare to look at the boy's parents – he quickly turned around and walked to the other side of the ship, staring blindly down into the dark blue water. This journey had turned into something far beyond his youthful imagination in the log cabin at home in Nannestad. He bent over the rail and vomited violently, his stomach cramping and tears running from his eyes.

LAND OHOI!! – The two words rang out across the ship from the crow's nest - two words that everybody aboard the Northern Light had longed to hear more than anything else the last few days. They knew they were getting close to the coast – sea gulls had been following the ship for five or six days, but to actually see it.......... Some of the immigrants had almost lost faith in ever setting their feet on land again. The bark stood down on a southeasterly course, heading for the Strait of Belle Isle. Little did the travelers know that they were sailing along the exact same route as Norwegian Viking explorer Leiv Eiriksson and his thirty five man crew, 860 years earlier. The Vikings had cut across the strait and made landfall at Lance Aux Meadows, on the northern tip of Newfoundland. There they founded the very first European settlement in the Americas. Another hundred years would pass after Olaus' journey before the settlement was rediscovered.

As darkness fell, the storm battered bark stood further out to sea. Although heading directly through the Strait of Belle Isle would have saved considerable time and greatly diminished the sufferings of the passengers, it was far too dangerous. In the strong currents and sudden storms occurring in the narrow strait there was not sufficient space to maneuver for ships under sail. On the other hand, the Newfoundland coast was not much of an improvement over the Strait of Belle Isle. It was broken into deep bays divided by rocky capes, and strong currents set towards the shore. But keeping well out to sea, the long trek circumventing the southern tip of the island was still a much safer choice.

Almost a week later, south of the island, Olaus climbed up through one of the hatches to get some fresh air. Anchored up on the banks in front was a fleet of large sloops fishing for cod. As the Northern Light made its way past the vessels the view of these symbols of civilization stirred the immigrants to cheers. Finally they had seen a significant sign telling them the journey was nearing its end. Two days later rocky coastlines rose on both sides of the ship – Cape Ray to starboard and Cape North to port. They were entering the Gulf of St. Lawrence. Above the flat shoreline of Newfoundland, covered with forests of spruce, pine and birch stretching up the mountain sides, undulating peaks were rising to almost 3000 feet. They reminded Olaus about the Norwegian coastal mountains he had read about in school, but never seen. Even if they seemed rugged, cold and uninviting, it gave the immigrants a feeling of safety to glide between two land masses. Finally they had contact with Mother Earth again, and it gave them a sense of security they had completely lost during the sea voyage. The craving to feel solid ground under their feet temporarily quelled other emotions – as long as they knew they would eventually stand on the docks of Quebec, somehow life seemed to have gotten a new start. However – the view of the capes was deceptive as a sign of soon being able to disembark from the ship. There was another 500 miles to go before they reached the quarantine station at Grosse Isle.

As they entered the gulf they passed the infamous St. Paul's Island. Numerous ship wrecks were strewn across the shores, victims of foggy weather, driven off course by strong currents and crushed upon the rocks. Human bones were scattered around the base of the island as memorials of times past. Meeting headwind and opposing currents, the Northern Light was successively tacking starboard and port to beat the forces pushing it back. As they passed Bird Island northern gannets – large, white birds with black wing tips and yellow heads – were seen feeding. Making high speed diagonal dives from more than 125 feet, the birds pulled their wings back just prior to hitting the surface, stunning small fish long enough to catch them with their long beaks. Two days later the bark approached the eastern tip of the island of Anticosti. Although the name sounded Italian, it was apparently a corruption of the Indian word Natiscotee. Stretching for 130 miles the island was surrounded by sunken reefs, and the captain ordered the crew to sheer off on the other tack to stay well clear of the dangerous coast.

Olaus spotted two headlands to the west, and learned it was capes Gaspe and Rosier. The capes signified the entrance to the St. Lawrence River. Long days of tacking back and forth became tedious as the Northern Light struggled against wind and current. Sometimes the ship could barely retain its position, and made no headway at all. One evening after nightfall, passing the river Mitis, Olaus was stirred to his feet by a loud, grinding sound followed by a shaking motion throughout the hull of the bark. Thinking they ran aground, he jumped up on deck just to find that the crew had dropped anchor. Even with sails reefed so not to be driven back by the wind, the current was so strong the ship had to lie at anchor.

The next morning the wind had abated and the Northern Light started tacking, this time in company with several ships that had come up during the night, fighting the same, unfavorable conditions. The bark had better luck than the day before, and gained some distance up the river. In the evening it was again pushed back by wind and current, and dropped anchor accordingly. This pattern repeated itself for several days, until they finally reached Trois-Pistols, opposite the mouth of the river Saguenay. There the ship came to a complete stop, due to the strong current aided by the massive discharge of water from the river, and no wind for support. However, at about 6 pm in the evening a few days later the wind veered and sails were quickly set. Within an hour the Northern Light was doing 7 knots, passing the three mile wide mouth of the river and getting beyond the grasp of its current.

Ships at anchor outside Grosse Isle about 1860, waiting to be inspected. Brouillet, Dr. C. / Library Archives of Canada/ PA 118086.

Upriver from the Saguenay the bark was subjected to the force of the tide and could easily get to Grosse Isle. Ships were always coming in to the quarantine station on the morning and evening tides – up to half a dozen at the time. Within a day the island was in sight.

Grosse Isle – Big Island – was one of twenty islands in the Isle-Aux-Grues archipelago, twenty eight miles downstream the St. Lawrence River from Quebec. It was certainly not the biggest island, as the name suggested – just one mile long and half a mile wide. The quarantine station was established in 1832 by then Lower Canada Government, to protect the continent against epidemics raging in Europe – especially cholera – brought across the Atlantic Ocean by immigrants. It later became a symbol of the horrific conditions during immigration on dilapidated sail ships. Some of the ships were old "slavers" having lost the slave trade, switching to human "cargo" on the way from Europe for a return trip from Canada with timber or wheat. A lot of them were so crowded, and the conditions so terrible, that they were called "coffin ships".

A crisis was reached in 1847, when over 100 000 Irish escaping the great Potato Famine came across the ocean. Thousands were infected with typhus. During the summer 5 400 succumbed at Grosse Isle – 2 200 of them on board the more than 400 ships waiting to be inspected - because of lack of quarantine facilities, hospital space, doctors and medical staff. 5 300 more had already been buried at sea. Healthy immigrants had to stay with the sick in the louse infested holds. Although nobody knew, lice were the arthropod vectors, spreading the disease. When the ships were finally ready to be inspected, corpses were pulled out of the holds with hooks and stacked on the beaches like cordwood, or simply dumped overboard in the river. Due to the overburdened quarantine facilities and lack of exact knowledge about the transmission of the disease, immigrants appearing to be healthy when inspected were allowed to continue inland. Subsequently thousands of fatalities were later registered beyond the quarantine station – about 2 700 in Quebec and 7 000 in and above Montreal.

Olaus was entirely ignorant of the events fourteen years earlier, although he found the excessively large cemetery on the tiny island quite puzzling. For him the twenty nine passengers – mostly children – he had seen slowly die on the Northern Light seemed a tragedy of immense proportions. Several years had passed since threats of dangerous epidemics had been imminent at Grosse Isle, and quarantine requirement were somewhat relaxed at the time the Norwegian ship anchored up downriver on the morning of July 6th, seventy days after leaving Christiania. The bark displayed its ensign at the peak, telling the medical personnel it was ready to be inspected. All the bunks had been dismantled and thrown in the river, followed by the straw mattresses. The ship had been scrubbed – both in the hold and on deck – to the extent the weakened passengers had been able to. Clothes and linen had been washed and when hung to dry, they added considerably to the colorfulness of the rigging and sails. This procedure was undertaken to easier pass inspection when the medical staff entered. A clean ship with immigrants looking free of disease was much more likely to avoid days of waiting for a clean bill of health, or even worse, to be put into quarantine.

Late in the afternoon they saw the doctor's boat coming towards the Northern Light. The first man to board the ship immediately started a conversation with the captain in Norwegian. Olaus could not hear the details of what was said, but the two men made gestures while talking indicating they were old acquaintances. What was a Norwegian doing at Grosse Isle? He later discovered that the man was

Andrew Andersen, who was invited to join the police force on the island in 1858 after the army had left the post. In1859 he was promoted to interpreter, a position he held for another twenty years. After a lengthy conversation the doctor appeared, ready to inspect the passengers. He inquired about the nature of illness encountered during the journey, how many immigrants had died at sea, and if there were sick or dead patients on board, to which the captain answered in the negative. Then he climbed down into the hold to take a closer look at the bark's interior. Apparently satisfied with what he saw, the doctor made his notes and gave the captain papers to fill in and sign as to the status of the ship. After another brief exchange between Captain Hansen and the interpreter, the medical inspectors disembarked. A clean bill of health would be issued within twenty four hours, provided the captain's papers were filled in properly. Next morning the doctor returned and the official papers were exchanged. The Northern Light weighed anchor and continued up the St. Lawrence River, leaving "The Isle of Death", as it was called during the Potato Famine. A river pilot boarded the ship to help them navigate safely through the last part of the journey.

At the time the immigrants from Nannestad arrived in Canada, Quebec was a city of about 51 000 inhabitants. The name was derived from an Algonquin Indian word – kebec – which meant "where the river narrows". As it was completely dependent on ship building and the square timber trade, the city would fare badly in years to come. Exports declined from eighteen million square feet of timber about 1860 to just seven million twenty years later. But for the passenger onboard the Northern Light, it was the largest city they had ever seen. When they anchored up outside the mouth of the river Charles, innumerable pilot boats were crisscrossing the harbor among a virtual armada of ships, some of which were a lot bigger than the ones they had seen in Christiania. They had dropped anchor close to the city on the side of Cape Diamond. On the opposite side was Point Levy with the village of D'Aubigne. The river banks were lined with wharves and timber ponds.

The immigrants were not allowed to disembark before the ship had been officially discharged from quarantine by the medical inspector and the harbor master. The two officials stood out from shore, approaching the Norwegian vessel in a boat rowed by six men. Upon arrival they demanded to see the clean bill of health and the ship's papers. After a thorough inspection of the papers the two serious looking men gave their consenting nods, and the ship was released. A steamer was already waiting to bring the travelers further up the St. Lawrence River, which would minimize the contact with one of the worst nuisances on the docks at immigrant arrivals – the runners. Runners were professional con artists and

Quebec about 1870. J.D. Woodward: Quebec. Picturesque Canada.

robbers, fleecing the naive newcomers in all kinds of ways. They would haul the luggage to filthy taverns for five to fifteen dollars, sell the unsuspecting travelers false or overpriced railway- or steamer tickets or simply rob them of their luggage, leaving them penniless on the street. To make matters worse – the runners were often of the same nationality as the people they robbed, giving them a sense of security in an unfamiliar environment where everybody else spoke a language they did not understand.

Olaus and Hans were well prepared for this part of the journey. Ole had warned them more than once not to engage in any kind of small talk or transactions with strangers approaching them after landing. They saw it happening to others all around them as they transferred to the steamer, but anybody approaching the two brothers was simply met by gazing stares, easily understandable in all languages. A brief look at the two men – one 5'9 ½" tall, the other with bulging muscles from years of striking the anvil – was enough to discourage the most rapacious runner.

While on the docks in Quebec they got the impression that something out of the ordinary was happening. Townspeople were looking in newspapers and talking loud, showing each other large headlines. The brothers tried to find somebody to tell them what the excitement was all about. Picking up bits and pieces from French and English, a Swede boarding the same steamer as Olaus and Hans put it together:
"There's a war on!"
"Where?" Olaus was at a loss of what the man was saying.
"A war! - There's a civil war in America!"
Olaus and Hans looked at each other.
"A war.........in Iowa?"
"No", said the Swede. "Washington."
Hans shrugged his shoulders. Well – war or no war – he was going to Iowa to Ole's farm. Washington was far away. They could worry about that later.

The steamer left at five in the afternoon, heading for Montreal. It was a new experience for Oluas to be mixed in with so many unfamiliar nationalities and cultures, and listening to the different languages – all of them completely incomprehensible – made him almost dizzy. He felt very out of place, and kept with his friends from Nannestad. Arriving at Montreal, the baggage was hauled to a canal where another steamer was waiting. The canal had twenty locks. Olaus found the first four interesting to watch, by the fifth he just wanted to get to the end of the canal. After an uneventful journey with many stops along the way they reached Kingston, where the travelers boarded a much larger steamer taking them across Lake Ontario. Stopping along a chain of similar looking ports – Olaus could not distinguish one from the other except the large city of Toronto – the steamer finally anchored up at Hamilton. There they transferred to a train on the Grand Trunk Railroad. The tickets did not provide seats in passenger cars. Sitting on the top of their luggage, they traveled on the beds of cattle cars.

The immigrants felt they were finally making headway towards their destination. They reached Port Huron, which was quickly becoming the second largest immigration point in the United States, trailing only New York City. Just two years prior the Grand Trunk Railroad had completed its 800 mile track from Portland, Maine to Sarina, Ontario. Another track was laid from Port Huron to Detroit, Michigan. To connect the two tracks, a "swing ferry" was introduced, capable of transporting railway cars across the St. Clair River from Sarina to Port Huron. The ferry made it unnecessary to unload and reload cargo. It was the first of its kind in the world, and it was propelled across the river by the strong current while extended from a cable at Fort Gratoit.

From Port Huron the journey continued via Lansing to Chicago on the Grand Trunk Western. As they got off the train in Chicago, it was no longer possible to ignore the fact that the Civil War was on. The city was a hotbed both politically, socially and economically, and it had been the springboard for Lincoln's presidency. The population had increased from 16 000 to 109 000 in just thirteen years, and it would double during the war. It was a stronghold for abolitionist sentiments, America's railroad capital, the greatest primary grain port and the largest lumber market in the world. The city boasted over 500 factories and dozens of mills, slaughterhouses and lumberyards went full tilt. War rumors were buzzing – a huge battle had been fought outside Washington, called the battle of Bull Run. Two incredibly large armies, said to have been 25 000 soldiers on each side, had stood face to face a whole day. The casualties were frightening – apparently in the thousands – and the capital was in immediate danger of being overrun by Rebel forces.

Olaus and Hans tried to ignore the fuss around them as they found their way to the next train, the Chicago and Northwestern, which would take them 85 miles north, to Milwaukee, Wisconsin. The locomotive pulled out of the station about 1 pm – cattle cars shaking and rattling, brakes screeching and bell tolling – with a long, black tail of smoke in its wake. As it sped up along Lake Michigan Olaus admired the view. Ships were crossing north and south on the dark, blue water, steamers and sail ships of all shapes and sizes.

Chicago about 1860. The city had grown from half a dozen log cabins to a modern metropolis of 109 000 inhabitants in just 40 years. The Library of Congress.

As the train puffed into Milwaukee, the travel weary immigrants entered the largest city in Wisconsin. The name derived from an Algonquin word meaning "The good land" and the city was built on the confluence of three rivers – the Milwaukee, the Menomenee and the Kinnickinnic. Just about a month earlier serious riots had broken out, called "the bank riots", and the citizens were still talking about it. A part of the work force had been paid in money some of the banks did not recognize, and violent riots had ensued where two banks were gutted. Now these events had been overshadowed by the Civil War. Olaus and Hans were regularly getting updates about the situation around Washington and in Virginia. Sentiments in Milwaukee were very much on the Union side. About 75 % of the population was of German descent, and the German-American community was strongly committed to the abolitionist cause.

Late in the afternoon the group from Nannestad boarded the last train on their seemingly unending journey. The transportation from Milwaukee was a slight improvement over the cattle cars. As they piled up their luggage for the last time, the La Crosse and Milwaukee Railroad provided boxcars the last 200 miles. Olaus took a short nap during the darkest part of the night, but he was too excited to sleep for long, and was up with the morning sun. Looking out on the Wisconsin prairie he marveled at its beauty – even if farms were dotting the countryside there was a definitive air of unspoiled wilderness about the scenery. With the wind blowing through his hair from the speed of the train, he was thinking about Ole's trek across the prairie to the Mississippi River six years prior. He had walked the whole distance! Now they could just sit on a train car and watch the countryside glide past.

While closing in on the Mississippi River valley forests became predominating. Trees were whizzing by along the sides of the boxcar, and with a screeching sound from metal on metal the train applied the brakes downhill, slowing down more and more, eventually rolling out on the flats outside La Crosse. The whistle blew a long, loud high pitched sound, and almost before Olaus knew it – like a shock – the long journey all the way from Norway came to an abrupt end. The train stood still. Releasing the brakes it let out a massive cloud of steam. They were in La Crosse. Olaus felt almost strange standing on the platform without any intention of boarding another ship or train – just a ferry across the Mississippi. He took a few steps, and it gave him a good feeling. He was used to walking, and it was good that he was, because he would be asked to excessively do just that for years to come.

Time had come to depart from their friends from Nannestad. The Bergs and Kaxrud were actually turning back. They were going twenty five miles east, to Cannon Valley in Monroe County, where they were going to stay with Nils Eggen, an uncle of Ole Berg. Olaus and Hans would walk thirty five miles to Highland Township where Ole and Maren were waiting. After a heartwarming good-bye the

LaCrosse in 1867. The Library of Congress.

two brothers boarded the first ferry across the Mississippi, and were soon on the trail towards northeast Iowa. After a long day's walk they passed a farm, and went by to ask for directions. The farmer came out on the steps, and – not surprisingly – he was Norwegian.

"Ole Hansen?" The farmer scratched his head, thinking.

"His wife's name is Maren", Hans said.

"Oh!" – Ole Aarnæs!" the man replied. "Over that hill and due west until you hit the old Indian trail from Spring Grove, Minnesota to Fort Atkinson. Follow the trail south until you get close to South Bear Creek – you're in Highland. Cross back east to the creek. Can't miss it. Nice place, too."

Shouldering their backpacks they set out for South Bear Creek. They spent the night under some large oak trees and early next morning they were back on the old Indian trail. The farmer's directions soon showed to be correct. As they were walking along the South Bear, through an opening in the forest they could see a farm answering to the man's description. Upon approaching the door a woman came out to greet them, and although they had never seen her before, they knew it had to be Maren. A girl about eight years old stood next to her. The woman took one look at the two men, smiled and turned to the open door.

"Ole!" she said. "Your brothers are here!"

TO WAR

The election of Abraham Lincoln for President in 1860 was the natural result of an ongoing cultural evolution in Iowa. Before1854 the state was heavily influenced by southern sentiments due to northward migration from Missouri along the Missouri and Mississippi rivers. Immigrants started to flow into the state in earnest after the Black Hawk War in 1832. These settlers moved in because of general population pressure in the south, but also because of economic competition with large plantation owners using field crews of slave labor. They brought traditional southern customs to their new homeland, especially in regards to politics and attitudes to slavery. Some of them even brought slaves into the free state, thinking they were still in Missouri. Strong links with the South was maintained through commerce, as before the coming of the railroads goods was mainly shipped north-south on the two big rivers. These cultural and commercial bonds had two decades to solidify before mass migration came underway from the northeast. The southerners' core values became influential in shaping the politics of Iowa, and also embodied in the state constitution.

Slavery had been on everybody's lips from the early 1850s. It seemed impossible to go to a river town without hearing about it, or getting into some kind of verbal exchange on the subject. On boats traveling up and down the Mississippi joint discussions on the inflamed issue would carry on all day and into the night, and sometimes develop into real quarrels. It was almost surprising that the quarrels did not develop into more serious conflicts, as whiskey was exceedingly common. Everybody could make it, everybody could get it and everybody could drink it, and it was sold for 15 – 20 cents a gallon. Some stores kept a barrel available for the customers, with a moveable head and a tin cup hanging from a chain to enjoy whenever they pleased. Luckily handguns were not yet very common in Iowa – some people could be seen with holsters on their hips, but the quality of the guns often made them more dangerous to the owner than the target. The only quality handguns found were dueling pistols owned by farmers from Virginia and Kentucky.

In 1852 a book was published which would have a massive impact on attitudes towards slavery in America. Appearing first as a forty week serial in an eastern abolitionist publication called "National Era", it was later released as a book.

"Uncle Tom's Cabin" by Harriet Elisabeth Beecher Stove sold 300 000 copies the first year. According to one Iowan growing up in a Mississippi River town, publishing the book was like "pouring fuel on the fire".

The issue became even more inflamed when the Kansas-Nebraska Act was passed in 1854. This law allowed the white settlers in each new state to decide whether they wanted slavery or not. The law superseded the Missouri Compromise, passed in 1820. This law had drawn a line along 36 degrees 30 minutes northern latitude from the Mississippi River towards the Pacific Ocean, allowing slavery south of the line, but not to the north. Iowa, being north of the line, already had a slave state to the south. With the Kansas-Nebraska act they could suddenly have slave states to the west as well.

Then – from 1855 - a virtual onslaught of immigrants poured into the state and the political environment underwent radical changes. The northerners were people from the New England states, Ohio and the Middle Atlantic region mixed with European immigrants – among them Ole Hansen from Nannestad. They flooded out on the open prairie previously shunned by people from the South. They were clamoring for free homesteads, which became one of the standard issues of political campaigns throughout the 1850s. The prejudices and loyalties they brought with them were entirely different than those held by the original majority in southern parts of the state – a respect for education, a belief in the social proprieties and a distinct anti-slavery attitude. The Norwegians, Swedes, Danes, British, Irish and Germans did not need anybody to tell them about the effects of living in bondage. The semi-slavery conditions they had left in Europe was the very reason many of them had emigrated to the United States – the land of freedom and liberty.

A year later the population in Iowa stood at 512 000, of which 38% originated from the northeastern part of the U.S. and Europe. The Scandinavians alone increased almost seven fold towards 1860, and of the 7 700 inside the state borders 2 900 resided in Winneshiek County. The outcome was inevitable. The northerners replaced the southerners both in numbers and influence in all but the southernmost tier of counties. During the Presidential election on November 6th the Iowa republicans won a decisive victory over the democrats with a 13 500 vote margin. Lincoln carried Iowa with more votes than his opponents combined. Apparently northern sentiments in the state were now clearly stronger than southern sympathies.

In Kansas, a diehard abolitionist from Torrington, Connecticut took action against pro slavery forces in the struggle to keep the new addition to the Union a free state. John Brown was a descendant of Peter Brown, one of the pilgrims on the Mayflower, and the son of abolitionist Owen Brown. He knew that under the Kansas-Nebraska Act, every effort would be made to carry slavery across the border from Missouri. Kansas became a battle ground between free settlers and pro slavery raiders – "border ruffians". Brown, who saw himself as a religious crusader against slavery, would figure prominently in the fight and did not see any contradiction between armed force and prayer. He created his own little army where six of his sons were members. He had friends in Iowa, and used the state as refuge when needed. In addition, he was a driving force in the Underground Railroad, funneling fugitive slaves into Canada. He would later carry out an attack on the Federal Arsenal at Harpers Ferry, Virginia, in order to procure guns for his anti-slavery army. The attack failed and he was taken prisoner by a detachment of U.S. Marines led by a colonel destined to become the supreme commander of the Confederate forces during the Civil War – Robert E. Lee. Brown was hanged for treason, which effectively terminated his impact on events in Kansas, but made him a martyr for the anti-slavery cause.

Even if slavery was a hot subject in Iowa, there were not a lot of colored people on the streets. They were very much a minority, as were the Indians constantly seen roaming through the towns, trading handmade moccasins and ornamental work for food and drinks. Some slave owners had actually moved into the state and freed their slaves, and by doing so had also taken on the responsibility to protect them. It was virtually impossible for these prior slaves to exist independently - they needed a guardian, and to stay close to home. If they were discovered without protection, professional slave hunters would kidnap them and sell them back into slavery in the south.

Such was the situation when Olaus and Hans Hansen arrived in 1861. In late July the three brothers were gathered at Ole's home in Highland Township. The state was alive with news from the front ticking in over the wire. The Norwegian newcomers had suddenly been thrown into a conflict of which they had no history, no knowledge and did not know how to relate to. Ole, on the other hand, having lived ten years in Wisconsin and Iowa had a solid insight into the political development leading up to the current situation. During long evenings in Ole's living room they were puffing on one-cent cigars and enjoying coffee and tall drinks of chilled lemonade while talking about the state of affairs. Soon the younger brothers were quite familiar with the political changes in Ole's home state, as he reviewed the development he had seen since he arrived in America in 1851.

Iowans had already been in the fray. The 2nd Iowa Infantry Regiment was the first to depart from Camp Ellsworth at Keokuk into Missouri at 5 am on the morning of June 13th – without their uniforms, which had not yet been issued. Colonel Samuel Curtis had been ordered to take military control of the Hannibal, St. Joseph and North Missouri railroads. On July 9th and 11th the 3rd Iowa skirmished with Rebel forces in northern Missouri. These regiments were the first to be formed, and the response to calls for volunteers had been overwhelming. After the attack on Fort Sumter Secretary of War, Simon Cameron, had asked Iowa governor Samuel J. Kirkwood for one regiment numbering 780 able bodied men to serve for three months. Almost 10 000 Iowans came forward. Meetings were held in school houses and every recruit became a recruiting agent. On May 3rd Lincoln issued a new call for volunteers, this time for 42 034 men for three years. After the disastrous battle of Bull Run another call was made on July 23rd. A fourth call would go out in October. There was an underlying expectation of every unmarried man between 16 and 25 years of age to volunteer. If not, he did not meet his call of duty in the local community. Nationality did not matter. Newly arrived immigrants were welcomed with open arms along with natural born Americans.

Olaus and Hans did not need to dwell on their decision to volunteer. As young men just becoming members of a mostly Scandinavian community, it was blatantly obvious to them that the responsibility to protect the Union against what they perceived as southern aggression would fall on their shoulders. With the heated events affecting both Missouri, Kansas and Iowa over the Kansas-Nebraska Act, it appeared to them as if slavery was very much in the balance, and one of the major reasons for the ongoing war. The cotter conditions they left in Norway and the long nights in Ole's smoke filled living room put them solidly against that particular institution. By volunteering they also knew that they had covered the family's commitment to the Union cause – Ole would not have to volunteer, and neither was he expected to. A father or brother of dependent children under twelve was exempt, and if two men from the same family volunteered, the rest of the family was likewise exempt.

From the latest development it did not take a lot of imagination to understand that Lincoln's three months war was entirely unrealistic – because it was already becoming past tense. The two Hansen brothers realized that, upon volunteering, they would not be back for a long time. Iowa was raising regiment after regiment, but they decided to stay on the farm and help Ole with the harvest before they

Decorah, Iowa about 1875. The Author's collection.

enlisted. In the earliest part of the war farm boys and sons of farmers had left pell-mell for the front, leaving crops in the fields to rot. Olaus and Hans saw no reason to follow suit, as the war was apparently going to last, and the initial fear of not getting to the front before it was over quickly faded. They cut the wheat and oat, and during the first two weeks of august were busy stacking the grain.

Saturday august 10th news came over the wire about the battle of Wilson's Creek, where the 1st Iowa had fought, and General Nathaniel Lyons was killed. During the following days everybody talked about the battle as the work in the fields was finished up – the preacher even mentioned it in church during the following Sunday's service. Ole urged his younger brothers to go if they felt it was the right thing to do, but they wanted to stay until the harvest was in. The three of them capped the grain for protection against rain storms and started mowing wild grass for hay. Then cordwood was stacked for the winter. By early October all the heavy work was done, and Hans' skills as blacksmith if anything went wrong with the farm equipment was no longer needed.

The 12th Iowa Volunteer Infantry Regiment had been under formation since September 14th. Throughout the month of October young Norwegians in Winneshiek rallied to enlist, most of them from Decorah, Highland and Calmar. Of the fifty four Norwegian recruits, forty four would eventually be mustered together in one single unit – Company G. On a Monday trip to Decorah on October 14th Hans attended a recruitment rally. It was an opportune time to enlist. The recruiting officer was Captain Charles Tupper, and when Hans returned to Highland he carried a document in his backpack, committing him to serve "three years or during the war". There were several Norwegian families with multiple brothers enlisting from Iowa. From Decorah came three Steen brothers from a family of seven – Theodore, John and Henry. They were born at Grorud in Christiania and came to Iowa in 1853. They all enlisted on October 21st in the 12th Iowa, Company G. Three more brothers enlisted - in the 1st Minnesota (Charles), the 38th Iowa (Martin) and Otto was the youngest recruit in the 15th Wisconsin. The Iowa companies were ordered to report at the training camp – Camp Union in Dubuque - as soon as they were enlisted. Hans made his way to the camp together with a large contingent of new recruits. They were all mustered in on Sunday, November 5th.

Olaus stayed on the farm helping Ole, wrapping up the work which needed to be done before winter set in. On Sunday, November 6th, as the family went to church in Decorah, another rally was running after the service was over, trying to secure young, unmarried men from the parish. Olaus wasted no time in getting to the table, Ole following close behind in case his help was needed. When the enlistment papers were duly filled in, Tupper pointed at the dotted line.

"Put your mark there."
Olaus looked at Ole.
"He says to put your name on the dotted line", Ole said in Norwegian.
Olaus signed his name.
Tupper looked at him.
"You can write?"
"Of course" Ole said.
The captain was notably surprised.
He turned the document around and read the name out loud.
"Olans Hanson."
"Olaus Hansen", Olaus corrected him.
The captain looked at him and nodded.
"Yes. Olans Hanson."

Olaus looked at Ole, who shrugged his shoulders. "Just leave it. He doesn't know how to read or pronounce you name. From now on you are Olans Hanson".

Tupper asked him to swear the oath, and with Ole's help he pledged himself "to support and obey the President of these United States, and defend the Constitution against all its enemies and opposers whomsoever they might be". Olaus thought he had just committed himself to three years of service. As the war progressed it would be January of 1866 – more than four years later - before he was finally discharged.

He traveled to Dubuque the following week, and was mustered into Company G on Friday November 11th. Arriving at camp, he quickly learned that this was a young man's war. With few exceptions the recruits were all unmarried men, and the average age of the Norwegians was twenty three years. Several of them were only eighteen years old - the oldest one by far was Søren Sørensen from Decorah. He was forty four. Nearly all were farm boys, sons of early settlers and used to pioneer life. Common bonds were strong patriotism and a hatred for slavery which had been intensified during the Kansas-Nebraska trouble. Once in camp, clannishness within the different ethnic groups soon surfaced. The Germans showed to be the most extreme, and aggravations between two companies led to a murder even before the regiment left basic training camp..........

Camp Union was located on a sand bluff about fifty feet above the Mississippi River. It was built for summer weather and showed to be a miserable place in winter. At no time during the war were they living under worse conditions than in the early part of the rigorous winter of 1861. The recruits suffering the most were the ones with rheumatism, and some of them could barely move around on their own. There was no kitchen, no shelter where to cook, no fuel to warm the barracks and a camp guard prevented them from bringing in any kind of extra provisions or conveniences. The harsh conditions inevitably led to desertions. This was not the glorious war the young recruits had envisioned at the recruitment rallies in Decorah. At the end of October Ansel Dodge and Lawrence Griffin took off a day apart, and just a week before Olaus arrived William Blackman and Joseph Hodges jumped camp the same day.

62

Olaus Hansen in the company descriptive book, 12th Iowa Volunteer Infantry Regiment. The National Archives.

Drills were incessant – squad drill, company drill and battalion drill in rapid succession – interrupted by runs on the double quick to the top of the bluffs, and bayonet charges on unsuspecting tree stumps. The instructor – "Little Major" Brodtbeck from Switzerland – became a favorite among the recruits with his drilling of the officers, who were as green in military doctrine as the raw recruits. His exasperated shouts could be heard across the parade ground as he corrected the officers muddling the troop movements: "Officers all wrong! Men all right!"

In the middle of November supplies were issued – blankets, knapsacks, canteens and fatigue uniforms. A full garrison of camp equipage was provided, consisting of Sibley tents, mess chests, axes, spades, picks, kettles and pans. In addition there were twelve wagons drawn by six mules each and two ambulances drawn by four horses. It was said that the regiment set out with more baggage and a larger train than would have been allowed three years later for the whole 16th Army Corps, with 50 000 men.

On November 27th, having cooked five days rations and spent the night waiting for transport with no fuel to build fires, the regiment was marched towards the city to be taken downriver to St. Louis, Missouri. A message came saying they would be transported on open barges. Colonel Joseph J. Woods, who had assumed command a month before, refused to expose his regiment to such conditions, and marched them back to camp. Olaus was used to low temperatures and freezing conditions from Norway. It took a certain mental and physical tolerance to endure it, and that tolerance was often sustained by the thought of eventually being able to build fires. Back in camp he could only blow warm air into his cupped hands, and that was a very poor substitute for a crackling fire.

In the afternoon the regiment was again ordered into the city and spent the night in public halls. On Thanksgiving Day – November 28th – the 12th Iowa crossed the river and boarded two trains on the Illinois Central Railroad at Dunlieth. At 10 pm they were rolling towards St. Louis 375 miles distant, where they disembarked thirty two hours later. At 2 pm on the 30th they marched into the recently created Benton Barracks through the old fair grounds. The weather was a radical improvement from when they left Iowa. It was warm and pleasant.

Benton Barracks – or Camp Benton - consisted of two long, parallel rows of frame buildings stretching for a mile in length for company quarters, with warehouses and other structures closing off the ends. Frame partitions closed off the company barracks. The buildings enclosed a mile square parade ground and the camp included a hospital capable of serving between 2000 and 3000 patients. Too much

Hans Hansen in Civil War uniform. Courtesy of John Murray.

rain would inevitably turn the parade ground into an ocean of mud, useless for drill and other exercises. Drainage was poor and time was wasted waiting for the ground to absorb the water. The 12th Iowa was assigned their barracks – two companies to a barrack, although it was intended for only one. At the rear of each company quarter was a separate frame structure containing a kitchen with brick furnaces. The dining room had a roof, but no walls. In camp, cooking was usually done by company cooks, and dished out to the men filing past in long lines. When out campaigning, everyone was expected to be their own cook.

Behind the cook houses were the cavalry stables – a very bad combination of facilities indeed. Although Olaus was used to flies from the farms in Nannestad, the number of six legged pests walking all over his food at Benton Barracks defied description. It was a constant battle to be able to eat while keeping the scavenging competitors away. If plates, cutlery or food were left unattended for a few minutes, fly droppings quickly appeared. Cold weather slowed the activity down somewhat, but as soon as the temperature rose, the battle was on again.

About 40 000 men were stationed at the camp, mostly raw recruits who had never

The old fairground in St. Louis where Benton Barracks was located. The Library of Congress.

before seen an army musket. On December 1st a grand review took place. Just a few hours after the 12th Iowa arrived in camp the nice weather had given way for a snow storm. Now about half of the soldiers at Benton Barracks marched over the snow covered ground in a line 2 ¼ miles long. The Hansen brothers were mightily impressed. Never before had they seen a parade of such immense size, and they felt convinced that once in the field the Rebel forces would stand no chance against such a formidable military power as the Union could muster. Within a few months that conviction would be shaken to its core, but even before then casualties would quickly mount from completely unexpected causes.

The cramped quarters soon resulted in outbreaks of contagious diseases ravaging the ranks. January of 1862 was cold and rainy, and instead of being occupied with drill half the regiment was on the sick list. Measles, pneumonia and mumps spread like wildfire and within two months of arrival 75 men of the 12th Iowa had died. The regiment suffered heavier losses at Benton Barracks than they did in any engagement during the whole war.

From the onset of the war it had been a general opinion among the Iowans that eastern regiments were issued better equipment than the recruits from the Hawkeye state. Guns issued to the first regiments were described as a cross between a blunderbuss and a Chinese matchlock, and Starr revolvers caused more fear within the regiments themselves than among the enemy. They either failed to work or went off at the wrong moment. Many regiments had to settle for Harper's Ferry muskets altered from old flintlocks. European imports were often standard issue among western regiments – Austrian muskets or Belgian smooth-bores – described as heavy, cumbersome, awkward and unsatisfactory in every way. The heir to the French throne, Louis Phillipe Albert, fled France for the United States before the revolution in 1848. While serving as an adjutant general on General George McClellan's staff, commander of the Army of the Potomac, he expressed that the refuse of all European arms passed into the hands of American volunteers.

Colonel Woods made sure the 12th Iowa was issued the best arms available. Persistent effort by governor Kirkwood and the state's militia commanders had paid off, and Olaus and Hans looked at each other when the result of this effort was put in their hands – new Enfield rifles! The bluish black barrels of the sleek guns dimly reflected the sunlight, and they gave off a scent of light oil enhancing the impression of pristine gunsmith artwork. The order was issued to immediately clean and dry them, and keep the metal parts covered with a fine layer of oil during storage and transportation. Preceding battles the inside of the barrels had to be wiped thoroughly dry for the oil not to be burned into the surface.

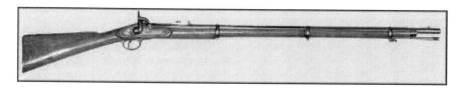

Caliber .577 model 1853 English pattern Enfield rifle-musket. Wikipedia.org.

While handling the arms the dangerous mix of untrained recruits and loaded guns soon became apparent. To load a musket or a rifle was a nine step process requiring the use of both the hands, teeth and a ramrod. Green recruits interrupted during the process had a hard time remembering if they had an empty or a loaded gun in their hands, and accidents started to happen. On the west side of the camp a soldier accidently discharged his gun, instantly killing another soldier across the parade ground. A 7th Iowa recruit had the top of his head shot off during a sham fight. A boy in the 2nd Iowa took a bullet through the head from a comrade jokingly pointing his gun at him pulling the trigger, thinking it was empty. And so it continued, accident after accident.

The Hansen brothers were inundated with army paraphernalia at Benton Barracks – there was no end to the useless knickknack the regulations required the soldiers to wear. Felt hats with black plumes, in desperate need of redesigning to be of practical use in the field. Brass eagles for the sides of the hat, a brass bugle for the front and brass letters and figures denoting company and regiment. "Dog collars" were issued to teach the soldiers how to keep their heads straight and raised during marches. A sign of definite improvement in a regiment's appearance on the parade ground was when the recruits could march perfect and unrestrained, without the dog collars.

On January 6th the soldiers received their first pay. The monthly pay for a private was thirteen dollars, and they were back paid from the day of enlistment. This was the only time the regiment was paid in gold and silver. There were rumors of a possible move out of camp on Saturday the 11th, and three days later 2nd Lieutenant Moir of company A and Commissary Sergeant Edgington went to the Good Samaritan hospital in St. Louis, where some of the soldiers from the 12th Iowa was admitted. They wanted to bid them all good-bye. However, the river was said to be full of ice, and not before after midnight on the 26th would the regiment get marching orders. By then, some of the soldiers had been released from the hospital and taken the street car back to camp.

On the afternoon of the 24th Hans came into the company barracks looking very disturbed.

"Har du hørt nyheten om kaptein Tupper?" (Have you heard the news about Captain Tupper?)
"Nei – hva har skjedd med ham?" (No – what has happened to him?) Olaus said.
"Han er død!" (He's dead!)
"Død?"
"Ja – død av sykdom!" (Yes, dead from disease!)
Olaus was shocked – less than three months had passed since he looked across the table at the captain when he enlisted, and he could still hear the words echo in his mind – "Yes. Olans Hanson"...........

From all the children dying on the ship to soldiers fading away on their bunks at Benton Barracks or in hospital in St. Louis, Olaus had witnessed more death and disease in the short time since he left Norway than during his whole life. Growing up at Nannestadteiet in a peaceful environment among family and friends had not prepared him well for the developing carnage. It slowly started to take a mental toll not yet noticeable to him, but it would escalate with each horrific battle he fought throughout his life as a soldier. Eventually it would become a condition not to be shaken off.

THE ARMY OF
THE TENNESSEE

About September of 1861 the Confederate commander of the Western Military Department, Albert Sidney Johnson, had established several forts along a line from Columbus to Bowling Green, Kentucky. Four months later plans were developing to have general P.G.T. Beauregard – of Fort Sumter fame – move west with fifteen regiments from the Confederate Army in Virginia, to reinforce this defensive line. Simultaneously the Union Commander of the District of Cairo, in the Department of Missouri, had realized that to break this line and take control of the waterways – the Tennessee, Ohio and Cumberland rivers - would provide open access to the heart of the Confederacy. This commander, with military experience from the Mexican War and several failed ventures in later military and civilian life, had reinvented his career with the onset of the Civil War. Known as Ulysses Simpson Grant – although his name was actually Hiram Ulysses Grant – he had just repeated his request from early January for permission to attack Fort Henry on the Tennessee River to his superior, general Henry Wager "Old Brains" Halleck. Grant felt that his plan had fallen on deaf ears, and followed up with a telegram on January 28th, after returning to his headquarter: "If permitted, I could take and hold Fort Henry on the Tennessee. If this is not done soon, there is but little doubt that the defenses on both the Tennessee and Cumberland rivers will be materially strengthened".

Although Halleck from personal reasons was slow to take action – something he had in common with other Union generals like George McClellan and Don Carlos Buell - Grant's appeal was aided by General War Order No. 1 from President Abraham Lincoln. This order urged a concerted movement against Confederate forces in the Department of Missouri by February 22nd. Lincoln felt that it was an absolute necessity to take control of the state of Kentucky. A loss of Kentucky would in his opinion mean losing the war. May be Grant had anticipated that an approval of the request was just a matter of time, because already on January 27th – the day before he sent his follow up telegram to Halleck - the 12th Iowa was ordered to march down to the ferry at Benton Barracks, cross the river and enter a train for Cairo, Illinois. Arriving at Cairo about noon on the 28th they waited until night, then boarded the steamer City of Memphis. Olaus was not very impressed

A flooded Cairo, Illinois 1862. Miller: The Photographic History of the Civil War.

with Cairo. The city faced the Ohio River which ran very high with flood water, as did the Mississippi. Levees had been built against the water, hiding most of the town from river view. Still the streets and surrounding areas were just a foul, stagnant swamp. Pumps were running to empty the surface water into the river.

The steamer backed away from the mooring and turned the stem south heading for Smithland, Kentucky at the mouth of the Cumberland River. That night Olaus got his first impression of the preferential treatment extended to commissioned officers compared to the common soldier. Enlisted men were always required to sleep on the hurricane deck or lower deck among the filth from mules and horses, sacks of coal, barrels and rubbish. This particular night the brothers were sleeping wrapped in their blankets at the base of a structure called "Texas", on which the pilot house stood. Around the base of the structure was a row of small windows, allowing them to look into the cabin down below. Olaus could smell the food through the windows. Officers sat in cushioned chairs or were wandering about in carpeted and brilliantly lit rooms while their supper was prepared. Colored servants in white uniforms brought food to the tables, and when a gong was sounded, the officers came over to enjoy. They were served ham and steak, boiled Irish potatoes, hot biscuits, butter, molasses and hot coffee served with cream and different kinds of preserves. When the time came to retire, warm and comfortable mattresses and quilts were waiting, keeping the officers utterly oblivious to the conditions outside. Olaus compared the scene with his own surroundings: A dark and cold night spent lying on the planks on deck in drizzling rain, soot and cinders slowly drifting down on the brothers from the smoke stacks. Supper had consisted of the army staple – hardtack and a piece of raw bacon. For beverage they had river water.

The steamer drifted slowly into Smithland. It was another shabby looking town. On January 30th the first camp in the field was established on a high hill overlooking both the city and the two rivers. A thin layer of snow covered the frozen, muddy ground. Three days of cold and stormy weather passed before everything was ready. The mules had to be harnessed in six-teams and sufficiently broken to haul all the unloaded stores to the camp site. In the meantime the soldiers were quartered in churches, masonic halls and the like. The large, tee-pee like Sibley tents – with a cone shaped stove under a tripod supporting the center pole – were pitched. They soon showed to be impractical for active service and were replaced by "pup-tents" - or "dog-shelters" - where the soldiers carried half a tent each. Fusing the two half-tents by a row of buttons, the men slept two together. The heavy mess chest was divided up, each soldier carrying his own cup and cutlery in his haversack, thus providing the opportunity to instantly turn in for the night when the regiment halted after a march.

Olaus slowly got used to camp fare. He was by no means spoiled by the food in the cotter's cabin at home in Nannestad, but this was still a few prongs down the ladder as far as quality was concerned. No more Irish potatoes for dinner and no more bread. Rations were drawn from the orderly sergeant via the cook – each soldier got his hardtack, bacon, sugar, salt, pepper, soap and candles. Coffee was enjoyed at every opportunity, and although in civilian life it was invariably taken with milk, that commodity was not available in the field unless they were able to milk a cow. Sugar was used excessively when available, both in coffee and on its own. The bacon was eaten with hardtack, often as a raw slice of meat between two pieces of the rock hard biscuits. Hardtack was a staple of army rations. A water-and-flour biscuit nearly half an inch thick, it was eaten in at least a dozen different ways. Most commonly it was crumbled in coffee, and often – due to long and improper storage – it was infested with grain eating weevils. A layer of the adult beetles would be found floating dead and dying on top of the hot liquid, but they could easily be skimmed off, and left no after taste. Olaus learned other ways of preparing the flour-tile that seemed even less appealing. However, he would later find that during a campaign – after long marches in cold weather and snow – he craved fat, and would eat that before anything else. Subsequently one of his favorite dishes was something the soldiers called "Skillygallee", hardtack soaked in cold water and then fried in pork fat, salting to taste.

No drill had been carried out since he arrived at Smithland, but the comforts of camp were of short duration. The regiment had barely gotten into bed on February 3rd when they were called back out, asked to cook two days rations and be ready to march. No sooner were they out of bed before an order came to return to the tents. On the morning of February 5th the order was repeated, and this this time the tents were broken down, rations cooked and the regiment on a boat before noon. The steamer returned downriver to Paducah, a town with low black brick walls giving Olaus an impression of smoke and dirt. The City of Memphis proceeded southwards up the Tennessee River towards Fort Henry.

Fort Henry was one of three forts designed to cover the important middle sector of the defense line between Columbus and Bowling Green. Sitting on the east side of the Tennessee it had the unfinished Fort Heiman on the opposite bank, and fort Donelson twelve miles across a strip of land called "The land between the rivers", on the banks of the Cumberland. The commander of the fort was Brigadier General Lloyd Tilghman, a Marylander who had moved to Paducah in 1852. Under his command he had about 3 400 men, many of them armed with only hunting rifles, shotguns and 1812 flintlocks. Grant's plan was to take both of the active forts, and force the Confederate Army to withdraw from Kentucky and the northern part of Tennessee. Fort Henry suffered from monumental errors made during the construction. It was built on low bottom ground near the river and flood water covered the land all around. This made the inside look more or less like a hog pen, the water in some places being waist deep. During January the Tennessee rose fourteen feet. In early February only nine of the seventeen guns were still

Fort Henry in 1862. The Library of Congress.

above water. It became a race as to who was going to conquer the fort first – the Union Army or the Tennessee River.

Grant planned to take Fort Henry by a combined attack of land- and naval forces, led by four ironclad gunboats invented and built by James B. Eads of Lawrenceburg, Indiana. Technically they were still Eads' property, since the Government had not yet paid for them. Three wooden gunboats would close up the rear. The gunboats carried a formidable fire power – fifty four guns to be brought to bear on Fort Henry's nine guns. In support of the naval attack under flag officer Andrew Hull Foote, twenty three regiments of infantry – 15 000 men - was to be taken by nine steamers up the river and disembarked at Bailey's Landing north of Panther Creek, out of range of the fort's guns. This force was to encircle the fort on the land side and make sure the garrison did not escape towards Fort Donelsen. Some of the regiments also made landfall on the west bank of the Tennessee, later to be ferried over from the unfinished and unprotected Fort Heiman.

The Hansen brothers had slept on deck all night in pelting rain when the steamers came to a stop downriver from the fort early in the morning of Thursday, February 6th. Everything was soaking wet, the ground thoroughly covered in mud and the water continued to rise. In spite of the overnight rain the morning was clear and mild. The regiment was ordered out on the flooded landing place, struggling and wading in the ice cold water, trying to form. There was little place to form by regiment, and absolutely none by brigade, unless they moved out along the road. By noon they were ready to march

PUM!! PUM!!

They had barely gotten underway when Olaus heard the thundering reports from the gun boats. The cannonade soon became incessant, hundreds of shrieking and exploding shells being launched across the water from both sides. Infantry officers urged the soldiers on, ordering march on the double quick. Regiments struggled to keep up in the waterlogged, muddy marshland. Olaus was sometimes crawling in mud, sometimes running, to close ranks with the rest of the regiment. The ground was soft and spongy, quickly draining energy from every muscle in his body. Rapid streams were crossed on single foot logs. Water backing up in ravines forced the soldiers to backtrack and make long detours, sometimes wading in water up to their waists, sometimes up the their necks.

74

Union gunboats approaching Fort Henry on the morning of February 6th, 1862, led by the ironclads St. Louis, Carondelet, Essex and Cincinnati. The Library of Congress.

An hour passed and Olaus was still fighting the muddy marshland. Then almost an hour and a half passed. He suddenly realized that an imposing silence had settled over the river. No more reports from the gun boats. No more shrieking shells. No more explosions. What was happening? He was close to exhaustion when they finally reached the rear of the fort. While he was mentally preparing himself for his first infantry attack – although he had no idea how to prepare for it – the anticipated attack was suddenly aborted. There was nobody to attack. General Tilghman had sent the infantry on its way to Fort Donelson and surrendered with eleven officers and eighty two men. Olaus felt almost cheated. He was prepared to jump into the inferno of war, urged on by the exploding hell created by the gunboats, and then – nothing. He turned to Hans who stared back at him, and Olaus could see felt the same way, a mixture of relief and disappointment. Now they had to start all over – prepare for the next battle – nerves frayed and nothing to show for it.

Lighting his pipe he drifted in between the bastions with the other soldiers. It was his first encounter with a western fort. He had imagined it would look something like the ones he has seen in pictures from the British Isles – or may be with palisades and block houses, which you would expect to find in the depths of Kentucky. To his amazement he saw just some kind of earth fortification, not in the slightest similar to what he had envisioned in his mind. However - its five bastions with fifteen guns had effectively covered a part of the Tennessee River several miles long. As he entered the fort he found that one of the guns had been blown up by the defenders themselves and another had been knocked off the carriage by a gun boat. A third had been disabled by dirt being knocked into it by an over exited gunner, and in the confusion of the barrage a charge had been rammed on top of the dirt, with predictable result. The dirt would not fire the charge.

The enemy had left everything behind – tents, cannons, commissary goods and other valuables. Olaus quickly forgot about the abandoned stores when he saw what was also left behind – horribly mangled corpses and fragments of human beings spread all over the fort – the result of the bombardment from the gun boats. He shuddered. He was not yet used to the violent death and destruction he faced in the theater of war. His mind had subconsciously sidestepped that link in the chain of events when he volunteered for three years in the 12th Iowa. He had been blinded by idealism, glory, future victories – and peer pressure. Now he stared stark reality in the face. Death could be instant. And quick. Or slow, and painful. He may be able to see it coming – and then again – maybe not. He turned away from the gruesome sight. Grinding his teeth on the stem of his pipe he started to fill his pockets with what he found useful among the wreckage on the ground.

The night was spent without overcoats and blankets, and the following day was cold and cloudy. Again Olaus and Hans struggled to haul equipment from the boats to build a camp. Due to the high water no wagons could be used, so everything had to be carried. It took two full days in continuous rain, and the fog and mist hung low throughout the timber in the river bottom where the soldiers were plodding through knee deep mud. No sooner was the camp ready, before the regiment on February 10th was told to move another half a mile from the river. Troops were arriving by the thousands. Another two nights passed with low temperatures and the ground became covered in heavy frost. Fort Henry was completely submerged in the river.

Olaus enjoyed a few days of camp life. The iron clads, badly damaged from Fort Henry's guns had drifted downriver to Cairo for necessary repairs, bringing with them general Tilghman and about sixty prisoners. General John. A. McClernand had issued strict orders that there was to be no harassment of the civilian population in the area around the battlefield, and to punish all depredators upon persons or property of peaceful citizens. On the other hand, it was made clear that all the local citizens were to be regarded as enemies. These mixed messages led to severe depredations in the countryside around the fort, and company F of the 12th Iowa was mentioned as one of the perpetrators foraging for farm animals. The soldiers of the company swore an oath stating "If any cow, sheep, chicken, goose, lamb, duck or other ferocious animal should bite a member of the 12th Iowa, it should surely die". They later claimed that no edible animal escaped the execution of the solemn oath on a technicality, or for want of evidence. Other Federal army units disintegrated into unorganized mobs, looting surrounding properties for any useful stores they could find and destroying the rest. Several of them were so out of control, Grant ordered them back to Cairo.

On Wednesday, February 12th Olaus' regiment was ordered to move out in light marching order with three days' rations. They set out for the next Confederate stronghold - which was regarded as impregnable - Fort Donelson. Generals McClernand and Charles F. Smith were commanding the 15 000 men overland attack force, while Lew Wallace – of later fame as the author of Ben Hur - was kept in reserve with about 2 500 men at Fort Henry. 10 000 more soldiers were on board steamers making the roundtrip by the rivers to join up at Fort Donelson. Marching just after daybreak they got beyond the river lowlands. Entering a hilly scrub-oak country a lot of the marching was up and down, and from the hilltops the soldiers looked forward and back along the lines, at the largest army they had ever seen.

The temperature increased considerably and sweat was soon rolling from their faces. On the spring like day most of the men in the column became over confident because of the nice weather - they interpreted it as an extended forecast. While the tunes of the band music rolled back and forth they began to shed their heavy, blue overcoats and blankets, leaving them along the road. They were in the sunny South, Daffodils pressed through previous year's layer of dead leaves, crocuses opened to the sun and sounds of frogs filled the air. Who needed winter clothes? With the ever changing weather conditions during the Tennessee winter of 1862, that would show to be a very bad decision………

The march was hampered by a Rebel cavalry screen under the command of Colonel Nathan Bedford Forrest, a southern planter, real estate investor and slave trader with a knack for warfare. After the Civil War he would become famous – or infamous – for his association with the founders of the first Ku Klux Klan, and known as "The Wizard of the Saddle" and "The Devil Forrest". Unaffected by the

Federal gun boats firing at Fort Donelson. The Library of Congress.

harassment from the Confederate cavalry, Olaus arrived with the 12th Iowa in front of Fort Donelson about sundown, where they went into bivouac. This time he was not surprised by the appearance of the fort. It was a formidable earthwork on a hill about a hundred feet above the water enclosing some hundred acres of land. At the base of the hill he could see two heavy water batteries. Rifle pits encircled the fort about a mile out. Slaves had been hard at work for days both inside and outside the rifle pits cutting trees about breast high and turning the tops with sharpened branches outwards, creating almost insurmountable abatisses. Fort Donelson was garrisoned by 20 000 men, strongly supported by eight batteries of artillery, and they had all been driven inside the fort.

The men slept on their arms overnight, got up to a clear morning and fell into line of battle. Some of them climbed to the tops of trees to get a better look at the Rebel fort. Three miles below the fort twenty steamers with reinforcements from Cairo were moored to trees along the banks. Closer to the fort four Iron clads were anchored up in the middle of the river. White steam slowly curled out of the stacks, but all human activity was hidden beneath their dark decks. In the bright morning sun the forest along the river sparkled with snow and the warm water from the Cumberland steamed up the air. For the second consecutive day Flag Officer Foote's fastest gunboat, the Carondelet appeared in front of the fort. The previous day she had shelled the fort without reaction from within the earthworks. Now she lobbed a few shells to see if she could locate the fort's guns – and drew instant return fire from the batteries. The fort opened up a terrific barrage, answering the long range guns of the boat. The exchange lasted for about an hour, seriously damaging the gunboat's machinery by a solid shot through one of the port holes. She withdrew down the river with multiple casualties.

The Carondelet – the fastest Union gunboat – was the first to open fire on Fort Donelson. The author's collection.

Although General Grant had specifically ordered his commanders not to bring on an engagement, several unsuccessful infantry assaults were launched on confederate positions, all of them with bloody repulse and heavy casualties. The 12th Iowa was in position with regiments from Iowa, Illinois, Indiana and Missouri on the left flank. In one of the unauthorized attacks they moved towards the brink of a hill overlooking the fort. It was within easy reach of the entrenchment, but separated from it by a ravine full of abatisses. Confederate sharpshooters were targeting Union soldiers from behind the abatiss, and Company A was detailed as skirmishers to drive them out. It was a dangerous mission. Olaus suddenly noticed commotion in the direction of the skirmish line, and saw a body being pulled to the rear.

"Who was that!?"

"Private Buckner!"

"What happened!?"

"Ball in the eye socket, straight through the head! Dead before he hit the ground!"

Olaus peeked over at the dead body when artillery shells suddenly came shrieking out of the fort, exploding with thunderous shock waves. Dirt and dust was like a cloud around him, shrapnel whizzing in all directions. He pressed his forehead against a moss covered rock while the firestorm passed over him with the scariest sound he had ever heard. Lying on top of his rifle he hugged the shaking ground as if he was afraid he was going to be pushed under an exploding shell. He glanced

over at Hans, who looked back at him with a reflection of his own expression –
shock and astonishment. This was indeed their baptism by fire. Olaus felt like all
the guns had drawn a bead on him alone, aiming to rip him apart at any second.
Splinters of rock were hailing down, nipping at his shirt and pants. Everything
happened in a flash – he heard the shell come hissing down, then a loud explosion
– and it was all over. He was dead – or safe.

The shelling stopped as quickly as it started. Olaus failed to comprehend that it
was over. He felt like in a vacuum, expecting the next shell to explode. He looked
up, and the dust was settling. He turned his head towards Hans to make sure he
was not hurt, and saw his blue shirt and pants covered in grey clay dust – but no
red blood. He quickly crawled to a safer position in case the guns inside the fort
would open up on the same spot. He pulled out the pipe and tobacco pouch from
his pocket. Trying to light it, he realized how much his hands were shaking. He
stuck the pipe in his mouth and kept it there, not to have to use his hands. While
they were pinned down by artillery fire regiments on the left flank had been
probing the defenses of the fort – with heavy casualties. The ground was strewn
with dead and wounded soldiers.

About a mile to the right Olaus could hear the sound of rapid fire from muskets. It
sounded perfectly like fire crackers as single shots and volleys were mixed
together – R-r-r-r-r-r-r-r-r-r-rap! Rap! Rap! Rrrrrap! Rap! Rap! He could see
something appearing to be blue columns advancing uphill on the extreme right,
and then recoiling down the hill repulsed by musketry and artillery. A few minutes
later he spotted a rapidly growing brushfire on the hillside. The wind carried faint
sounds he thought were screams in pain and agony. He later learned that artillery
shells had put the vegetation ablaze, and the screams were from wounded soldiers
not being able to move. Burning to death their horrific screams could be heard
from the hillside. Some of the confederate soldiers not able to stand their suffering
leaped over the earthwork and pulled a few of them to safety.

The standoff on the left flank continued for about eight hours when in the
afternoon rain started to fall. By dark it changed to freezing rain and sleet. Olaus,
having left his overcoat at Fort Henry, wrapped his blanket around him. Soon it
was soaking wet. The wind turned north and it started to snow. Large, wet flakes
fell until it covered everything to a depth of six inches. The temperature dropped
below ten degrees and the wind picked up until he had difficulties standing up

A wounded Union soldier burns to death in the brush fire caused by exploding shells in No Man's Land at Fort Donelson, February 15th 1862. The Library of Congress.

against it. On the front line fires could not be built, due to the danger of becoming a target for the Confederate snipers inside the fort.

Olaus could feel his body reacting to the intensely cold weather – he was exceedingly familiar with the symptoms from Norway. Staying completely still everything felt normal, but as he tried to move, he noticed that he had lost control of his finer motor skills. His fingers were stiff and numb, and he could not light his pipe. The fingers would not hold something as small as a match, and they were not strong enough to light it. Nothing could be buttoned or unbuttoned, and he could barely hold a knife to carve off some frozen bacon. Speaking properly was impossible, as the muscles around his lips were paralyzed, and he could not form words. It felt like a pair of pliers was pinching his ears and soon his teeth started to rattle from the uncontrollable shivering of his jaws. When trying to walk he could only stagger awkwardly along. He knew that there was only one thing to do – get moving. He started to walk in a circle as fast as he could, but without breaking a sweat. He had to find a speed where he could continue to move indefinitely, and not stop and sit down. It was not going to help his hands or lips, but it would keep him alive and prevent frostbites to his feet. Most of the soldiers in the 12th Iowa had come to the same conclusion as Olaus and circled around more or less all night long.

In No Man's Land between the Union and Confederate lines wounded soldiers who were not able to move were slowly covered by a blanket of snow. Some were groaning, some screaming in agony, some swearing – and some calling out "Mother!" As the temperature sank and the snow got deeper, the sounds grew fainter. Wet uniforms and hair froze to the ground. Hypothermia set in and the helpless soldiers slowly perished. They froze to death.

About daylight on the 14th the regiment was relieved and sent to the rear to build fires and dry their clothes. The blankets were like sheets of ice and the men were leaning them up against trees near the fires to thaw out. The bacon was frozen solid, and to be able to eat it they had to hold it on a stick over the fire to broil. Olaus noticed that General Lew Wallace had arrived from Fort Henry with his force of 2 500 men, after a quick and cold overland march. They fell in between the two divisions already on the field, the right flank resting on a hill looking down into the valley of Indian Creek. The Iowa men made coffee, soaked some hard tack in water and ate it with a slice of raw bacon. By noon they were back on the front line. Everything around them was covered in ice and crusty snow, and they huddled together blowing warm air into their hands.

The 12th Iowa kept their position all day waiting for the gun boats to come up and reduce the fort, for the three divisions to take it by storm. About 3 pm Olaus could hear the report from batteries on the river side of the earth works, and see massive clouds of gun smoke billowing up. The battle between the boats and the fort had opened. It sounded like rolling thunder for little more than an hour as hundreds of exploding shells flew in each direction – then it suddenly stopped. Had the fort surrendered? Were they about to storm it? An orderly came riding along the lines with a message: All gunboats damaged, drifting downriver with an injured Flag Officer Foote and heavy casualties. They were expected to be out of the fight for good.

Olaus and Hans shook their heads. Incredible! Now what? How long were they going to be stuck in this ice box? Olaus pulled out his pipe with hands numb from the cold and managed to light it. He was leaning up against a tree, inhaling tobacco smoke and letting it slowly seep out through his nostrils. They were not going to move. It had been a long, cold day. It would be an even colder night. Luckily an order soon came to retreat to the ravine where they had breakfast in the morning, and they were able to build fires and make coffee. Another storm mounted, wind howling and snow falling. That night the two brothers were reasonably comfortable. Covered by their blankets, finally dried by the fire, they slept with the enemy just fifteen minutes away while the snow kept building on top of them, inch by inch. Two companies were on the picket line, watching for Confederate movements.

On Saturday 15th the sun rose in a clear sky, shining brightly on the glittering, snow covered landscape. Olaus had breakfast – the usual raw bacon, hardtack and coffee - the latter made with water from melted snow. Suddenly, about 6 o'clock, he heard the din of battle from the extreme right flank. Something big was going on, and it appeared to slowly be coming his way. The division was not moving, however – Grant had ridden off before dawn to a conference with the injured Flag Officer Foote, and had given strict orders not to move or bring on an engagement. So they waited – and waited.

In charge of the 2nd Division was Grant's commander from West Point, Charles Ferguson Smith, a fifty five year old general with and oversized, white mustache who unflinchingly obeyed orders. Hour after hour passed, and Olaus could still hear the battle raging on the right flank. Cannons were thundering with a continuous roar, volleys from muskets echoing between the hill sides and massive, thick, grey clouds of gun smoke drifting on the wind out of the ice crusted forest. Suddenly a mounted orderly came rushing down the line, shouting the Rebels had launched a full scale attack. Lew Wallace had been urged by McClernand to come to his support. Taking matters into his own hands Wallace established a defense line of howitzers across Wynn's Ferry Road where McClernand's men came racing to the rear.

When Grant finally arrived from his conference about 1 pm General Smith was sitting under a tree, and as Grant rode past the waiting soldiers Olaus saw him up close for the first time. In a brief second he got the impression of a man about forty years of age with an almost sad expression on his face and a cold cigar sticking out of a graying beard – and he was gone. After a brief conversation between the generals, Colonel Joseph J. Woods approached the regiment waiting under arms. "Forward march!" he yelled at the top of his lungs, warm breath drifting as a transparent fog around his head in the cold air. At about 2:15 pm they moved out across the snow covered ground in column of two abreast.

Olaus looked around at the other soldiers. This was their first frontal assault. Some of them would die today. May be many. Would it be him? Hans? In a flash his thoughts went back to the log cabin in Nannestad. It was like looking back at a previous life, something he could not quite relate to. Reality was here, now, the din of battle, gun smoke, the hill they had to scale, the lethal monster sitting on top

Brigadier General U. S. Grant, the Army of the Tennessee. Wikipedia.org.

of it which in a few minutes would be pouring a hail storm of lead and iron down on them. They had to either conquer it – or die. He was ready.

Emerging onto an open field the task before them quickly became apparent. The left wing of the 2nd Iowa under Colonel James M. Tuttle was already heading down the ravine in front, moving by the flank and pouring over a rail fence which quickly fell down under the pressure from the advancing soldiers. They had removed the percussion caps from their rifles to make sure nobody fired before they reached the top of the breastwork. This was a frontal assault carried out with cold steel. The right wing under Lieutenant Colonel James Baker was close on their heels about 150 yards to the rear. The 12th was part of a large movement making a feint attack to the right to draw fire and allow the 2nd to storm the parapet. As the two wings of the 2nd started the uphill climb they moved quickly about 200 yards through a wooded area before passing through an almost impenetrable abatiss of felled trees stretching for another 150 yards. The two

Brigadier General Charles Ferguson Smith leading the bayonet charge of the 2nd Iowa at Fort Donelson February 15th, 1862. The Library of Congress.

wings merged on the far side and fell into line of battle, the regimental lines doubled to have more impact during the final assault. The fire from the breastwork grew to a hailstorm of musket balls, shots and shells raking the hillside, the parapet almost obscured in clouds of gun smoke.

At the head of the 2nd Iowa Olaus saw the 6 feet 3 inches tall General Smith towering on top of his horse. Waving his sword with his hat at the tip, he was yelling something in English Olaus did not understand - but he could distinguish some of the words: "- VOLUNTEERED TO BE KILLED, AND NOW YOU CAN BE!! The rest of the sentence disappeared in the "Rrrrrrrrrrrap! Rrrrap! Rap!" from Rebel muskets and the explosions of shells. The regiment set off in a reckless charge over the last hundred yards of slippery, icy, muddy uphill slope, bayonets fixed.

Of the 300 soldiers initially in the charge, about 150 became instant casualties. The dead and dying were strewn in the regiment's path along the broken hillside. As he watched the carnage in front of him, Olaus felt as if the hair at the back of his neck slowly rose. He was scared, but would not admit it – even to himself. The

12th had set off at a dead run to divert attention from the 2nd. They came under intense fire from the front and right, and started to veer left, towards the remnants of the 2nd. Musket balls were hissing around their heads, and Olaus jumped over dead soldiers – and some live dragging themselves down the slope in search of cover. Suddenly he realized he was no longer scared. As long as he kept moving he felt perfectly calm and detached, as if the slaughter on the hillside was completely irrelevant to the challenge ahead of him. The bullets zipping past his head with stinging sounds might as well have been rubber balls. He discovered that he could think clearly, and his entire focus was to get to the top of the earthwork, then over it, and put an end to the monster creating the havoc around him.

Men were falling exclaiming "Oh Lord!" – "Oh, My God!" at the instant they knew they were struck – may be fatally. Suddenly the hostile fire stopped – the 2nd Iowa had carried the breastwork, pushing the enemy back during their headlong bayonet charge. As the 12th Iowa leaped over the earthwork, Color Sergeant Henry Grannis – a "university recruit" from Upper Iowa University, and brave to total recklessness – stormed over the parapet and planted the first regimental flag inside the fort itself. The enemy tried to reform a hundred yards back, but the Iowa soldiers quickly capped their guns and poured a devastating volley into them, then continued their charge. Another five hundred yards to the rear, the defenders got behind the next breastwork.

To his astonishment Oaus noticed that some of the men in the 2nd Iowa seemed to be struck by bullets from behind. He turned his head and saw an Indiana regiment appear over the breastwork they had just scaled, opening fire on the Iowa soldiers in front of them. He screamed at the top of his lungs, waving his arms for them to cease fire, but in the chaos of smoke, gunfire and yelling from the other soldiers, he might as well have been a mute. The mistake was apparently discovered, because the boys from Indiana held their fire.

Confederate forces previously diverted to the right flank during the battle earlier in the day were now reassigned to positions in front of the Iowa regiments. After coming under heavy fire from the Rebels the Iowans were forced to withdraw to the outer breastwork. Still they were now holding the high ground at the fort, and could bring enfilade fire to bear on the rest of the entrenchments. The time was 3 pm. The assault had lasted only forty five minutes.

For the first time Olaus knew he had killed a man. As he jumped down inside the outer parapet he knelt down, aimed deliberately at a Rebel soldier and carefully

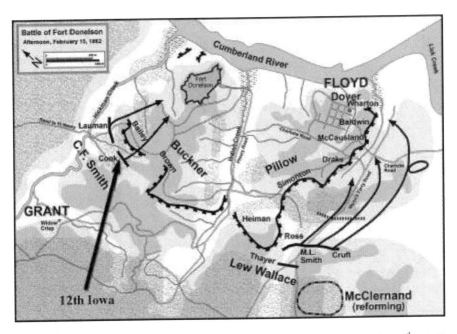

The 12th Iowa's position during the assault on Fort Donelson February 15th, 1862. Map by Hal Jespersen www.posix.com/CW.

pulled the trigger. The impact of the musket ball was like a brush of wind through the soldier's shirt and he instantly threw his arms up and went crashing down, muddy water splashing around him. During the assault Olaus had no time to reflect on the kill – the charge was going full speed and there was no time to think. Now it all came back. He was not at all sure what he felt about it, but knew he had no choice. In war, it was the enemy or him. No gray zones, no thinking, no evaluation – just do it, or die.

He did not feel like seeing the fallen soldier at all, but during the retreat to the outer works it was as if he developed an overwhelming urge to view the result of his own undoing of a human life. He moved slowly over to the dead body. The Confederate was just a boy – may be seventeen – caught up in a war far away from home, just like himself. He had an almost peaceful expression on his face, as if he had resigned to his fate when Olaus bullet struck him. One of them had to die, and today it was not Olaus. He turned quickly away, climbed to the outside of the parapet and pulled out his pipe. His hands were shaking again.

Hans was suddenly in front of him, and the sight of his brother brought him back from his trance like condition. Hans was unhurt. Olaus was unhurt. They looked at each other.

"You okay?" Hans felt that something had changed in his young brother's demeanor.

"Yep", Olaus replied, inhaling the heavy tobacco smoke. Hans knew not to probe any further.

"Did you hear about Stillman?"

"Nope." Olaus kept answering in one word sentences, blowing half a dozen smoke rings.

"Shot is the head by a sniper from half a mile away, after the Rebels retreated".

Olaus looked down at his boots. John Stillman, from Waukon, Makee. Nice guy. Now he was lying in a gun box, ready to be shipped back to Iowa. Well, at least that was better than being buried on the battlefield, like poor Buckner. A thought suddenly struck him. Where would he be buried? In an unmarked, shallow trench together with 150 other mangled bodies on a muddy battlefield somewhere? He inhaled deeply again, keeping his hands in his pockets. Better not go there.

Another long, cold night was approaching. Olaus could hear sounds from the battlefield – unnerving groans from wounded soldiers - but there was nothing he could do to help them. As it grew colder he got up to move around for his feet not to suffer frost bite, and noticed that his clothes had frozen to the ground. He wanted to get some sleep, but knew he was between battles, as they were still just at the outer breastworks. Tomorrow a new challenge would be put upon him and the 12th Iowa – to take the inner works. The thought of it did not induce much sleep, but at last he drifted off from sheer exhaustion.

About 4 am next morning – at the other end of the Confederate lines, under cover of darkness and hidden from the Union pickets – Colonel Nathan Bedford Forrest made his way out of the little town of Dover just south of the battlefield. He set out along River Road and escaped through the icy water across the flooded Lick Creek at Smith's Ford with 500 cavalrymen and at least another 300 infantrymen. Olaus would encounter him again in the not too distant future.....

On February 16th Olaus woke up to a morning a bit warmer than the previous. He soaked some hardtack in water and chewed it slowly together with raw bacon. He tried to calm his churning stomach with black coffee. This was a sign he would always notice during later campaigns – his stomach would churn as if he was nervous for an upcoming battle, but once he got into the action, he felt no fear. After breakfast they marched back up to the entrenchments. General Grant's orders for the day were straight forward and to the point: An all-out assault on the inner works of the fort along the whole line of battle. Upon reaching the breastwork just after 9 am they spotted white flags sticking up along the inner parapets, and orderlies were riding to and from with the message that the fort had surrendered. Thundering cheers rose among the Union soldiers – there would not be a desperate and deadly frontal assault mounted that Sunday morning after all.

Olaus looked down the hillside to the rear, where the 2nd Iowa had made their desperate assault the previous day. He saw blue coats scattered between the trees and stumps, each of them signifying a dead soldier. They had advanced in a column up the slope and then spread out along the breastwork for the final assault. The dead soldiers' positions indicated this march as looking strangely like a broom. Many of them had been carried off during the night, but he could still count nearly twenty bodies in one spot below the parapet, and one – or sometimes two together – in a line down the hillside. Immediately within the works he could see six more bodies. He found it somewhat peculiar that of all the casualties he saw, the soldiers at the bottom of the slope were hit in the legs, halfway up the hill in the body, but by the parapet everybody was hit in the head – and all of them dead.

Later he walked across the battle field and the carnage made a lasting impression on him, adding to his experience from Fort Henry. There were puddles of blood, canteens, blankets, weapons, clothing, dead horses, dead and mangled soldiers, bloody mud and snow, and hats – lots of hats – with hair and brain tissue still stuck to the inside. He noticed similarities in a lot of the casualties. The rifled and smooth bore muskets had done unprecedented damage during the battle. Both the dead and surviving soldiers had suffered ghastly head injuries, and some had their jaws shot clear away.

The Union Army marched in and took possession of Fort Donelson. Bands were playing "The Star Spangled Banner", "Hail Columbia", "Yankee Doodle" – and even "Dixie". Between twelve and fifteen thousand Confederate soldiers were captured, the largest number ever to surrender as prisoners of war on the North American continent. In addition, the capture included about 20 000 stands of arms, forty three cannons, fourteen heavy guns, ammunition, between 2 000 and 4 000 horses and commissary stores, at a value of several millions of dollars. In Dover, every citizen had fled the Union forces. In spite of orders from General Grant, throughout the day private and public stores all over town were looted by Federal soldiers, and what could not be used was destroyed. In an attempt to prevent the

Musket balls caused many severe head injuries at the battle of Fort Donelson.
The author's collection.

soldiers from getting away with their loot, Grant ordered all the steamers searched before they left Fort Donelson. Guards were stationed on all the vessels to stop the men from carrying their plunder aboard.

As casualty lists were prepared and sent north to Union newspapers, friends and relatives appeared on the battle field to claim the bodies of their loved ones and take them home. Virtually no relatives of Confederate soldiers could do the same, as friends and commanders of fallen Rebel soldiers had been sent north to Federal prisons, such as Camp Douglas in Chicago. Most of the Confederate dead were simply dumped into unmarked mass graves and covered over.

Inside the fort the 12th Iowa was assigned log cabins, a major improvement from sleeping out in the snow. The cabins had "stick-and-mud" fireplaces at one end and bunks at the other. They were furnished with Dutch bake ovens and split log benches. The Dutch ovens gave the soldiers opportunity to bake corn bread and hot biscuits, a welcome change in diet from the raw, salted pork. Olaus settled down for camp life and rest. The exposure the soldiers had endured during the days of siege and attacks had resulted in a lot of sickness. Young men of not yet thirty years of age already experienced severe cases of rheumatism, not being able to move around without help from their fellow soldiers. Apparently the water also contained sulfur and caused a scourge of diarrhea. Many of the men were too sick to eat. In addition, they were plagued with large populations of lice – "graybacks" – which they had annexed together with the sleeping quarters of the Confederate defenders. The 12th suffered far more casualties from exposure and disease at Fort Donelson, than from hostile fire.

On February 21st the 2nd, 7th, 12th and 14th Iowa regiments were brigaded together and designated as the First Brigade of the Second Division of the Army of the Tennessee. This was the first brigade organized entirely of regiments from Iowa. The Union troops initially drawn loosely together for a common purpose on the Cumberland River had now become an army of almost 30 000 men. This army would go from victory to victory throughout the Western Theater of the Civil War, and never face defeat. At the center of the action were Olaus and Hans Hansen, two brothers from Nannestad, Norway. During the battle of Fort Donelson they had certainly had a first rate opportunity to "see the elephant" – the soldiers' expression for being introduced to combat. However, there was a much larger "elephant" ahead, where they would be at the nucleus of events.........

THE HORNETS' NEST

After the fall of Forts Henry and Donelson the Confederate commander, Albert Sidney Johnson, fell back from Kentucky and the west and middle Tennessee. He established a staging area for an offensive against the Federal forces at the railroad hub Corinth in Mississippi. The Federal troops at Fort Donelson, after resting for about three weeks, were ready to move by steamers to the west side of the Tennessee River to engage Johnson at Corinth.

Friday, March 7th dawned with a clear sky. The temperature was increasing by the hour, giving every indication of a nice, warm day. By 10 o'clock General C. F. Smith's Division with the 12th Iowa Regiment left Fort Donelson and marched to Metal Landing on the Tennessee River about four miles north of Fort Henry. During the march they got a thorough lesson in what to keep and what to dispose of before the upcoming campaigns. They drove ten teams with camp equipage, and the men themselves were loaded down with knapsacks, haversacks, canteens, overcoats, blankets, arms – in short, everything needed for any kind of situation in warfare. In addition some of the soldiers had brought all kinds of relics like cannon balls from the battlefield, as they firmly believed that they were probably going home.

After a long, hot, muddy march they reached Metal Landing about sundown, built big fires and slept the night in the open. The 12th stayed in camp at the landing, enjoying the warm spring weather with just an occasional thunder storm. On the 11th they received orders to leave at a moment's notice, but not before the 13th was the order executed. A flotilla of fifty eight steamers had come up to load the 15 000 men and 3 000 horses aboard, and the men now realized they were not going home. They were going upriver, deeper into enemy territory. All of the heavy and unnecessary equipment was deliberately discarded. From now on the Iowans regarded themselves fully equipped when dressed in blue fatigue suits, blankets rolled into thin, long rolls, ends tied together and thrown over the shoulder, canteen and haversack with three days' rations and a musket with forty rounds of cartridges in the box and many more in their pockets.

The newly formed Iowa Brigade was the last to be transported and they boarded the steamer John Warner about noon. It was dark before all the equipment and animals were on board. The horses and batteries of the 1st Minnesota filled the lower deck together with all the mules and camp equipage, leaving just the upper deck to crowd together for the men. There was no space for cooking, and coffee could only be had with hot water from the ship's boilers. As the convoy made its way upriver Olaus was leaning on the railing looking at the magnificent spectacle of all the steamers. Black smoke was pouring out of the tall funnels, flags and banners flying. The bright sunlight was reflected from thousands upon thousands of bayonets on the stacked guns, and bands were playing "Hail Columbia" and "The Star Spangled Banner". The decks were crowded with men taking off their long blue coats in the warm spring weather. The bluffs along the river were heavily wooded, the flood water covering the bottoms up to thirty feet deep, making it look like the trees grew out of the water. Long, gray moss hung from the limbs interspersed with mistletoe. That night, as they pulled in to Savannah, the weather had changed radically and rain was pouring down on the Army of the Tennessee. They stayed at Savannah until they were ready to move the last eight miles to their destination.

On March 19th John Warner drifted in to the moorings at Pittsburg Landing. The site – named after "Pitts" Tucker who operated a tavern during the years preceding the Civil War – had for a long time been an important distribution center for both the city of Corinth and the farms in surrounding Hardin County. The many roads crisscrossing the area made it possible to move a large army in concert towards Corinth. The 12th Iowa disembarked and was immediately marched about one mile out, forming the extreme right flank of the Union line. As other regiments arrived they were thrown out in a semi-circle around the landing. The camp ground was situated between Lick Creek and Snake Creek, emptying into the Tennessee River above and below Pittsburg. The terrain was wooded and rolling, broken up by swamps, ravines and clearings with a few farm houses.

The camp was intended for rest and training before a battle was launched. Never had so many green troops been gathered in the same place at the same time. Eight Ohio regiments had been issued their guns within the last two weeks, one regiment right before they boarded the steamer, and some of the soldiers did not get their guns before disembarking at the camp site. The Army of the Tennessee – growing to six divisions at Pittsburg Landing – had only about thirty regiments with battle experience, either at Belmont or at forts Henry and Donelson.

Olaus settled into a life of leisure in the huge camp. 5 000 Sibley tents dotted "The Plains at Pittsburg Landing". The food transported up the river to the idling army was incredible – seafood, meat, dried vegetables, cheeses, biscuits, soda crackers,

Pittsburg Landing on the Tennessee River. The Library of Congress.

roasted coffee - and bread was baked continuously – thousands upon thousands of loaves. The U.S. Government sure had money to spend on their soldiers, as long as logistics made the commissary stores readily available. The 12th was situated on a dry ridge with a small stream running by the left flank emptying into a bayou behind the camp, giving unlimited access to fresh water.

Spring quickly approached and the budding trees gave the forest a shade of green. More and more frequent Olaus spotted wildlife – rabbits, squirrels, raccoons and opossums. Even reptiles like snakes and lizards - depending on increasing temperature in the air for physical movement – began to appear. When the soldiers were not drilling – which they did excessively every day in anticipation of battle – they enjoyed all kinds of sports and games in the beautiful spring weather.

Hardtack, bacon, sugar and coffee. Miller: The Photographic History of the Civil War.

Throwing horse shoes and playing baseball and cricket were some of the favorite pastimes. They went fishing when time allowed, and some hunted squirrels or picked wild onions and turkey peas for a variation in diet. Not all of the men were up to outdoor activities – some were sick, and John Bradford of Company E had contracted smallpox. He died from the disease just three weeks later, and Olaus was happy he had already been vaccinated.

General Charles F. Smith picked the camp site at Pittsburg Landing. Rumors had been afloat in camp that the old warrior had been disabled by a leg injury and was hospitalized in Savannah. Smith would gradually get worse from his injury, and eventually die from infection and chronic dysentery. Due to the circumstances Ulysses S. Grant – promoted to Major General after the battles of forts Henry and Donelson – had arrived two days before the 12th Iowa and assumed overall command.

During the first days of April Olaus heard the sound of musket fire several times a day, about two miles from the 12th Iowa camp. He thought it was some of the other regiments doing shooting drills, but Hans said Sergeant Sumbardo had talked to his friends in the cavalry. They had encountered Rebel forces just three miles outside the Union camp, and skirmishing went on continuously. Olaus found it strange that life in camp went on like nothing had happened. However, he trusted that the general officers knew what they were doing. That was certainly not the case.

The Union camp was laid out with more regard to sanitary conditions and open space for drilling than to defense. The top brass was so convinced that the

Confederate army was sitting still waiting at Corinth, that any report from lower level officers about Rebel movements in close proximity was scoffed at and dismissed. The commander of the 5th Division, William Tecumseh Sherman, was particularly dismissive - at least officially. He probably had his personal reasons. He had become famous all the way to Washington, D.C. for his exaggerated view on the size of the enemy forces when he claimed that 200 000 Federal soldiers were needed to hold Kentucky alone. Samuel Wilkerson of the New York Tribune, who had been present at a meeting with Sherman, would later declare him insane and on November 9th, 1861 Sherman was relieved of command. This time he would downplay the danger, something that would cause irreparable damage to the initial defense, once the battle opened. For a large part his division contained green regiments. They had not yet seen Confederate soldiers, not to mention engaged them in pitched battle. These green regiments were camped farthest out in front towards Corinth and the Rebel army, at a Methodist log meeting house called Shiloh – ironically meaning "place of peace". Veteran regiments like the 2nd and 12th Iowa were camped to the rear.

As it was, Albert Sidney Johnson had no intentions of being a sitting duck for Ulysses S. Grant. He knew that Major General Don Carlos Buell with the Army of the Ohio was heading towards Pittsburg Landing to support Grant, and Johnson wanted to strike before the two separate armies merged into one huge, unified army. The early April weather was forever changing between heavy thunderstorms at night and sunny days with light rain showers. Thursday April 3rd started out cool, but by midday it was scorching hot. Olaus saw General Grant close up for the second time, as he reviewed the 1st Brigade consisting of the four Iowa regiments.

On the morning of April 6th Olaus and Hans were out of the tent after reveille, enjoying a hearty breakfast of bread, ham, coffee and biscuits. Like the rest of the boys in the regiment they were attending to everyday chores – cleaning their guns and shining their shoes for the morning inspection. Some were washing dishes after breakfast, others shaving for the Sunday morning service. Birds were singing in the balmy spring weather, the oak trees budding and the peach trees were in full bloom. It was like a May morning in Iowa, and some of the men had ceased the opportunity to take a swim in the creek behind the regimental camp.

The time was about 7 am when Olaus heard a familiar sound.
PUM!! PUM!!
Artillery! He jumped to his feet and listened.
PUM!! PUM!! PUM!!

The sound was coming from southwest, followed by intense rattling from "firecrackers" - volleys from muskets - and he could tell by the volume of the sound and speed of the firing that this was no drill. Some of the Iowa boys held out for the possibility that this was just another skirmish between pickets. They had heard enough of those the last few days. However, Olaus was in no doubt as to what was developing, and when an hour had passed the discharges from the artillery developed into a continuous, thundering roar. The forces were engaged. A battle was on.

The men of the 12th Iowa came running from wherever they had been doing leisurely Sunday morning activities, most of them with gun in hand and cartridge box strapped on. A loud cry rang out: "Fall in 12th Iowa! Fall in!" The sharp sound of the long roll sounded from a snare drum and within a few moments the whole regiment – about 485 privates and 26 officers - fell into line on the parade ground and joined the rest of the brigade as it moved towards the front on the double-quick.

At the head of the 1st Brigade Olaus saw Colonel James M. Tuttle mounted on his horse. Tuttle was still not feeling well after an injury at Fort Donelson, and had slept late. Looking to the rear Olaus could see the 3rd Brigade following close on their heels. They ran as fast as their equipment allowed along the Hamburg-Savannah Road, veering onto the Pittsburg-Corinth Road. Not all of the boys could keep up. After running full speed for a mile Olaus saw John Gaston of Company G, 14th Iowa hanging over a stump while throwing up.

No sooner were they out on the Pittsburg - Corinth Road before they were met by hundreds of stragglers and all kinds of camp followers breaking for the rear. Some were injured, bloody from head to foot and grimed with gun powder. Many were hatless and had thrown away their guns, knapsacks, caps, blankets - anything that could slow them down. It was a flood of panicked soldiers streaming in the opposite direction of the advancing Iowa Brigade, and Olaus could hear them scream: "We are cut to pieces! The Rebels are coming!" One soldier stood next to the road with his hands thrown up, shouting: "For God's sake, don't go out there, you will all be killed. Come back! Come back!" Some were completely overcome with heat, dust and fatigue and had just dropped to the ground, lying scattered throughout the forest.

Amidst the stragglers heavy six-team mule wagons and ambulances loaded with wounded were heading for the temporary hospitals at the landing. Some of the soldiers were carried on stretchers. Cavalry horses with empty saddles were

Deserters running in panic back to Pittsburg Landing. The Library of Congress.

running in all directions while escaped artillery teams pulled caissons at full speed through the forest, crashing them into trees causing the percussion shells to explode, blowing up both the caissons and the horses. The deserters would not stop before they reached Pittsburg Landing where several commissary boats were almost sunk by the masses of boarding soldiers. The boats had to push off from shore and cross to the other side of the river. Dozens of men drowned from being pushed into the water by stragglers crowding from behind. In the course of the day the number of deserters huddling together in cover under the bluffs on the banks of the Tennessee River reached between 5 000 and 10 000. There was little or nothing the officers could do to make them return to the front line.

As the Iowa Brigade moved through the retreating stragglers Olaus could hear the incessant storm of infantry fire ahead and feel the thunder of artillery while shells were shrieking and bursting overhead. The air was thick with dust and burnt gun powder taking all the moisture from the mouth and creating a burning feeling all the way down the throat. He was in no doubt about what he was in for. A veteran from Donelson, he knew he had never seen an "elephant" this size before. But he was on the move, and felt no fear. He just wanted to get to the center of the action. His wish would be thoroughly fulfilled.

The brigade veered onto the Eastern Corinth Road and with his binoculars Colonel Tuttle spotted the enemy in the woods beyond an open cotton field. He turned the 2nd Iowa down an old wagon trace running near the crest of a small hill towards the Pittsburg - Corinth Road. It was Joseph Duncan's farm road, worn down in such a way as to form a natural breastwork for lying defenders. The other regiments followed in order of increasing numbers. Finally in position the 12th Iowa stretched across the Eastern Corinth Road. The artillery was placed on an elevation to the rear. Although nobody knew on that fateful day, the 600 yard stretch at the center of the Union line would become one of the most iconic stands of the Civil War. Olaus Hansen had just been deployed in the Hornets' Nest.

From his position he faced dense forest and undergrowth to the left in front of the

Colonel James Tuttle. Wikipedia.org.

14th Iowa. The thicket would not allow for much of a view of the approaching enemy or a good field of fire. Looking to his right he had the cotton field where the 12th, 7th and 2nd was positioned behind a split rail fence along the edge, with a ravine to their rear. Colonel Tuttle was riding along the line addressing each regiment separately: "Remember you are from Iowa! The eyes of your friends are upon you! I expect every man to do his full duty, and hold your ground at all hazard!"

About ten o'clock reflex from metal flashed in the sunlight, somewhere in the woods across the field. Olaus suddenly heard clattering of different Norwegian dialects along the line of defenders – he was not the only one who had spotted the ominous flashes. His eyebrows were already dripping with sweat in the hot morning sun and he wiped his forehead as he squinted his eyes and looked at the spot where he had seen the flash. Colonel Tuttle and Major Cavender, having scouted the edge of the woods from the cotton field on horseback, came rushing back to the line.

Suddenly a field battery opened up behind Olaus with a deafening roar. It was Prussian born Captain Emil Munch's 1st Minnesota pounding away at a Rebel battery about to unlimber on the other side of the cotton field. Several horses of the Confederate battery were splattered in a bloody mess on the ground, effectively halting its preparation. When it finally managed to counter fire, the shells from the somewhat inaccurate smoothbore went largely overhead, moving down trees and cutting limbs, falling down on the Iowa soldiers. Other Rebel batteries drew a more accurate bead on the Hornets' Nest and launched an incessant hailstorm of exploding shells. Some of the men were standing behind the posts of the split rail fence. They were instantly cut down by the flying shrapnel, demonstrating for rest of the brigade the necessity of staying on the ground behind the bottom rail.

The artillery duel lasted for about an hour. Through the blazing inferno the Iowa soldiers hugged the ground to avoid the shots and shells shrieking through the air and bouncing across the field and through the forest. When the barrage stopped, Olaus lifted his head and watched the edge of the woods some 300 yards away. Something gray in color emerged from the forest line – long lines of soldiers under the Confederate flag bearing directly down on the 12th and 14th Iowa. The flashing reflex he had seen earlier was hanging like a permanent gleam of sunlight above them – from innumerable fixed bayonets. Olaus stared. This was not Donelson.

Modern day Hornets' Nest with Olaus Hansen's approximate position, facing right, on April 6th, 1862.Tennessee History for Kids.

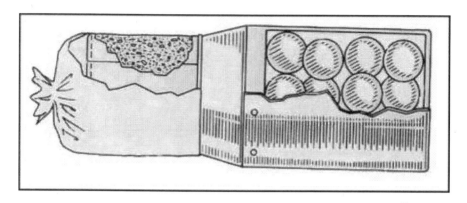

Canister – a can filled with lead- or iron balls used as an artillery shell against frontal assault by infantry. The Library of Congress.

This was not a massed attack on the run. He was not the aggressor, rushed by an overwhelming feeling of wanting to destroy the danger threatening him. Instead, for the first time, he saw a monster coming for him. Deliberately and unstoppable, it was moving towards him, and he had to lay in wait for a whizzing hail storm of lead balls and the cold, sharp steel of the bayonets. He did not have to look at his hands to know they were shaking. He clasped his Enfield, his knuckles turning white.

The Confederate column drew nearer on the double quick. To his right Olaus could hear Colonel Tuttle yell an order: "Ready! Aim! Fire!" A coordinated volley from the 12th and 14th sent a burst of smoke and flames from the muskets along the left wing of the First Brigade. Olaus could see Rebel soldiers be hit by bullets in several places simultaneously, collapsing in bloody piles on the ground. He loaded and shot at full speed. Nine-steps-load, aim-shoot! Nine-steps-load, aim-shoot! When reloading he had to roll over on his back and hold the gun along his side. To get up on his knees or assume a standing position to push the ramrod down the barrel meant certain death. He rolled back on his belly and fired. He had no misgivings about killing this time. When firing the first shot he had taken careful aim at one of the approaching Confederates, drawing a bead on his second coat button. After the first volley the smoke from the gun powder drifted like thunder clouds across the front of the brigade. Olaus eyes were burning from the smoke and the view of the approaching enemy was completely obscured. He could see nothing to shoot at. He just aimed low, firing into the thick clouds in the general direction of screams from wounded and dying men.

Munch's battery belched behind him. The four guns were raking the cotton field

The Union line of defense along Joseph Duncan's farm road in the Hornets' Nest on April 6th, 1862. Lossing: The History of the Civil War.

with double canister – cans filled with iron- or lead balls spreading out from the cannon's muzzle, making it into a giant, short range shot gun. The gunners were loading and firing non-stop, hurling themselves out of the way and to the ground at every shot, not to get hurt by the wildly recoiling cannons jumping back six feet at the discharge. The right wing of the Iowa brigade opened a terrific crossfire upon the advancing gray lines from a ravine extending onto the field. The Rebels who so far miraculously had escaped injury made a hasty retreat and took cover in the forest to reform, leaving scores of dead and dying behind.

During a lull in the artillery fire Olaus could hear sounds he subconsciously had been aware of, but not paid attention to. As an ironic counterbalance to the Hell of bursting shells, rattle from musketry and screams of wounded and dying men – birds were singing! On a branch right above him a bright red northern cardinal male was claiming its territory, as if it wanted to make perfectly clear that either side of the apocalyptic inferno was actually intruding on its personal domain. Olaus looked at Hans, who shrugged his shoulders and looked back out on the battlefield. The piles of mangled, bloody, dead and dying men littering the cotton field and the red crested bird with the beautiful song created an incomprehensible contrast.

A renewed artillery barrage was suddenly launched at the Iowa line. A perpetual hail storm of iron and lead ravaged the forest and dirt was thrown in all directions from the exploding shells. Suddenly it stopped. Olaus could see that Hans was saying something. His lips were moving. Olaus shook his head and pointed to his ears. He was almost deaf from Munch's battery and bursting confederate shells. However, he knew what Hans tried to say. An infantry attack was imminent.

Through the forest to his left a Federal regiment from Missouri approached on the run, shouting the Rebels were coming in heavy columns. They raced past the lying 14th Iowa and to the rear. Olaus could still not see the enemy, just hear them barging through the underbrush. Lying flat on the ground, they let the Rebels close in to about thirty paces. Colonel Tuttle gave the order: "Ready! Aim! Fire!" The 12th and 14th rose and unleashed a point blank volley completely destroying the first line of the attacking force. The Confederate soldiers were falling like corn for the scythe, the dead and wounded lying in a perfect row, riddled with bullets. Simultaneously the artillery joined in the fray, breaking up the rest of the attacking column with volleys of canister. The scattered remnants of the force retreated and broke off to the left, disappearing through the thicket.

Flushed by victory the 14th Iowa and the left wing of the 12th pursued in a bayonet charge, but could not find anybody to fight. The Confederate battle flag was captured, lying on the ground just twenty yards from the Union line. For a short while Olaus was part of an extreme left flank hanging unprotected in the air, but the counter attack force soon returned and took up their previous positions. Sometime after their return Olaus saw a horseman in full major general's uniform complete with buff sash appear behind the lines, chewing on a cold cigar. General Grant was on the battlefield, addressing his division commanders.

As long as the firing continued massive clouds of gun powder had been hanging throughout the forest, the thick canopies preventing the wind from blowing them away. After the firing stopped the clouds slowly drifted off, revealing the carnage on the battlefield in all its horror and gore. A cavalry horse came storming into view, snorting in panic. The guts were trailing behind it from a wound in the belly, getting snagged on trees and branches as it ran. Eventually it got entangled in its own entrails and fell to the ground. Unrecognizable piles of bloody substance lay scattered in the thickets and on the cotton field - Confederate soldiers moved down by solid shots, shrapnel and canister - some headless, some shot in half, some with arms and legs shot off and most in grotesque, impossible positions. Screams and groans could be heard from the ones still alive, many fatally wounded and knowing it. There was no recovery from a piece of shrapnel through the bowels.

Olaus spotted a dead Rebel with something appearing to be an arrow in his body sticking straight up towards the sky. He pointed it out to Hans.

"Ramrod", Hans concluded. "Somebody forgot to pull the ramrod out of the barrel before he fired".
Olaus shuddered. Ramrod! Of all the ways to be killed............

"Look at that!"
Hans nodded towards the cotton field. Masses of men were filing into line in the forest on the opposite side. The attack force looked formidable, stretching all the way from Eastern Corinth Road across the entire cotton field ending at the Corinth Road. Olaus' ears were still filled with a loud, humming sound from the artillery barrage, but this time he heard Hans talking to him.
"Yep. How many, do you think?"
"Don't know." Hans was guessing: "Four thousand. Many, anyway. Too many."
Olaus could feel the hair at the back of his neck bristling. The sight of the enemy together with the immobility of the Iowa line was fraying his nerves.

A long, gray line of soldiers started to move out of the forest, proceeding steadily towards them. Piercing yells rose from thousands of throats as the attack force poured across the field. Olaus was all too familiar with the sound – the Rebel Yell. He had heard it on several occasions, and it did nothing to reduce the prickly feeling at the back of his neck. The Iowa regiments let loose with all the fire power they had. Olaus fired as rapidly as he could - three shots a minute - against the wall of marching Confederates. Munch's battery – now under the command of Lieutenant William Pfender - spewed a hail storm of double canister over his head, taking a fearful toll in the advancing columns. Through the dense, grey clouds of gun smoke Olaus could see the Rebel line suddenly hesitate. The volleys from the Hornets' Nest made the gray line sway - made it look like someone shook a rope from one end. It got jumbled, like no officers were in charge, some parts advancing, others retreating. Suddenly the whole line crumbled and dissolved, failing to press home the expected, decisive charge.

Olaus was astonished.
"What was that?"
"No idea". Hans looked at the retreating Confederates. "I think they could have made it."
"No question. I was expecting hand–to-hand." Olaus stroked the back of his head. The prickly feeling persisted.

It was about noon and the heat was scorching from the midday sun shining mercilessly down on the Shiloh battlefield. Olaus wiped his forehead for which time he did not know, squinting his grey eyes as he aimed down the gun barrel pointing out on Duncan Field. He moved a little to keep in the shade from trees overhanging the split rail fence. He had not had a drink since breakfast and his tongue felt swollen from thirst. He pulled his canteen out, took a sip and let it roll around in his mouth before swallowing. He had to do it a few more times before his mouth felt somewhat normal. By luck he had grabbed a few extra lumps of sugar on his way out of the tent when the long roll sounded, but his stash was almost out. He put one in his mouth and let it slowly melt. That helped.

The 8th Iowa had joined the 1st Brigade, shoring up a conspicuous gap at the left of the Union line between the 14th Iowa and some remnants of different brigades under the command of General Benjamin Prentiss. They were soon to see some severe fighting. Olaus suddenly spotted movements in the scrub oak thickets to his left. Although he could not see them clearly, he took the rustling in the brush to be Confederate soldiers making their way towards the 8th Iowa and Prentiss' forces. Captain Andrew Hickenlooper's 5th Ohio Battery of brass 6-pounders opened up at a furious firing rate of one shot every 30 seconds. Changing from shrapnel to canister and double canister, Hickenlooper's four guns fired so fast it almost sounded like one long, continuous explosion. A deadly hail storm of nearly 450 lead balls every minute covered the field of fire in front of the battery. Immediately following the artillery the 8th Iowa delivered a crackling volley from 800 muskets. The 12th and 14th poured in supporting crossfire at any Rebel they could see moving through the underbrush. Some of the struggling attack force was virtually annihilated at point blank range, but the remaining survivors still rushed all the way up to the battery and killed most of the gunners and the cavalry horses.

For a few moments the battery was in Confederate hands before men from the 8th Iowa swarmed forward in hand to hand combat, retaking the guns – at a frightening cost. One hundred men were killed or wounded in the counter attack. The Rebels also paid a terrible price for the failed assault. Not only had most of the front line been wiped out by the Iowa Brigade – the rear of the attack column had been so over excited and confused in the impenetrable oak thickets, they fired into their own comrades at the front, killing several of them.

For hundreds of yards the brush was cut by flying bullets and shrapnel, giving it the appearance of a topped cornfield. The large trees behind the Duncan farm road were riddled with bullets up to a height of a hundred feet. The woods had caught fire from burning artillery-cartridge flannel, and Olaus relived the horrors from

Fort Donelson at close range. In No Man's Land more than a hundred wounded soldiers were quickly engulfed by the raging brush fire, and screams from the dying men could clearly be heard above the crackling sound from the blaze. Nobody ran out to help, as a steady stream of bullets were whizzing through the shrubs. Olaus felt like holding his hands over his ears, but instead he stared like paralyzed at the flames racing across the ground and licking up along the tree trunks. He would never forget the appalling sights and sounds of wounded men screaming and struggling to get away from the inferno.

The Confederates who were still able to fell back and Olaus ceased the opportunity to clean out his musket. The gun powder had been a notorious problem throughout the whole campaign. The quality was so inferior it literally choked up the gun barrel after continuous, heavy firing – and the firing along Joseph Duncan's farm road had indeed been heavy. Contrary to some of the other officers Colonel Tuttle had done an excellent job in bringing up a sufficient supply of ammunition to the front - the road was almost completely covered in a blanket of paper from discarded cartridges.

Olaus poured some water from the canteen down the barrel to clean it out. Tearing paper cartridges filled with charcoal, sulfur and potassium nitrate open with his teeth created a burning thirst. Sharing his water with his gun was something he resented, but there was no other way. He would rather have a working gun than quenching his thirst. The rifled Enfield had the advantage of a longer range and a more accurate shot than a smoothbore, but required a higher frequency of cleaning. When the barrel heated up the lead balls swelled as he rammed them home, and the rifled twist made it extra difficult. He cleaned the barrel thoroughly, rammed home a new ball and was ready.

Again the blackjack oak thickets started to rustle, and Rebels could be seen approaching the defenders along the farm road. They instantly took a hailstorm of lead and iron from the Hornets' Nest, and reeled back with heavy losses. Olaus was puzzled by the frontal attacks through the impenetrable thicket. He thought the first attempt would have taught them a lesson. How did they expect to reach defenders lying in hiding waiting for them by floundering for a long distance through brush they could not even see through? He kept firing in the general direction of the enemy, not knowing if he hit anybody or not. The gun smoke and dense forest made it impossible to ascertain any kills, but keeping up the barrage would pin the attackers down. After an exceedingly sharp contest, the rebels again fell back across the fields.

It did not take long before a new attack was underway. The gray line came barging through the oak thicket for the third time, with the same predictable result. This time they held back at a longer range, some units well hidden, others badly exposed to the storm of shrapnel and canister from the Federal batteries. It was bloody murder – Olaus kept firing at soldiers barely able to fire back, the only thing saving some of them during the suicidal assault was their obscurity from view behind gun smoke and thick underbrush. The firing suddenly abated from the oak forest in front, and he could see nothing to shoot at. The rebels had melted away in retreat.

Olaus had lost count of the attacks – if he ever tried to count them. There were continuous firefights all along the Union line as Rebel units were thrown piecemeal across the field and through the thickets. After the war survivors would claim there were eight charges upon the Hornets' Nest, some even said ten or twelve. For the defenders behind the split rail fence it just appeared to be successive tidal waves of Rebel soldiers pouring in from different directions, each wave more dangerous and deadly than the previous. There was no time to keep track of who, where, and how many. Every man fought desperate to save his life, and the lives of his comrades in arms.

A fragmented column appeared directly in front of the Nest. The blue line along the farm road erupted in sheets of flames, but in spite of the heavy firing the Confederates managed to get within fifty feet of the defenders. There they were pinned down in the brush for ten minutes. As they rose to push on, one of them was struck by a cannon ball tearing away half of his head in a cascade of blood. Olaus watched in horror as the man walked a few steps like nothing had happened - and then suddenly dropped to the ground. The fighting was furious before the Rebels finally fell back amidst explosions of shrapnel and canister aided by steady fire from muskets.

Olaus rolled over on his back and cleaned out his gun barrel again – he had a hard time with the ramrod almost getting stuck during reloading. Next to him Hans was doing the same operation, grinding his teeth at the inferior ammunition.
"Garbage gunpowder!" Hans ripped the ramrod out and started reloading.
Olaus watched the cotton field, but nothing happened before about 2:30 pm – and the attack did not come across the field. The three Steen brothers were lying just a few feet away, and John looked at Olaus, silently pointing to the left, towards the forest. Sounds could be heard from approaching columns, but as before nothing could be seen through the scrub oak thickets. Olaus nodded and swung his gun around, Hans quickly following suit.

The wood clad gun boat U.S.S. Tyler was shelling the Shiloh battlefield with its 8 inch naval guns on the afternoon of April 6th. The author's collection.

A flashing hedge of bayonets suddenly appeared in the undergrowth, making its way towards the 12th and 14th Iowa. The men held their fire, waiting with their fingers on the triggers until the attackers were about fifty yards away. Olaus spotted a Confederate lieutenant colonel at the same instant he shouted "forward" – and the Iowa line exploded in a wall of musket fire, while Munch's battery was raking the thickets with canister. The burst of flames came as a total shock to the Rebel attackers. Not only did they take fire from the front, but a heavy and unsuspected fusillade was poured into their left flank by the 7th and 58th Illinois. The two Illinois regiments had wheeled left out onto the field, hiding behind Duncan's log cabin and some cotton bales. The conspicuous lieutenant colonel fell with a musket ball through the neck and the attack force reeled back in confusion, not stopping before they had run a quarter mile.

During the attack Olaus heard reports from massive guns in the direction of Pittsburg Landing. He knew that only the gun boats carried that kind of artillery. It was the wood clad U.S.S. Tyler lobbing 53 pound shells from its 8 inch naval guns all the way in on the Shiloh battlefield. It was overshooting its target by a wide margin, but added to the general confusion in the Confederate ranks moving up to attack the Union defenses. After the Rebels retreated Olaus saw Colonel William

Shaw of the 14th Iowa moving out on the battle field with one of his captains. He walked over to the lieutenant colonel who had fallen in front of his regiment during the suicidal frontal attack. As the captain exchanged a few words with the dying man, he rolled him on over on his back and put his arms across his chest. A pocket handkerchief placed over his face a few moments later told Olaus that the officer was dead.

The time was almost 3:30 pm, and Olaus was ravenous with hunger. The sugar was long gone, and his water almost exhausted. He was on his back loading the gun when somebody pitched a small pebble at him. He looked up, and John Steen was pointing again. An enemy force was coming through the forest up along the Eastern Corinth Road – directly towards Olaus' position. As before the previous attack the Iowa regiments waited, their fingers on the triggers, until the rebels were at close range. Almost simultaneously they rose and poured a volley of small arms fire into the attackers, keeping the firing up at will. The artillery quickly followed up, spewing canister into the rapidly falling confederate ranks. Olaus feverishly loaded and shot through the thick, black smoke from the howitzer batteries driving through the forest, not knowing if he hit anything or not. The rebel force split up in fragments and retreated, shooting as they went back behind a slight elevation about a hundred yards distant. As the gun smoke slowly drifted away Olaus could see a Confederate officer galloping around trying to rally the men, but they were not about to resume the attack. They had had enough.

Olaus rolled over on his back, mentally exhausted. He had been lying in the Hornets' Nest under a scorching sun for almost six hours. Right in the middle of the chaos of screaming, whimpering, dying men, burning underbrush, sound of gun fire and thick gun smoke making it hard to breathe – he wanted to sleep. Just close his eyes for a spilt second and drift away - away from it all..........The birds were still singing in the trees above. "Incredible" he thought – the last thought to flash through his mind before a shower of Confederate shells exploded all along the Iowa line, blowing mangled corpses sky high. The largest concentration of field artillery ever gathered on the North American continent – almost sixty guns – had been brought to bear on the Hornets' Nest. Without the Iowans' knowledge, the Federal flanks on both sides had fallen back towards the Tennessee River, leaving the Nest like an island of blue in a converging sea of gray. The final destruction of the invincible stand had begun.

There was no time to load guns – and it would have been utterly pointless. There was nobody to shoot at. Olaus could clearly see the shells - they came screaming across Duncan Field like a hailstorm of lead and iron. They seemed to come from

John Steen. Vesterheim Norwegian-American
Museum, Decorah, Iowa.

two different locations – one somewhere out along the Pittsburg-Corinth Road to the north, and one down the road they were deployed across. As the incoming shells exploded it was like a hurricane pushing everything in front of it – men and horses were dying amidst flying shrapnel and bouncing solid shots. Trees were shot down, limbs falling, showers of earth and splintered rocks filling the air. Olaus threw himself behind the thick log of a fallen tree at the side of the road with his arms over his head. He had already seen casualties - Ole Olesen, Alfred Fuller and John Steen were down, all of them injured. Ole was beyond help. He had also seen a very, very long and menacing line of confederate gray slowly emerge from the forest line across Duncan Field. He knew it would be on top of them in a few minutes, if the artillery barrage forced them to stay behind cover.

Olaus and the 12th Iowa slowly became aware of the untenable situation they were in. The Federal fire had faded on both flanks. The Army of the Tennessee was retreating. At least seven Confederate brigades – about 15 000 men – almost completely encircled their position. Parts of General W.H.L. Wallace's 2nd Division had already started to withdraw. The 2nd and 7th Iowa were preparing to move out, the orders to follow never reached the 12th and 14th other than as a message, with no location on which to rally. About twenty minutes after the artillery barrage commenced Hans tapped Olaus on the shoulder and pointed to the rear. Munch's Minnesota battery had conspicuously disappeared. That was not a good sign. Olaus saw Captain John Stibbs of Co. D running over to Colonel Woods, pointing towards the rear of the disappearing 7th Iowa. Colonel Woods still hesitated to retreat, and Stibbs started to take D out on his own. Woods finally gave up hope of getting support and gave the order to retreat. The time had come to extricate the 12th Iowa from the Hornets' Nest.

As they quickly marched back along the Eastern Corinth Road the Rebels were hot on their heels and they had to about face and take a brief stand before continuing. They ran into fleeing soldiers from Prentiss' division which had crumbled on their left. Advancing another two hundred yards towards the Pittsburg-Corinth road, they suddenly realized Confederate soldiers were blocking the retreat. As they were making their way up a hill, at least two regiments were waiting for them, drawn up across their line of escape. Olaus threw his Enfield to the shoulder, everybody in the 12th Iowa making the same move. Colonel Woods barely had time to give the order before the entire front of the 12th was a sheet of flames. After about a dozen well aimed volleys the Confederates scampered behind the hill, lying down for protection.

Veering off along the knoll the 12th continued on the double quick. Young Henry Steen - helping his brother along - shouted something while waving his arm. Looking over his shoulder Olaus spotted another detachment of Rebels racing over the hill, closing in on their flank at a dead run. Under a heavy crossfire the Iowa soldiers ran headlong into the depression later to be known as "Hell's Hollow", when the regiment they had just put away behind the knoll came sweeping around the bottom of the hill from the right. Abruptly stopping to pour a murderous volley of musket fire into the 12th, they were so close Olaus could hear the clicks from the hammers as they cocked their guns. Simultaneously the Confederates coming down the hill fired into their rear. Colonel Woods took two bullets, one in the leg and one in the hand, immediately putting him out of action. As the Confederate regiments converged on the 12th from both sides, they were so close together the musket balls missing the Iowans took effect in their own ranks. From then everybody fought on their own account, firing at will at any gray jacket they happened to spot. They were not hard to find.......

The regiment had stopped in close vicinity of some huts to use them for protection from the Rebel fire. Colonel Woods was lying in a tent, severely wounded, and

112

Colonel Joseph Jackson Woods, 12th Iowa. The State Historical Society of Iowa.

none of the captains seemed determined about what to do. Quartermaster Joseph B. Dorr – as the only officer on horseback - went on a sweeping ride around the rear of the regiment to bring up stragglers who had been cut off. Miraculously he was not hit by the withering crossfire. When he returned to the regiment perceiving the complete stall, he jumped on a box and urged the officers to get their men into line and cut their way through before it was too late. Olaus could clearly hear his appeal when Dorr shouted that if they did not want to be slaughtered where they stood or rot in southern prisons – to get out. Some of the officers made efforts to get their men into line, when a white flag was hoisted. Dorr immediately had it brought down.

Suddenly Colonel Shaw of the 14th Iowa appeared about fifty yards away, walking bare headed in company with some other officers. Olaus saw Dorr running over to talk to him, and in an instant he realized that something was wrong with the officers' uniforms. They were Confederate. Shaw had surrendered.

Olaus was dumbfounded. He could not believe it – all that fighting, for nothing? As he watched two joyful Rebel cavalry troopers dragging the 12th Iowa regimental banner through the mud, he clasped his Enfield as if he would never let it out of his hands. Confederate soldiers were pointing their guns at everybody who had not stacked their weapons. "Stack your gun!" Hans whispered in Norwegian. "Stack your gun! Do you want to be killed? Stack your gun, boy!!" Reluctantly Olaus followed suit with the other 428 Iowa soldiers. A long day of fighting was over. They were prisoners of war.

Olaus felt ashamed about the capture – it was an inglorious end to the long and furious battle along Joseph Duncan's farm road. However, future would show that the 12th Iowa Infantry Regiment and the Iowa Brigade's determined stand in the Hornets' Nest had created a reputation of invincibility among both friend and foe which grew over time to become almost mythic.

PRISONER OF WAR

As the prisoners were led under guard towards Corinth, they left a battlefield behind which by the next day would count the largest amount of casualties in any battle the United States had ever been involved. Almost 24 000 soldiers were dead, wounded or missing – more than during the Revolution, the War of 1812 and the Mexican War combined. Shiloh was depicted as an indescribable scene of horror, where the wounded and dead were almost buried in mud and trampled upon by men and beast. At Pittsburg Landing commissary stores, ammunition, cannons, horses, mules and men were piled together. Hospital tents were overflowing and the wounded left unattended on the muddy ground. Surgeons were amputating arms and legs with bone saws and knives making the blood splattered operating rooms resemble butcher's shops. The limbs were thrown in large boxes to be taken away. Row after row of fresh graves marked with shingles were dug for the dead who could be identified. The unidentified were unceremoniously dumped in a large pit, covered with lime and dug over. The battlefield was reeking with the smell of dead and putrefying horses, mules and men, and the stench was peculiar when mixed with the sweet smell of peach blossoms. The animals were surrounded with cordwood and set on fire, adding another repugnant odor to the mixture.

Immediately after the surrender some of the Iowa boys fell into conversation with the Rebels keeping them under guard. Olaus did not know enough English to follow the exchange, so he paid no attention to it. Darkness was falling as they were marched back across the battlefield in front of the area previously held by General Prentiss. They met Confederate forces pushing to the front, taunting the Federal prisoners as they passed. About nine o'clock at night, after a heavy march through the mud, they were ordered to halt in an old, plowed cornfield by General Braxton Braggs' headquarter just outside Monterey. The cornfield - about three acres in size – was eight miles from Pittsburg Landing. A double line of guards was posted around the perimeter and there was no chance of escape.

Olaus dropped to the ground between the furrows, trying to get some sleep. It was not to last. A torrential rain storm washed over the field, forcing the men to stand all night. Since their coats and blankets were back at the landing, they had no cover against the downpour. When the bright morning sun finally rose, it found the

2 200 prisoners cold, soaking wet and standing in deep mud. For breakfast they were provided with two moldy crackers and a small piece of bacon. Much more beneficial for Olaus' spirit was a cup of hot coffee he managed to get his hands on from one of the fires. They were ordered to give up their small arms, but neither Olaus nor Hans had any handguns to surrender.

Several Company G soldiers were wounded – Carl Kittelson, Gilbert Anderson, Peter Larson, Nels Peterson and John Steen - but they had all managed to march along. All five of the Hansen - and Steen brothers stood together having a rapid fire conversation in Norwegian about the circumstances and the future. They could talk freely, as none of the Rebel guards could understand a single word they said. About 9 am the prisoners had waited for two hours to move out, when a detachment of Rebel cavalry armed with double barreled shotguns rode up, claiming Federal horsemen were in hot pursuit. They were in favor of shooting all the prisoners, rather than letting them be recaptured. The captives were immediately set in motion towards Corinth, seventeen miles distant. The road was lined with wounded, and Rebel units were continuously moving to and from the front, almost invariably armed with shotguns.

The prisoners plodded through mud all day. The progress of the sick and wounded marching along was so slow they did not reach their destination before about 4 pm. Olaus became aware of a procession slowly making its way through town. It was the body of fallen Confederate General Albert Sidney Johnson and his guard, and the event caused quite a stir, with much hostile talk against the Federal prisoners. Just after dark, in the middle of a heavy rainstorm with gale force wind, they were marched into boxcars on the Memphis and Charleston Railroad to be transported to Memphis. There were between forty and sixty men in each car, which made it impossible to lie down. Even if they had been able to, they probably would have preferred to stand, as the boxcars had not been cleaned since the last transport of cattle and the floors were covered in several inches of cow manure. The rain wet the manure enough to make the cars reek with the smell.

It was well after 10 pm when the train pulled out of Corinth, and the prisoners had not had anything to eat since the scanty breakfast about fourteen hours earlier. Olaus tried to ignore the hunger which had become a dull pain of variable intensity. He knew there was no point in anticipating when the next meal would occur. It rained all through the night and the leaking roofs in the dilapidated cars made them all soaking wet. About noon the following day they arrived at Grand Junction. Three miles further on, at La Grange, they were held up for three hours while trains with troops from the battle of Island No. 10 passed on their way to

Corinth. At about 5pm on April 8th they arrived at the Memphis and Charleston railway depot at Memphis. A large crowd had gathered to gawk at the Federal prisoners, and Oaus felt as if he was an animal on display at a circus. However, they were not all yelling and screaming at the captives – there were quite a few sympathizers in the city who brought provisions, cigars and tobacco. The prisoners were kept on the train until about 2 am Wednesday morning, when they were marched two miles down to the river in a pelting rainstorm. The rest of the night was spent in a three story brick tobacco warehouse on "The Bradley Block". For breakfast the following morning - their first meal in forty eight hours – they got some boiled ham and hard bread.

Olaus peeked out of the window. He did not know what he was looking at, but some of the other prisoners told him that the shoreline across the Mississippi River was the state of Arkansas. He saw several steamers flying a flag he had only encountered on battlefields – the flag of the Confederate States of America. About 9 am next morning they were marched back up to the railroad and boarded a train. Theodore Steen was not joining his two brothers and the Hansens. Due to his rank of 3rd corporal, he was sent elsewhere – either to Tuscaloosa, Alabama or Macon, Georgia.

For some reason they could never work out the train stood at the depot all day, and the prisoners passed the time singing old Union songs like the Star Spangled Banner, Hail Columbia and Yankee Doodle. Arriving at Grenada on April 10th they were transferred to the Northern Railroad, continuing to Jackson, Mississippi where they pulled into the station on the morning of the 11th. After another transfer, to the Meridian and Jackson Railroad, they left Jackson about midnight to arrive at Meridian at 10 am on the 12th. Olaus was amazed at the large crowds gathered to stare at the captured Federals at every the stop. At Meridian even a detachment of Rebel cavalry had shown up. The last change of trains was made at 3 pm the same day, when they were transferred to the Mobile and Ohio Railroad.

The long and arduous train journey ended at Mobile, where they arrived about 9 pm that night. The prisoners were divided into squads for further transport to makeshift prisons within the Confederacy. Olaus and Hans were intent on staying together, as were the Steen brothers. They managed to slip into the same unit without any idea as to where they were going, but it was much better to stay together with family, than to be alone. The different squads were marched down to the wharf and aboard steamers. Upon boarding the James Battle the Steen brothers – proficient in English after eight years in Iowa – soon discovered their final destination. It was Montgomery, Alabama.

That night they slept on the steamer. About 2 pm the next afternoon James Battle slipped away from the moorings and turned the prow upriver, the prisoners crowded on the hurricane deck. It was Sunday April 13th. Two other boats carried prisoners destined for Tuscaloosa. Olaus found the scenery along the Alabama River monotonous and dreary – forests stretching back from the shoreline and dead bottomland covered in Spanish moss. It was certainly not as appealing as the river valley along the upper Mississippi. As they passed Selma, they made a stop to let General Prentiss and the colonels, majors and captains ashore. They were to be taken to Talladega, with the intent of separating officers and privates so no organized resistance would occur. Without officers the privates would become pacified and not create trouble for the prison guards. Except for a short stop to fix the wheel on the steamer they arrived at Montgomery about 11 pm, and stayed on the boat overnight.

At 9 o'clock in the morning on Wednesday, April 16th a tired, dirty, smelly and ragged Olaus disembarked after the ten day journey. With the rest of the prisoners he marched to a cotton warehouse near Tallapoosa Street.
"Montgomery, Alabama", John Steen commented as they were closing in on the warehouse.
"This is the cradle of the Confederacy. Jefferson Davis was inaugurated here last February. Can't get any deeper in than this."
They filed in through the massive wooden double doors at the end of the warehouse. Olaus looked around to get an impression of the prison he would be confined to for the foreseeable future. The structure was about 300 x 200 feet with a railroad running through the center, entering and leaving through the double doors at each end. The sides of the building were sheds, with slate, iron and tin roofs. A wall about twenty feet high ran around the whole perimeter. There were no floors, and no bedding was provided for sleeping quarters. Olaus watched the rest of the prisoners as they crowded in through the double doors. Looking at John Steen he could see that his lips were moving. He was counting. Finally they were all packed inside the shed, like sardines in a tin.
"How many?" Hans asked.
"Seven hundred or so", John replied. "About two hundred from the 12th".
Olaus threw himself on the floor. No bedding, no blanket, no food. But at least he could rest or sleep whenever he felt like it. There was not much else to do.

Prison life got monotonous within a day or two. Rations were drawn once a day – they were miniscule and grew even smaller over time. The food consisted of corn pone without salt, made of un-sifted meal – corn and cob ground together - some days mixed with black beans normally used for cow feed and with the occasional bit of silk in it. The beef had a "fishy" smell from being badly preserved in the warm weather, and the prisoners called it "mule beef". Moldy crackers, a little rice, sugar, may be some molasses and no coffee summed up the menu, making it altogether half a ration. Over a few weeks it dwindled down to a quarter ration. The men made fires of coal on the floor of the prison. When sweet potatoes could be purchased from the poor white population in the vicinity, they would slice them thin and brown them very dark. This made an acceptable substitute for coffee. Water could be had by filling the canteens in an outside well. A guard would take two or three prisoners at the time. Latrines were dug in a corner of the warehouse, and with 700 prisoners confined to a small area, the stench quickly became imposing.

The four brothers stopped talking about the battle – things were bad enough in the cotton shed already. The day after their arrival there had been talk about the men they had not seen since April 6th, and names were continuously brought up as casualties. One of the Norwegians, Charles Larson, was definitely dead. Other names were added to the list – Israel Fuller, Thomas Wilson, William Pauley, Reuben King, John Moran, Thomas Henderson............ and of course, 2nd Lieutenant George W. Moir. Olaus stopped listening. The sights and sounds from

A tobacco warehouse used as a military prison, similar to the one where Olaus Hansen was detained. Wikipedia.org.

the battlefield were still imprinted on his mind. He did not have to dwell on the horrors any further.

On April 20th the temperature dropped and it stayed cold and rainy for about a week. Everybody slept on the dirt floor with no cover for protection against the low temperatures at night. Some of the prisoners had found a pine plank to lie on, but Olaus had a hard time understanding how that would create much improvement in the level of comfort. One morning he woke up he was itching all over his body. He did not ponder very long what the reason might be – experience from Fort Donelson told him that he had been invaded by "the southern grayback" – the body louse. Some of the university recruits even knew its scientific name – Pediculus vestimenti. Olaus could see little difference in the condition by knowing the name of its cause. He was still itching, all the same. In the crowded quarters infestations of lice became a major nuisance, and all the prisoners could be seen "skirmishing" – sitting cross legged on the floor removing lice from their clothing. This became one of the most time consuming pastimes during the imprisonment. Olaus heard that up to fifty of the persistent pests could be removed from a jacket in one single sitting.

Skirmishing, however, could not compare to soaking the clothes in boiling water, the possibility of which was far removed from the situation they were in. When the weather was warm they were allowed to swim in the Alabama River, and a thorough body wash provided temporary relief from the stinging parasites. Olaus found that he would rather stay inside and skirmish – a 200 man guard took the enjoyment out of the swim, since some of them were pointing their guns at him. He was surprised by the primitive weaponry brandished by the guards. Most of them were armed with nothing but pikes – long spears trailing back in history to medieval times - but lethal enough, if used with determination.....

During the first few days there was a steady stream of visitors bringing in pamphlets and magazines like Harper's Weekly, Eclectic Magazine, Atlantic Magazine and The Knickerbocker. Olaus was a bit surprised that they were allowed to read these Yankee publications, but the line was drawn at newspapers. They were regarded as contraband and kept strictly out of the prison, although the men managed to smuggle them in to keep track of the development of the war. When they were not reading the men kept busy playing ball and cricket, running, jumping and pitching quoits. They tried to make some money to buy extra food by obtaining sweet briar roots, making them into pipes and selling them. During an attempt to dig a well within the confines of the prison they came upon a heavy layer of clay just a few inches below the surface of the floor. This became raw material for pipes, rings, mugs etc. providing the prisoners with some extra "shinplasters" - low currency money – helping them to survive in spite of the sub-sufficient rations.

The crowded, unsanitary quarters inevitably led to outbreaks of disease. The first death occurred already on April 30th, when Julius Ward of Co. H died in the hospital from typhoid fever. He was the first of 198 soldiers to die in the cotton shed at Montgomery. Nobody wanted to go to hospital unless it was absolutely necessary, as the treatment there was even worse than in prison. The food consisted of nothing but coarse corn bread and water.

On the evening of May 1st, young Henry Steen came running across the floor from the big double doors straight towards his brother. John was chatting in his native tongue with the Hansen brothers, as they usually did to be able to speak freely in front of the guards. Henry's face had the color of white ashes. He stopped in front of them, not uttering a word. John looked at him.
"Hva er det, Henry?" (What's the matter Henry?) John said.
"Si noe da, Henry. Hva er iveien?" (Say something, Henry! What's up?)
"Løytnant Bliss er død!" (Lieutenant Bliss is dead!) Henry blurted out. "Skutt! Myrdet med kaldt blod!" (Shot! Murdered in cold blood!)
Olaus got a sinking feeling in his stomach. Murdered?
"Some guard just shot him! – straight through the heart, for nothing! Just for getting his milk!" Henry was almost crying.
"Slow down, Henry!" John put his hand on his shoulder. "Slow down! Pull yourself together - tell me what happened!"

Henry related the story the way he had heard it, put together in bits and pieces from other prisoners. Apparently Lieut. William S. Bliss from the 2nd Michigan Battery together with Lieut. Winslow of the 58th Illinois had gone to the well under guard about 5 pm. Since they had some money they used to buy milk and cakes in a house about ten yards away from the well. Bliss walked over to the back window of the house to pick up his milk, but was ordered away by the guard. Replying that he was just going to get his milk, he handed over a shinplaster to the woman in the window. The guard, standing about six yards away repeated the order, to which Bliss replied "in a minute" while he received his change. Instantly the guard leveled his gun at Bliss, who exclaimed "Good God, you will not shoot me, will you?" Calmly stating that he had to do his duty, the guard shot Bliss through the heart at almost point blank range. The lieutenant died instantly, dropping to the ground without a sound.

Henry Steen. Vesterheim Norwegian-American Museum, Decorah, Iowa.

News about the cold blooded murder ran like wildfire through the cotton shed. Olaus could hear oaths of vengeance being sworn all around him.

"Remember the murder of Bliss!"

Prisoners exclaimed this would be their war cry.

"Remember the murder of Bliss!!"

The shed was humming with excitement, and instant vengeance prevented only because nobody was armed. The Rebels could feel the suppressed tension in the crowd, and the same night they ordered two pieces of artillery hauled to the site. They were aimed at the doors to make sure nobody instigated a full blown riot.

Olaus was furious. He had held no premonition as to how he would react to such news, but he was raging inside. The war was getting to him. Battle after battle, gruesome sights of dead and dying soldiers - friends wasting away in beds or sprawled out in the mud on the battlefield, guts protruding through blood drenched uniforms, blood and brains splattered all over the ground, stench from charred and bloated bodies - death wherever he turned his face. Death.

In the Alabama cotton shed Olaus discovered a new side of himself – war became personal. He wanted to kill that Sesech – kill all Sesech. He wanted to get that guard and execute him with his own hands – destroy everything and everybody creating the hell he was living in. His mind had turned to accepting the horrors of war – to become a part of it - the only way he could survive while preserving his sanity. He had taken his first step on the road to become a professional soldier - and he would suffer the consequences.

Bliss war buried at 9 am on Saturday, May 3rd. He was identified – as were all the prisoners - on the list among the funerals of slaves in the Montgomery Advertiser: "Died, a Yankee prisoner." In the shed Olaus noticed the soldiers keeping diaries writing feverishly. Bliss' murder would not be forgotten. Disease continued to ravage the ranks. Hospital space and medical supplies were entirely inadequate. Dr. W.A. Morse, lieutenant in the 12th Iowa, was treating diarrhea, malaria and less severe diseases. He always had at least 150 cases and it was not unusual to be completely without medicines for several days. Prisoners continued to die at an alarming rate.

On May 5th Olaus heard rumors of a possible parole. After three weeks in the cotton shed on half to one quarter rations, the prisoners became over exited by the news. Just three days later it became apparent that a lack of railroad cars would prevent such a move. All cars were busy transporting either cotton or Rebel soldiers. After the first rumors of an exchange, it was like time slowed down. The days became an extremely long wait for news about the release. There were also rumors about a Federal campaign against Corinth, but the conflicting stories made it hard to get a good picture of the events taking place. On May 16th a catalyst for their release came from an unexpected angle. The citizens of Montgomery held a meeting and made a statement to the effect that they simply could not keep the prisoners any longer – there was such scarcity of food in the city, they needed it themselves.

On Monday, May 19th the prison camp was buzzing. Henry Steen came over to his three comrades sitting on the ground leaning up against the wall.
"Have you heard about the petition?" he asked.
They shook their heads.
"There's a petition going around to be signed, asking the Rebels for a parole. Would you sign it?"

"Hell, no!" Olaus did not even look up. "No way! I'm not disgracing myself by asking those Sesech murderers for anything!"

Hans and John shook their heads again, agreeing.

"The 12th Iowa is in unison" Henry said. "The petition has been signed by almost all the other privates, but everybody in the 12th is refusing".

"Good!" Olaus nodded. "Good! Excellent!!"

The same night the steamers John Delett and Cherokee arrived with prisoners from Tuscaloosa. They were marched off the boats and confined to a machine shop in the city until the next morning.

Olaus woke up to a clear and cool day. The prisoners were always woken up to roll call while it was still dark, so if it was clear, they would watch the sun rise. This day the Rebel sergeants came in to take descriptive rolls of the privates. Every prisoner knew what that meant – the rolls would be compared to their military records for identification before release. Information about age, height, color of eyes, complexion and profession of each soldier was carefully collected, and they all had to give their name, rank, company and regiment. Olaus could feel the anticipation grow. Would they soon be able to get out of this place? Eighteen year old Elijah Overcoker of Co. F would not be joining the paroled prisoners. He died during the day in hospital.

On May 22nd the privates were called out to compare the descriptive rolls. Release was imminent. The paroling was a slow process, going letter by letter. During the stay in prison they had learned that less than 20% of the Confederate soldiers were literate, and they surprised the Rebel officers by showing their ability to write when signing the following statement:

Montgomery, Ala.
May 22nd, 1862.

"I pledge my most sacred word of honor that I will not, during the existing war, between the Confederate States and the United States of America, bear arms or aid or abet the enemy of said Confederate States, or their friends, either directly or indirectly in any form whatsoever, until regularly exchanged, or otherwise discharged"

The next day the provost marshal declared that the privates would be sent to Atlanta on Saturday the 24th and from there be transported to Knoxville. The non-commissioned officers were to be transferred to Macon, Georgia the following day. At roll call on Saturday morning it was cloudy. By 8 am rain was pouring down, lightning flashing and thunder rolling across the sky. Olaus hardly noticed the thunderclaps - today he was getting out! The day dragged and dragged, but who really cared about a few more hours when they were finally going to see the last of this louse infested camp of starvation? About 6 pm more than 500 privates were marched out of the cotton shed on their way to the railway depot of the West Point and Montgomery Railroad. An hour later they were speeding towards West Point, Georgia in freight cars.

The train arrived at West Point about 4 am next morning and stayed for 3 hours. The town was completely destitute of provisions of any kind. Passing through LaGrange the train made it to Atlanta by 3 pm the same afternoon. After a meal of half a ration of bread and meat the soldiers were on their way to Chattanooga by 7 pm. Olaus could not sleep. He listened to the clatter from the wheels against the tracks while staring out into the dark night. He noticed that all the wood bridges were guarded. About 6 am on May 26th the train finally rolled into Chattanooga. Again the soldiers got half a ration of food before they were marched to an old shed.

About 10 am on the morning of the 27th they found themselves on yet another train, this time on the Memphis and Charleston Railroad heading for Bridgeport, Alabama. Olaus noticed that many bridges had been burned and rebuilt, and all of them were guarded. During the run the train broke in two, and while it was being repaired the soldiers scattered all over the surrounding hills. After arriving in Bridgeport at 4 pm they stayed until the 28th. The men ceased the opportunity to swim in the river and feast on mulberries and parched corn.

On the morning of May 29th each name was called out as they boarded the steamer Paint Rock, which took them thirty miles down the Tennessee River to Bellefonte Landing. Here they were marched off the boat in a part of the country which was claimed to be foraged by both armies, but held by none of them. They proceeded to Bellefonte Station on the Memphis and Charleston railroad some five miles away. There was no food, and the men began to scour the countryside, some even setting out for the Union lines. They knew that the receiving General – Ormsby Mitchel – had refused to receive the last third of the parolees. They would be sent back to a stockade in Macon, Georgia extending their imprisonment with four months. Almost half of them would never return, but end up in the prison's burial trenches.

The parolees at Bellefonte now started to fear that they were stuck in No Man's Land, with nobody coming for them from behind their own lines. To everybody's immense relief a train from Huntsville, Alabama showed up on the morning of the 30th, carrying a detachment of the 10th Wisconsin Infantry. They set up a post and received the prisoners who boarded the train and arrived in Huntsville about 3 pm. The Hansen- and Steen brothers quietly shook hands, trying to suppress the feelings overwhelming them. They had made it. However – this was not the time for joyous celebration – Theodore was still in captivity.

On the morning of May 31st they boarded a train at Huntsville to be taken to Nashville, Tennessee. A message came through the train: *They had to disembark and march there.* Olaus looked at Hans.
"March there?? That is a hundred miles! Some of these men will not get there alive – they are starved and weak – there is no way they can take a hundred mile march!"
It seemed like the generals were going to finish the job the Rebels had not been able to do – to kill even more prisoners.

Rescue came in the form of Quartermaster Joseph Dorr of the 12th Iowa, who had showed real leadership before the surrender at Shiloh, and now stepped up to the plate again. He had some mules roaming the countryside caught and hitched them up to ten old Government wagons. Men who had experience with four- and six mule teams were selected as drivers. Soon the column was on its way convoyed by the 10th Ohio Infantry and a company of cavalry. They proceeded through Elkton, Elliston and Pulaski, and reached the banks of the Duck River at Columbia on June 3rd. Just after dark they boarded a train on the Louisville, Nashville and Great Southern Railroad arriving at Nashville by 11 pm. The next day they were quartered in an amphi theatre at the fairgrounds. There they disposed of their ragged clothes and spent a long time with water and soap in a small creek getting rid of dirt and graybacks. After drawing new clothes on June 10th they went into camp on the 11th which they named Camp Jackson. Guards were stationed around the perimeter to keep the parolees inside. Olaus could never understand why.

Even if they had suffered severely in prison, the men at Camp Jackson were more fortunate than prisoners captured later in the war. The mounting problem with imprisonment and exchange of tens of thousands of captives would create an almost insurmountable obstacle for both the North and the South. A parole system called the Dix-Hill Cartel was signed on July 22nd, 1862. It was created during a series of meetings at Haxall's Landing on the James River between generals John Adams Dix for the United States and Daniel Harvey Hill for the Confederacy. This would provide for a relatively smooth exchange of prisoners for some time, but it eventually broke down, making it hard to return prisoners from either side of the lines. The prisoners at Camp Jackson had been released by a unilateral act on the part of the Confederacy – even before the cartel was in effect - probably more rooted in the lack of being able to feed them rather than from a political or military evaluation.

After signing their written oath in Montgomery the prisoners took their parole seriously, and did not expect to do military service before duly exchanged. On June 26th there was a threatening rumor of an attack on Nashville, and they were asked if they would arm to defend the city, if need be. Olaus and Hans had not even contemplated service while on parole. The prisoners expected to be granted a furlough and go home before they were exchanged and put back into the unit. They refused. On the 28th the War Department issued General Order No. 72, stating that furloughs would not be issued to paroled prisoners. Instead they were to report at one of the three parole camps – Camp Parole in Annapolis, Camp Chase near Columbus, Ohio and Benton Barracks in St. Louis.

Subsequently, after breakfast on June 29th they were expelled from Camp Jackson and put on a train on the Louisville and Nashville Railroad bound for Louisville, Kentucky. Upon arrival the next night they were marched to the levee and taken on board the steamer Atlanta, arriving at Cairo, Illinois about 6 pm on July 2nd. The destination was some old, deserted, louse infested barracks in the hot, malarial Cairo swamps where they received idle threats from the post commander, General Stone, for not doing military service. Six days later they were put on board the steamer Southwestern and taken up the Mississippi River to St. Louis.

During the march to Benton Barracks they were under guard by the Dutch state militia, who thought they were guarding Rebel prisoners. Upon entering the fairground there was no way of restraining "the prisoners" any longer. With a yell the 12th Iowa stormed towards the best barracks to a long night with no taps. Colonel Benjamin Louis Eulalie de Bonneville of the regular army was in charge at Benton Barracks, and Captain Brown of the 23rd Missouri was in command of the guard. They ordered the parolees to do guard duty. Under the leadership of King and Zuver the 12th Iowa flatly refused - probably because the 8th Iowa men had stated that, as long as they had gone on duty, the 12th would not dare to refuse. Taunting Brown with his running record at Shiloh and daring him to shoot, they drove him and the guard off by stoning them with pieces of coal.

On July 26th Major McChennis from Iowa took over command at Benton Barracks. General Frank P. Blair made a speech to the parolees to try to ease the tempers. He was met by hooting. Together with the rest of the men the Hansen - and Steen brothers were waiting to get paid. On August 5th they finally received their $ 50.00 each, and started to take their leave, even if not granted. Olaus and Hans left for home - Ole's farm in Highland. In no time the 12th Iowa was reduced from 138 soldiers to 40. None of the men on "French leave" were ever reported as deserters or absent without leave by King or Zuver. Olaus' and Hans' military records showed them as being present.

The brothers had not seen Ole for nine months. Staying at the farm was like coming to a different world – the war was certainly on people's minds and lips, but Iowa had not been subjected to any Confederate campaigning. They were far removed from death and destruction. Ole was anxious to hear about the war first hand, and he quickly realized that the glorious war they read about in the papers and the one his brothers fought on the battlefield were vastly different. Olaus could hardly believe that it was just thirteen months since he left the quiet and peaceful community of Nannestad. It felt like a lifetime ago. There were some Norwegian immigrants who felt that they should probably never have left at all. An anonymous letter appeared in the Norwegian newspaper Morgenposten (The Morning Mail) in Christiania just a couple of months later, penned by a Norwegian in Dodge County, Minnesota. It told a story about the carrot and the stick used to make the immigrants enlist for war – a bonus of $ 225.00 to enlist, or to be sure to be back at the next levy if they did not do it this time. They were forbidden to leave the country without special permission, and they would not be granted a passport. Squashed between hostile Sioux Indians and Federal commissioners, they felt like prisoners of war in the free country they had come to live in.

During the long, mild and beautiful fall in Winneshiek Olaus and Hans spent quiet and rejuvenating nights in Ole's home, smoking and talking about the past and the future. Maren kept them with food and drinks they had only been able to fantasize about in the service. They helped Ole with the harvest like the previous year. There was never time to sit idle on a farm, and it felt good to think about and do something productive and work on the land instead of dealing with blood and death. The summer of 1862 had been long and warm, and the crops were good. On October 6th Theodore Steen was paroled at Aikens Landing on the James River, twelve miles from Richmond, Virginia. He was ill after his imprisonment in the South. In November and December he was on the sick list at Benton Barracks before he was sent to Decorah in early January.

Paroled prisoners from the 12th Iowa Volunteer Infantry Regiment at Benton Barracks. From Clark and Bowen: University Recruits.

On April 21st the previous spring the soldiers in the Iowa "Hornets' Nest Brigade" who had escaped capture by being sick or otherwise detached, were formed into one brigade – The Union Brigade. This unit was kept together until the different regiments could be reorganized upon the exchange of the prisoners. After taking part in the battle of Corinth they were sent to Davenport, Iowa on December 17th to await reorganization. Almost all of the parolees were on French leave when they were exchanged in December of 1862. General Curtis issued an order stating that all soldiers had to be back at Benton Barracks by January 1st, 1863. They would have free transportation and no charges would be leveled against them.

The exchanged prisoners rushed to St. Louis to be present at the muster on December 31st. Some were still absent, and on January 2nd Capt. John Stibbs issued an order declaring that everybody who did not return immediately would be regarded as deserters. Charles Fenerabend and Jasper Wagner had seen their share of bloodshed. They did not return.

Instead of doing reorganization the exchanged prisoners were immediately sent to Rolla, Missouri to protect the city against a raid by Confederate Brigadier General John S. Marmaduke, who tried to destroy the Federal supply depot at Springfield and disrupt the supply line which connected Springfield with Rolla and St. Louis. The Hansen brothers did not mind the trip – the rush to Rolla got them quickly back into action. On January 26th the Steen brothers told Olaus they were leaving on detached service. They were detailed to escort prisoners to Columbus, Ohio and left the next day. On March 26th the men lined up to meet someone they had been waiting for, for a long time – the paymaster. The previous payment from the Federal Government to the Iowa soldiers had been made in St. Louis more than a year ago. Olaus walked away patting his pocket. A year's pay! Two days later he was aboard a steamer on his way to St. Louis. The disbanded Union Brigade was waiting - the old regiments were to be restored. On March 31st – after almost a full year's separation – the two parts of the 12th Iowa were finally reunited.

THE VICKSBURG CAMPAIGN

" – What a lot of land these fellows hold, of which Vicksburg is the key. The war can never be brought to a close unless that key is in our pocket.......we can take all the northern ports of the Confederacy, and they can defy us from Vicksburg." This was Abraham Lincoln's opinion of the importance of Vicksburg. The Mississippi River was the main artery for domestic and international commerce. Whoever controlled the river controlled the access to the interior of the American continent and the batteries at Vicksburg were the deciding factor as to who could enter and leave. European powers were sitting on the fence watching the outcome of the American Civil War. England, dependent on resources from the South, could intervene on the part of the Confederacy and the mighty British Navy could dismantle the Union war machine. A victory for the Union at Vicksburg would split the Confederacy in two and decide the outcome of the war in favor of the North. If the Confederacy lost, the chance of recognition as an independent country by European powers was lost. President Abraham Lincoln knew this, and so did Major General Ulysses S. Grant – and he set out to win the most important battle of the Civil War.

The battle started literally in the trenches. Grant devised different schemes to circumvent Vicksburg with material and supplies, and they were resting on the ability to dig canals between the Mississippi and the surrounding bayous to bring ships through. One of the canals was "Pride's Ditch" in Duckport, Louisiana, nine miles above Vicksburg. Olaus and Hans were soon to be acquainted with that particular canal. About 1 pm on April 9th they boarded the steamer Planet at St. Louis, bound for Duckport. The steamer was loaded with supplies for the army near Vicksburg, among them a large number of coffins. While the new recruits looked at the coffins with decidedly mixed feelings, Olaus and Hans found them to be excellent sleeping quarters. During a stop in Memphis, Tennessee, the Hansen brothers disembarked and managed to be late for the steamer's departure. They were left behind. On the roll call April 15th at Duckport they were reported as AWOL – absent without leave. Upon arriving at their destination they were set to

Major General William Tecumseh Sherman. Wikipedia.org.

work on the canal together with 3 500 soldiers detached for this duty. The 12th Iowa was assigned to the 3rd Brigade of the 3rd Division of the 15th Army Corps under Major General William Tecumseh Sherman. The 3rd Brigade was made up of the 8th, 12th and 35th Iowa Infantry Regiments under Brigadier General Charles L. Matthies, and Colonel Joseph Woods was in charge of the 12th. The regiment camped in a cornfield behind the levee where the ground was at least six feet lower than the surface of the Mississippi. There was standing water between the corn rows and the only way to keep the tents semi-dry was to dig holes in the ground to drain the water away, and use the dirt from the holes to level up the tents.

"Pride's Ditch" – named for the colonel in charge of the project, George D. Pride - was an attempt to connect Duckport Landing with the Walnut Bayou by dredging a three mile canal through the cottonwood swamp to a place near Dr. David H Dancy's Crescent Plantation. This would enable travel to Carthage by flatboat and supply the army as it moved south through Louisiana. At noon on April 13th the levee was cut and four steam dredges started to deepen the channel. The work went rapidly ahead, creating a canal forty feet wide and seven feet deep. At the same time fatigue parties were removing trees and stumps from the Walnut Bayou. It was backbreaking work.

"How did we get into this?"
Olaus dragged and pushed a heavy log up on the bank, standing in muddy, waist deep water, sweat pouring off his face and mosquitos swarming all around him.
It was like working in a Norwegian sauna.
"By enlisting in the army" Hans replied from the opposite end of the log.
"I think I'd rather be shot at." With a groan Olaus dropped the end of the log. Hans lit his pipe and took a few, long puffs before he answered. His hazel brown eyes rested on the face of his little brother.
"There will be plenty of opportunity for that. We are going to Vicksburg. No matter how this canal business works out – we'll be going in there for an assault. There is no way we are going to win this war by pussyfooting around those batteries on flatboats. That city needs to be taken, and held."
Hans knocked his pipe against the log to clean it out. He looked at Olaus.
"Well – until then – here's the next log!"

During the night of April 16th four transports and seven gunboats managed to slip past the batteries at Vicksburg. One of the transports was sunk, but the successful attempt showed that supplies could indeed be sent through. Six days later another seven transports passed Vicksburg, and Grant decided to link up with General John McClernand, already camped below the city. The 15th Corps was detailed to make a wagon road along the banks of the canal across to Walnut Bayou. Olaus and Hans found themselves yet again with shovels in their hands in a muddy Louisiana swamp while the rest of the army marched overland towards Vicksburg. On April 30th Grant crossed the Mississippi River below Grand Gulf and ordered Sherman to follow. Sherman was gravely concerned about Grant's plan of attack against Vicksburg, and said as much to one of his division commanders. But as usual he was loyal to his commander's dispositions and promptly got underway.

The 3rd Division under Brigadier General James Tuttle – promoted after Shiloh - left Duckport in light marching order with no knapsacks at 3pm on Saturday, May 2nd. One of the five comrades was not coming. Theodore Steen was ill again, and was left in Duckport. John had a bright new stripe on his arm. He had been promoted to corporal on April 23rd. As Olaus walked along the canal he counted twenty barges stuck in the shallow water, together with two dredges. The only vessel to ever get through to Walnut Bayou was the tug Victor, eventually reaching Carthage. The weather was beautiful, the roads were good and Olaus felt relieved walking away from the intensive labor on the canal. Along the way he saw several well maintained plantations with corn growing about knee high. It puzzled him to see that the white population had abandoned the plantations, but the black servants were still there caring for the property. About 10 am on Thursday, May 7th, after almost a week's march, they reached Hard Times Landing opposite Grand Gulf and were immediately carried over on the steamer Chessman.

"What happened to the boat?" Olaus pointed to the bullet riddled smokestacks and wood. Without taking his eyes of what he was doing, one of the crew answered from the corner of his mouth – opposite of where his cigar was hanging:
"We ran the batteries at Vicksburg."
"Must have been a terrific fire" Olaus put his fingers in some of the holes.
"Didn't think we were gonna make it," the sailor replied. "One of us didn't."

When they disembarked at Grand Gulf, five days' ration of coffee and crackers were issued to be kept in the haversacks. With the crackers came the order that this was the entire supply, and they would be expected to live off the land to provide the additional supplies needed. At 10 am on May 8th the division moved out towards the east to join up with the rest of the army already at the rear of Vicksburg. On May 10th they made a halt at Rocky Springs to rest and wait for the different commands of the army to get into their assigned positions. No provisions of any kind could be found in the countryside. By the time they reached Rocky Springs the contents of the haversacks were already exhausted and they ate parched corn from the mules' rations for dinner.

During the night a herd of beef cattle was found and brought in on the hoof, one animal assigned to each company. After killing and dressing the animal each man got his share and broiled it over the fire on his ramrod or fried it in the half-canteen. This became supper and the next day's breakfast and dinner. Every night the men would go out and forage for cattle, sheep and hogs and repeat the procedure from the previous day. During long, hot marches the meat did not keep very well in the haversacks, and dinner would often consist of stale meat.

On Monday, May 11th the march resumed towards Edward Station, midway between Jackson and Vicksburg, and that night they bivouacked at Auburn. The next day General James McPherson's 17th Corps at the right of the marching army had an engagement with the enemy at Fourteen Mile Creek, driving the opposing force ahead of them and capturing several prisoners. From the prisoners they learned that Rebel forces were concentrating around Jackson and General Joseph E. Johnston was expected to come there and take command. Grant immediately decided to turn the army towards Jackson and gave the three corps commanders orders to converge on the city, Sherman with the 15th Corps by way of Mississippi Springs and from there directly to the destination.

On the 13th about 4 pm it started to rain. Upon reaching Raymond at 9 pm they encountered a Rebel force the Federal advance guard could not drive away. Advancing in line of battle the corps drove the enemy all the way through Mississippi Springs and went into bivouac on the east side of town.

Reveille sounded at 3 am next morning and Olaus was on his feet in a flash. He was soaking wet. It had not stopped raining all night, and it was still pouring down, accompanied by thunder and lightning. The foot deep dust on the roads had turned into a foot of mud, and where there was no mud – a foot of water. The men had a quick breakfast – beef cooked four to five hours earlier. Before 6 am they were on the road to Jackson. The two corps were continuously encountering Rebel resistance from about two miles outside the city, but drove the enemy advance guard in front of them. Olaus could hear cannon fire from McPherson's front, but the thunderclaps made it difficult to determine the intensity of the fight.

Sherman moved forward prepared to give battle with Tuttle's division directly in front of the Confederate works, the Iowa Brigade positioned on the right. Tuttle's artillery of twelve guns opened fire. The division had reached the defense perimeter about the same time as McPherson, and Company B and C of the 12th Iowa were sent forward across a low meadow as skirmishers. Olaus watched and waited as the two companies drove the Rebels ahead of them all the way inside their works. As he was staring trough the driving rain he discovered two riders passing just behind him, and recognized them instantly. It was Grant and Sherman, soaking wet but deeply involved in a conversation. Suddenly Olaus spotted Brigadier General Joseph "The Wolf" Mower of the neighboring Eagle Brigade riding towards the Confederate works. He wheeled around and came trotting back. Olaus could not hear a word of what he was yelling, but within minutes an order came for Tuttle's division to attack.

As the drenched Iowans stormed forward a yell rose from the line which could have scared the ghosts of the Confederacy. Olaus could hear somebody scream almost in his ear – and astonished he realized that it was himself. The Rebels took one look at the shouting, blue line rolling towards them and before it was even within musket range they fired a few shots from a field battery and took off across Pearl River, closely pursued by the Iowa skirmishers. The 12th jumped over the works and rushed through the Rebel camp, Olaus grabbing some ready cooked dinner on the run. While the Federal soldiers took over the city dispositions were made to protect themselves against attacks, then fires were lit and clothes hung to dry. Close to the camp a large number of cotton bales were discovered and brought back. They were opened and the cotton distributed, and for the first time in a long, long time Olaus was sleeping in a soft bed.

On Friday, May 15th Sherman's corps was ordered to hold Jackson and await orders. The United States flag was floating over the capitol. Company C, 12th Iowa was on picket duty. The 3rd Brigade with the rest of the 12th was marched four miles out on the Memphis railroad to destroy the tracks from there all the way in to Jackson. Even if they quickly developed an effective technique it was still very heavy work. The whole regiment lined up along the track and ripped up a section. The ties were piled up and set ablaze. The rails were laid across the ties and when the steel was red hot it was twisted into an angle from where it would have to be re-milled.

The following day the Eagle Brigade was provost guard in the city and responsible for destroying large amounts of commissary stores and the public buildings. Olaus heard a story about the Confederate House, a hotel where some prisoners from Shiloh had visited passing through Jackson en route to their place of detention the previous spring. They had tried to pay for their food in greenbacks, and the proprietor had refused to take their money, insulting them in the process. These soldiers happened to be a part of the force now destroying the public buildings, and their revenge was quickly executed when they unceremoniously torched the hotel. The marauding Federals brought in a lot of Confederate money found in town, but as they were worthless the men used the five hundred and thousand dollar bills to light their pipes and cigars. The men also enjoyed an abundance of cornmeal, peanuts, tobacco and whiskey although some of the soldiers claimed that the whiskey was of very bad quality......

At 1 pm Sherman received a message about a battle in progress at Champion Hill and with his usual effectiveness had the corps on the road within half an hour. After a forced ten mile march to Clinton the men were issued two hardtacks, the first ones Olaus had seen since they left Rocky Springs. The crackers were in high demand among the soldiers and priced at one dollar each. Very few were willing to sell. After a cup of coffee the march was resumed towards Bolton, another ten miles down the road. The corps made its way through the dark night delayed by ammunition trains, artillery and broken bridges. At every halt soldiers would drop to the ground and instantly fall asleep. At 2 am on May 17th, after a thirteen hour

Sherman's pontoon bridge at Bridgeport May 18th, 1863. Miller:The Photographic History of the Civil War.

march, they reached Bolton only to find that the battle had been fought and won by the 13th and 17th Corps.

The enemy had retreated to Black River, and after resting until daylight on the 17th the corps set out in a flanking movement northwest towards Bridgeport. Outside Bolton they passed the plantation of Jefferson Davis, President of the Confederate States of America. The black servants did not seem to mind when some of the soldiers swung by and snatched the cattle herd. The day was exceedingly hot, and water scarce. A lot of the soldiers fell out of line from pure exhaustion, and straggled into camp at Bridgeport by dark, after a march of twenty miles. At sunrise on May 18th the corps continued across the Big Black River on a pontoon bridge constructed during the night. Grant was riding with Sherman and as they approached Vicksburg he ordered Sherman to proceed to the right on Graveyard Road which brought them almost to the Mississippi River south of Haines' Bluff, effectively cutting Vicksburg off from the north. As they approached their destination Olaus could hear musket fire. The skirmishers had made contact with the Rebel defenders. Suddenly artillery mixed in with the musketry – Major General Frank P. Blair Jr.'s batteries were shelling the Rebels as the Federal columns filed into position. By 4 pm the 15th Corps was in line of battle along

Chickasaw Bayou. Miller: The Photographic History of the Civil War.

Graveyard Road just out of range from the heavy Rebel guns. At the same time the 13th and the 17th Corps were closing in from the east.

Early next morning Olaus was on the road again when at 9:30 he heard artillery fire from the front. It was Blair's sixteen guns pounding away at the triangular shaped log- and earthwork called Stockade Redan. Blair wanted to break down the walls to prepare for an infantry attack at 2 pm. The 3rd Brigade with the 12th Iowa had been ordered out on a reconnaissance mission to Chickasaw Bayou to open communication with the Yazoo River. During the night engineers had built a bridge across, and on the 19th wagon trains were moving up with supplies to the half-starved army. Food had become an extremely valuable commodity. Just the day before a colonel of the 20th Ohio had offered to buy a piece of corn bread from a soldier for five dollars - more than a third of a month's pay. The soldier refused to sell.

The 12th was back about noon, and received order for an attack at 2 pm. The 3rd Brigade was camped at the rear of the corps, and Tuttle's division was ordered to stay in reserve during the engagement. At 2 pm the artillery fired ceased, to be followed by three salvos – the signal for the infantry attack. Company C of the 12th

Iowa was detached as ammunition carriers, and during the afternoon Norton T. Smith – one of the carriers – was killed by Rebel fire. Olaus was listening to the intense musket fire. He had seen Stockade Redan and was happy the 12th Iowa was not taking part in the assault along Graveyard Road Ridge. It looked like a suicide mission. The sound of musketry went from a crescendo to slowly petering out - and so did the momentum of the assault. Soldiers in the attack force who had made it all the way up to the stockade were stuck lying in ditches, barely out of sight from Confederate snipers. They had to wait to withdraw until after dark.

Olaus did not know the number of casualties, but rumors said it was large. Hundreds. Early in the morning of May 20th the regiment moved closer to the front into some hastily prepared entrenchments from the previous day, covered behind the brow of a hill. On the 20th and 21st the weather was hot and dry and dust was filling the air until a thunderstorm during the afternoon of the 21st laid the dust and cooled the air. Grant had not given up the thought of taking Vicksburg by assault. Sherman and Grant was in agreement that the key to the failed assault lay in the difficult terrain and lack of preparation and equipment like ladders to scale the stockade.

The supply trains had finally begun to run smoothly, after a slow start on the 19th. On May 21st the Hansen- and Steen brothers were in camp talking and smoking their pipes when they suddenly heard loud chanting: "Hardtack! Hardtack! Hardtack!" Grant was riding along his lines and he had been spotted by one of the soldiers who commented loud enough for him to hear: "Hardtack!" Soon all the soldiers in the vicinity were yelling in unison: "Hardtack! Hardtack! Hardtack!" That night the menu was hardtack, beans and coffee.

Grant had decided on a new assault on the morning of May 22nd. Artillery was bombarding the city all night – 220 guns including Rear Admiral David D. Porter's naval guns on the river. After a lull during the darkest part of the night the shelling started again at 6 am and continued for four hours. The infantry was ready to attack on a three mile front along the perimeter of Vicksburg. The 2nd and 3rd Brigade of Tuttle's Division was again in reserve, massed in a ravine to the east of Graveyard Road. The Confederate artillery had come back to life, after being suppressed by Federal snipers during the last two days. As the infantry moved to attack loads of canister were shrieking overhead.

Messages from the front told Olaus that this assault did not progress any better than the one on the 19th. Grenades were being rolled down the slopes at the advancing Federals compounding the casualties caused by musket fire, and killed and wounded along Graveyard Road slowed the advance to a halt. Men were pinned down throughout the day in scorching sun and many felt victims to sun stroke and heat exhaustion.

Grant ordered Sherman to renew the attack at 3pm using the reserve brigades. Sherman picked the 2nd Brigade commanded by "Wolf" Mower – promoted to brigadier general two days before - to lead the advance. The brigades emerged from their reserve location and deployed on a sheltered part of Graveyard Road. Mower moved to the front closely followed by Colonel Woods' 3rd Brigade. The 12th Iowa was at the head of the brigade, Company C in the vanguard. Mower would attack the works directly in their front while Colonel Woods' brigade with the 12th deployed to the left and followed up the attack as they approached the Stockade Redan.

At exactly 3 pm the brigades charged up the road, bayonets fixed. As the head of Mowers brigade raced into view of the Rebel defenders they were met by volleys of lead and steel tearing into the first regiment. The roaring of cannons and rattling of small arms fire was unequal to anything Olaus had ever heard. Almost 130 men fell instant casualties to the fire. When he saw the breastwork Olaus knew they would never reach it. The top of the stockade was covered in massive clouds of gun smoke, penetrated by flashes of fire from the Rebels' muskets. He jumped over corpses at a dead run – Graveyard Road was strewn with casualties from different regiments having been pinned down in the same spot at the 10 o'clock assault. He had a familiar reaction to the gruesome display – mangled and bloody bodies stretched out in impossible positions, some of them looking like they were simply asleep, others with expressions on their faces telling him they died writhing in agony. The hair at the back of his neck bristled, but he ignored the feeling, screaming at the top of his lungs.

He saw Mower and a part of the 11th Missouri surge forward all the way to the breastwork and plant a flag. The 12th Iowa veered left and moved on the double quick to about four hundred yards from the breastwork. They came to a sudden halt running into clusters of troops from other regiments blocking the advance. Olaus spotted a staff officer rushing to the front making signs to the regiments of Mower's brigade to abort the attack. They were heading directly into a Rebel meat grinder, ready to slaughter anything moving towards the stockade. Not able to get any further the 12th Iowa deployed to the west of Graveyard Road with its left

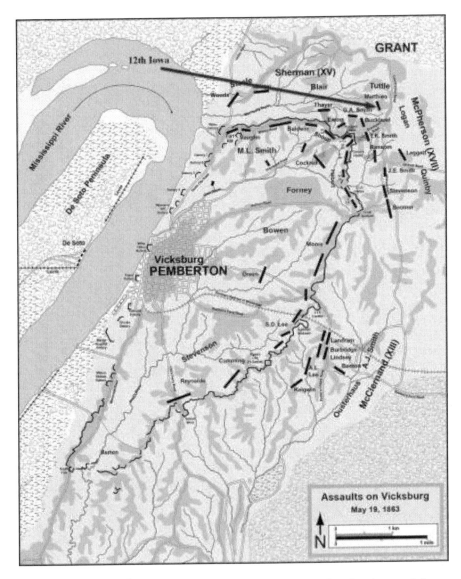

Vicksburg May 19th, 1863. The map shows the batteries, fortifications and the position of the 12th Iowa. Map by Hal Jespersen www.posix.com/CV.

resting on the road, in support of the 2nd Iowa Battery. From there they covered the other units as they retreated from the firing line. The fire died down on the parapet as the Federal detachments withdrew out of sight of the Rebels. Olaus knew there were men out there injured and in need of help, pinned down along the road and in ditches all the way over by the stockade. They would suffer intensely for hours from painful injuries, a scorching sun and lack of water – and there was no way to help them before darkness fell.

The assaults on the 22nd had convinced Grant and Sherman that Vicksburg could not be taken by massed infantry attacks. Although it was not in his original plan, Grant settled down for a siege. All communication to the city was cut off. It would only be a matter of time before the Rebels had to surrender, unless a Confederate army came to their rescue.

As the hostilities ceased on May 22nd the 12th Iowa went into bivouac in their position by the 2nd Iowa Battery. The regiment entrenched its bivouac for an extended stay. The hillside was leveled for sleeping quarters and in some cane brakes nearby canes were gathered for beds. It was exceedingly hot, and even if the beds were comfortable the soldiers were inundated with all kinds of insects and swarms of flies. Every day they were detailed for picket duty, which was very hazardous. Three soldiers from company C were injured in early June – the most severely wounded was Edward H. Adams, who lost his leg to a cannon shot. If they were not on picket duty the men were detailed to fatigue parties digging trenches and approaches, closer and closer to the Confederate works. Rebel sharpshooters tried to pick off Union soldiers sticking their heads above the trenches or moving about outside. Olaus found out first hand when he went for water, which was obtained from a spring between the lines at the left front of the regiment. He was in plain view and within shooting range of the Confederate sharp shooters as he approached the spring, and bullets were whizzing around him. To be able to get water during the day the soldiers had to run for their lives, and subsequently water was a valuable commodity in camp - the going price was 25 cents a canteen.

On May 24th the Rebels sent over a flag of truce to have the firing stopped for a few hours to bury the dead. The corpses of Federal soldiers were so near their breastworks they could not stand the stench any longer. The Union army sent details to gather the fallen solders along Graveyard Road, but they had been lying in the sun for so long they could not be moved. Two feet of dirt on top of the bodies was the best that could be done. After forty eight hours there were injured soldiers still alive. Two privates were brought in, one with an arm shot off, the

Union entrenchments at Vicksburg during the siege of 1863. Miller:
The Photographic History of the Civil War.

other one missing a leg. They had survived by taking food and water from their dead comrades. Both of them died a few days later. Olaus finally got information about the number of casualties. Four thousand. Four thousand in two days' assaults.

The 12th Iowa settled down to the siege. Cannons and mortars were thundering almost around the clock, showering the city with shots and exploding shells. During the siege Union gunboats lobbed more than 22 000 shells into Vicksburg, and Union artillery even more. The entire perimeter was crowded with rifle pits where Union sharpshooters took pot shots at Rebels moving along the top of the parapets. Olaus could easily fire fifty shots in just a few hours, and his skills steadily improved. He did not count any kills for several days, but as he learned the behavioral patterns of the defenders, and when and where they usually showed themselves, his kill rate improved. Sometimes he could not tell if his target was hit or just jumped out of sight, but a stretcher being rushed to the spot was always a sure sign of a bullseye. By the end of the siege Olaus was certain he had fired at least a thousand rounds from his rifle pit.

Grant realized that he did not have enough manpower to completely encircle the twelve mile perimeter of Vicksburg, even with an army which by now had grown to 50 000 men. The commander of the Vicksburg defenses, John C. Pemberton, still had a scant possibility of escaping along unguarded roads. To tighten the noose around the city Grant had General Francis J. Herron's division of 5 000 men transferred from the Department of the Missouri on June 11th to extend the Union's extreme left flank south of the city.

As expected the Confederates under General Joseph E. Johnston tried to organize an army to relieve Vicksburg. On the same day as Herron arrived a part of Johnston's force made a demonstration at Haines' Bluff. That night the 3rd Brigade was ordered out along Graveyard Road towards Haines' Bluff to resist any attack from the Rebels. The brigade stood at arms in the road all through the night, with no sign of the enemy. In the darkness Henry Steen leaned over towards Olaus and said in a low voice:
"Martin is at Vicksburg!"
"Your brother?"
"Yes! – he's here!"
"How do you know?"
"Just got a message. He's in the 38th Iowa – they came in south of the city today – Herron's division."
"So now you are four brothers at Vicksburg!? Are you going to see him?"
"I hope so – haven't seen him since the furlough in Iowa last year. He enlisted in November when I was home."

Henry's hope of seeing Martin would not be fulfilled. Next morning the 3rd Brigade established bivouac by the road and was kept in readiness to march at a moment's notice. While doing heavy fatigue duty during the day they stayed in this camp until June 22nd, when they marched to Bear Creek near Black River to guard the rear of the siege operation. As usual disease was ravaging the ranks, and Theodore Steen was ill again. He had to be left in the camp at Walnut Hills.

At Bear Creek half the regiment at the time was either on patrol- or picket duty, guarding the roads from Black River Bridge to Brownsville Road. Even if it was heavy duty, Olaus thought it was far better than lying in a gopher hole outside Vicksburg with the prospect of getting a bullet through his head every time he ventured outside. John Steen had been appointed acting sergeant major. His task was to oversee the appearance and performance of the non-commissioned officers of the regiment. Henry had been detailed on detached service at Walnut Hills. On July 2nd, exactly two months after they left Duckport, all the knapsacks, tents and camp equipage they had left behind arrived at Bear Creek. The 12th Iowa spent time pitching the tents and making bunks in a pleasant grove nearby. After having slept on the damp ground they enjoyed the new sleeping quarters immensely – for two days. On July 4th a message came that Vicksburg had surrendered. An order was issued to march immediately to Black River for an attack on Joe Johnston's army. Henry Steen would not be coming. He was still on detached service. By 3 pm Tuttle's division was on the road, again leaving all the camp equipment behind together with the ones who were too sick to march. Fifty hours later they crossed Black River driving the enemy in front of them. After pushing on for another five miles the division deployed in line and the men stacked their guns. It was 9 pm on July 6th.

After another day's march they bivouacked in a cornfield near Bolton. During the night Olaus woke up, soaked through and through. A torrential rainstorm forced him to move from the bottom of the flooded cornrows to the top. Soon the whole field was flooded, and they all had to climb a fence and perch on a rail for the remainder of the night. On July 8th the 15th Corps arrived at Clinton. The men watched somewhat amused as the 9th Corps passed moving north, a corps consisting of soldiers from eastern regiments. Clearly they had not yet gotten used to western campaigning, as they - with exhausted looks on their faces – wore full uniforms and heavy knapsacks. From Bolton to Jackson the Iowans suffered exceedingly from lack of drinking water. Water could only be had from cisterns or water holes, both of which had been destroyed by Johnston's retreating army. The water holes had been contaminated by worn out mules being driven into them and shot. Still soldiers could be spotted in the holes, standing on top of the carcasses of mules while they dipped their canteens in the water.

During the march on the 9th skirmishing was constant, continuing until they bivouacked after midnight by the entrenchments outside Jackson. The 12th Iowa went into line with the regiment's right resting on the Jackson and Vicksburg Road and – it came to show – within reach of a big gun in the Rebel entrenchments. A squad was standing by one of the camp kettles watching their dinner being cooked while the gun lobbed shot after shot across the camp. Suddenly the gunner got a perfect range and landed a ball directly in the kettle. The soldiers scattered with lightning speed, happy that it was a solid shot, and not a grenade.

On July 12th Olaus was on the road again, marching all day guarding a forage train of fifty wagons. Three days later General Tuttle reported sick and Colonel Woods assumed command of the 3rd Division. At daybreak on the 17th Jackson was abandoned by the Rebels, and Union forces moved into the city. The 3rd Division camped inside the city limits and was assured that it would be allowed several days to rest. The Hansen – and Steen brothers went to work on their quarters with more thoroughness than usual. After all – they would be staying for a while. They looked forward to a few days leisure time when a rumor ran through camp. A few hours later it was more than a rumor. An order was issued to report to General Frederick Steele the next morning in light marching order with three days' ration in the haversacks. About 6 pm on July 18th they left together with the 8th Iowa, 114th Illinois, 72nd Ohio and Captain A.C. Waterhouse's 1st Illinois Light Artillery. The regiments were a selected force of 5 000 men on a mopping up operation towards Meridian. The detachment moved out across Pearl River and pushed on about three miles before they went into bivouac.

The heat on the morning of the 19th was oppressive. Many of the soldiers were suffering severely as they marched along the road towards Brandon. The 12th Iowa was in advance when they encountered a considerable force of Rebels about noon, covering the road with artillery. Olaus spotted the discharge from a battery – at least three guns, probably a mile way. It was easy to distinguish because of the massive clouds of smoke. The gunners had an almost perfect range. The shells came shrieking over the column - barely missing – killing orderly Sergeant Duncan riding at the rear. The detachment instantly deployed off the road into a cornfield, the 12th Iowa moving forward in line of battle to the right of the road through corn reaching above their heads.

As they came past the cornfield the advance slowed down – the field ahead was intersected by ditches from eight to ten feet deep with briars and bushes on either side. Olaus climbed and crawled in and out of the ditches, all the time making sure he did not get dirt stuck in the gun barrel. That could prove catastrophic – the gun would explode in his face upon discharge, killing him instead of the Rebels. The enemy kept up a constant fire and the Federals had lost artillery support. Waterhouse's guns could not be dragged through the field intersected by all the ditches and they could not reach the rebel position, while the Rebels accurately dropped shells on the Union battery. As the infantry emerged from the thickets onto an open field the artillery and Rebel camp was within musket shot. Olaus took his cap off and looked at Hans while wiping the sweat off his forehead with the back of his hand – a hand that was not shaking. He was on the advance, and he wanted to get where he was going.
"Here we go."
"Yep."
Almost like they were on the parade ground the Iowans advanced in line of battle across the field, bullets whizzing around their heads. The Rebels had already seen

enough. They scrambled to get away through the forest at the rear of the camp. The Iowans stormed into the camp and through the thick forest, but the enemy had already managed to escape, retreating through the town of Brandon.

During a torrential thunder shower the Federal detachment took possession of Brandon, going into bivouac at the center of town. The next day, moving back towards Jackson, they destroyed the railway along their march. Back at camp in Jackson they stayed until July 23rd, when the army moved back to its previous position on the west side of Black River. The 12th Iowa returned to the camp at Bear Creek. The men had named it Camp Sherman. Olaus thought it was quite fitting. Sherman had come through on this campaign – Olaus was quite aware that he had his detractors, and he had heard a lot of reasons why. He was nervous. Unruly - but loyal. Intense. And apparently intensely intelligent. From what he had seen of the general throughout the last few months – he liked him. There was something about him and Grant that appealed to the men. They were down to earth. Unassuming. Meat and potatoes. But they knew who they were and what they wanted - and they got it. Olaus had seen other generals. Pompous and self-important. Full of talk and no action. Men wanted generals to lead them - not just talk about how great leaders they were. Just do it. Grant and Sherman did.

The Hansen- and Steen boys enjoyed Camp Sherman. After leaving Duckport on May 2nd they had slept almost every night on damp or soaking wet ground. Three months of sleeping in their clothes not even unfastening the belt. When they dropped to the ground it was with the expectation of possibly hearing the long roll before morning, and often they were woken up by the order "Fall in quickly!" At Camp Sherman life was running at a different pace, and it was doing so with excess leisure time and an abundance of food. Milk, honey, coffee, peach sauce, pickles, cod fish, potatoes, bread, butter, hot biscuits – Olaus had seen nothing like it in fifteen months, when he was back at Pittsburg landing. The camp was kept clean – the streets were swept and the dirt hauled away every day. At Sunday morning inspections everybody turned out in full uniform, with guns polished and shoes blackened.

One afternoon Hans came in to the tent, smiling from ear to ear.
"Yes? What?" Olaus was waiting for the good news – whatever it might be.
"Furlough!" Hans replied.
"Furlough?!!" Four pairs of eyes were staring at him.
"Furlough!" Hans was waving a piece of paper in the air. Olaus snapped it out of his hand, examining it carefully.
"Furlough! 30 days - Hans Hanson – from August 11th, 1863."

"Are you coming?" Hans asked with an innocent expression on his face.

"I don't think so."

Now four pairs of eyes were staring at Olaus.

"You don't think so?"

"Nah. I like it here. It's a good camp."

Theodore Steen looked at him. "Are you serious? You're not going?"

"No." Olaus studied his hands. "I've been travelling enough for a while. I want to stay here and recover. Don't feel like jumping on a steamer for Davenport right now."

For some reason he could not really explain Olaus had taken to military life. He felt comfortable in camp. He felt up to the challenges. He liked the routine, the hard physical labor and the long marches. What he had found most interesting was – he did not mind danger. As a matter of fact, he found it exiting. It was real, here and now – do or die. He already knew he would never be satisfied behind a plow. That would be like dropping back into the trough he came from. No – prowling the roads and countryside with a musket under the thundering roar of cannons – that was to be his lot. He could just feel it – it was the right thing for him to do. It came to show that John and Henry Steen also remained in camp. John had been appointed clerk in the regimental quartermaster department – he would not be granted a furlough. Hans and Theodore left for Iowa on August 12th. Three days later Olaus returned to his quarters after lunch. Henry Steen was waiting for him.

"Henry." Olaus sat down on his bunk, pulling his boots off.

"Corporal." Henry replied.

"What?" Olaus stopped pulling at his boot.

Henry pushed an envelope across the table. It was addressed to him: Corporal Olans Hanson, 12th Iowa Vol. Infty. He tore it open. It had a pair of corporal's stripes in it, and a letter. "Olans Hanson – you are promoted to 8th corporal in the 12th Iowa Volunteer Infantry Regiment........."

He had to read in again. "Olans Hanson – you are promoted....." He was promoted! A corporal! A smile appeared on his face.

"Congratulations, Olaus!" Henry was all smiles, too.

"Thanks! What do you think this is all about?"

"This is all about you, Olaus. Somebody has been watching you since Donelson. That's what I've heard. You have no fear. No fear at all. In a war, that will get you promoted."

Olaus settled down to life in camp with his new distinctions. Details were few – mainly picket duty and scouts for prowling guerillas. Brick ovens were built for

baking bread, which was a vast improvement over leathery slap jacks and moldy hardtack. Hans and Theodore were back from furlough, and they all obtained commutation of rations for the time they spent in Rebel prison from Lieutenant David W. Reed. When Hans walked into the tent upon his return to camp he took one look at Olaus' stripes, and put his hand on his shoulder.
"Very good little brother! Very Good! Congratulations!"

On September 16th the regimental camp was moved to the Harris Plantation, but within two days somebody got cold feet about the scattering of forces, and the camp was moved back to Bear Creek. On the 18th – the day Olaus returned to Bear Creek – a new letter was waiting for him. "Cpl. Olans Hanson – you have been promoted to 7th corporal in the 12th Iowa Volunteer Infantry Regiment........." He was not quite sure what had prompted the promotion this time, but it was certainly a verification of his status he felt very proud of.

In late September the 3rd Division was left on its own to guard the line along Black River, as the other two divisions were ordered to Chattanooga, Tennessee. The summer camp was broken on October 15th and the 3rd Division under General Mower together with a division from the 17th Corps and a brigade of cavalry was ordered to march against a Rebel force massing at Canton. After a two day march the enemy was encountered outside the city, and even if they were dislodged, they continued to harass the Union train on its return to camp. The 12th Iowa was assigned to guard the train on the way back on Monday the 19th, and did some heavy duty helping the wagons over bad places in the road. Olaus was exhausted when he arrived back at Black River. On the 20th "Camp Hebron" was set up at Clear Creek, nine miles from Vicksburg. Many of the men built fireplaces in their tents. They expected the campaign to be over and Hebron established as a winter camp. Confederate General Nathan Bedford Forrest thought otherwise.

VETERAN VOLUNTEER
AT TUPELO

Theodore was ill again. He had left for Decorah in September, and for Olaus that was not the worst of it: Hans was ill, too. They were both in Iowa. On the evening of Friday, November 6th an order came to break camp and march into Vicksburg the next morning. Less than three weeks of rest was over. They boarded the steamer Thomas E. Tutt - destination Chattanooga - to join the other divisions. The 12th was the only regiment on the boat, and the three remaining men in the Hansen/Steen team enjoyed the five day trip up the river under conditions far from crowded. At 11 am on the 12th the regiment disembarked at Memphis, where they were held up for six days waiting for railroad transportation. No cars ever showed up, so on November 19th they were ordered to march fifty miles to LaGrange. Three days later they bivouacked on College Hill outside the town. Due to the delay plans had been changed. Sherman had summoned another division to Chattanooga, and the 3rd would be stationed on duty guarding the railroads from Memphis to Corinth. The 12th Iowa regimental headquarter was established at Chewalla under the command of John H. Stibbs, promoted to lieutenant colonel. In addition to railroad guard duty they were ordered to suppress local guerilla operations.

During December the regiment held several meetings to discuss if they were going to reenlist after the expiration of service. The previous June the War Department had issued a general order offering furloughs, bounties and other inducements to make the three year men reenlist. One month's advance pay was offered, together with a two dollar premium and a four hundred dollar bounty, to be paid in installments of twenty five to seventy five dollars. If two thirds of the regiment reenlisted, it would retain its organization and be re-mustered as a regiment of veteran volunteers. On Christmas Eve John, Henry and Olaus was talking it over.
"I'm in". Olaus was in no doubt. He was in for the duration of the war.
"Hans is not".
"He's not?" John was surprised "How do you know?"
"He told me. I understand him well. He's thirty. I'm just twenty two. He came here to farm - to make a living. He's gotta get on with it. We never dreamed the

war would last this long. It becomes your life, and it really can't, because when it's over – then what?"

"Well, I'm in, no matter what", John said.

"So am I." It came like an echo from Henry.

Olaus leaned back on the bunk.

"OK. Settled."

On Christmas Day the required two thirds of the regiment – 298 men altogether – reenlisted for three more years or the duration of the war. The 12th Iowa Veteran Volunteer Infantry Regiment had been formed.

On December 28th Tennessee Scouts came in with information about a Rebel lieutenant being on furlough in the vicinity. At 4 pm companies I and G marched through the stockade under the command of Captain Charles L. Sumbardo striking out to capture the Rebel – or Rebels – whichever it turned out to be. Olaus marched south on muddy roads through the falling darkness, soon crossing from Tennessee into Mississippi. During the night the detachment searched several farms for their target, but had no luck before about 5 am next morning, when they closed in on Goose River after a thirteen hour march. Quietly surrounding a house where a party was apparently taking place, they were discovered by some of the participant trying to escape through doors and windows, some of them armed. After a short engagement the Federals rounded up nineteen prisoners, five of them wounded. One Rebel had been killed, none of the Iowans wounded.

On January 1st, 1864 Olaus was promoted for the third time, to 6th corporal. His participation in the raid into Mississippi and his determination to stay for the rest of the war had paid off. John Steen was assuming greater responsibility in the quartermaster department – on the same day as Olaus was promoted he was made quartermaster sergeant of the 12th Iowa. On January 5th everybody who had decided to reenlist was mustered into the veteran volunteer regiment.

With reenlistments and promotions came changes. About January 25th the 12th Iowa was ordered to burn and abandon the barracks on the Memphis and Corinth Railroad and take a train to Memphis and there to board the steamer Delaware destined for Vicksburg. The plan was to join General Sherman for an expedition to Meridian. Again they were delayed in joining Sherman – this time by lack of steamers to take the whole brigade downriver – and missed the opportunity to march with his army. On the upside the men received two months' pay and on February 1st set out for Vicksburg, arriving at 10 am on the 3rd. The regiment remained in camp at Black River Bridge for a month. It was almost like they were back at Camp Union. Company drills, regimental drills and brigade drills were

Olaus Hansen's reenlistment in the 12th Iowa Veteran Volunteer Infantry Regiment at Chewalla, Tennessee, on Christmas Day of 1863. The National Archives.

carried out daily, and both the Hansen- and Steen brothers got back into the routine after a year of constant campaigning. On March 6th Colonel Joseph J. Woods assumed command of the regiment. Under Special Field Order No. 14 he transferred the 12th Iowa non-veterans – about seventy all told, including Hans Hansen - to the 35th Iowa. The next day Woods boarded a dilapidated old tub called the Minnehaha for Memphis together with the veteran volunteers to turn over all the ordnance stores. From there they would proceed to Davenport, Iowa and report to the superintendent for recruiting service for thirty days' furlough.

Olaus and Hans had a talk before the Minnehaha left for Memphis.
"Are you going to Highland?" Hans asked.
"Nah – don't think so. It's far, even from Davenport. Furlough's just a month – I'll spend a long time just travelling there and back. Probably stay in Davenport. I know the Steen boys are going to Glenwood, but – that's different. Their parents are waiting. Gotta go home."
"Well – I'll see you soon, little brother. Be careful!"
It was actually Hans, himself, who was in need of the good wish. The next time Olaus saw him, he would be in a hospital bed in Memphis............

After turning in the stores at Memphis the Minnehaha continued upriver towards Davenport. The trip became a nightmare. The regiment used hawsers to pull the continuously stranded boat off sand bars so many times it felt like they were back digging the Duckport canal all over again. Finally she came to a permanent rest on one of the bars. The men pulled and pulled, but to no avail. The Minnehaha had done her duty. She was not going anywhere. Some of the officers went to Cairo on a passenger steamer securing the boat Island City to take the regiment off the Minnehaha and on to St. Louis. When they arrived it came to show that, due to the reenlistment, the St. Louis citizens had invited the whole regiment to a banquet. Olaus felt honored. This was a change from sleeping on wet, muddy ground eating hardtack and bacon. They were wined and dined with food and beverages he could not even pronounce the name of, but they certainly improved his general mood and he cheerfully enjoyed everything that was put in front of him.

Olaus was no stranger to alcohol. For someone born in Norway at the middle of the nineteenth century, that would have been impossible. Alcohol had a long and influential history in Norwegian society and in the Middle Ages important decisions in business and politics were commonly made at large parties or in taverns. After previous restrictions on alcohol production a law was enacted in 1816 making it a free for all. In 1835 - in Christiania County alone - more than half of the 2 036 registered businesses were liquor stills. Most of them were small, associated with farms with potato production and run by the workers. Every Norwegian older than 15 years of age drank an average of 3.8 gallons of pure alcohol annually. House servants and laborers often demanded an alcohol allowance as part of their contract when working for large farms – drinks for breakfast, dinner and supper. In addition – as in other countries – alcohol was heavily endorsed by physicians because of its perceived medicinal properties. There was no shame associated with drinking in Norway, but the habit certainly became a social problem, and a strong temperance movement grew between 1830 and 1855. In 1842 the Parliament proposed a law of prohibition, but King Carl Johan refused to sign it, as it would have put a large part of Norwegian industry out of business.

In the United States Olaus found a drinking pattern similar to the one in Norway, but with a much larger consumption. In 1790 the average American drank 5.8 gallons of pure alcohol annually, which rose to a historic high of 7.1 gallons in 1830. The habit of drinking throughout the day was well described from Virginia, where a gentleman would get out of bed at eight o'clock in the morning to a large glass of rum with sugar (Julep), then ride around his plantation having a cider at his ten o'clock breakfast, toddy before his two o'clock dinner, and then continuously more toddy until bedtime.

Olaus felt at home in St. Louis. The city had a distinct German influence. More than 20 000 came in 1852, and another 25 000 two years later. By 1860 one third of the city's population were natives of Germany. Like Olaus had fled the cotter system in Norway, the Germans had fled serfdom under feudal barons. The similarity between the cotter system, feudalism and slavery was easy to spot, and many of the German communities in St. Louis were radically against slavery. They were also generally against the temperance movement and more than forty breweries in the city told a story about a people who wanted to be left alone to enjoy their lager beer. These attitudes resonated with Olaus' train of thoughts. He felt very much at home.

On March 22nd the veteran volunteers arrived at Davenport on the Island City and thirty days' furlough was granted. Three weeks later Olaus got some very disturbing news through his army contacts in Davenport. Hans had been sent on detached service with Company K of the 35th Iowa Infantry joining the Red River Campaign to capture Shreveport, Louisiana. The campaign was apparently pretty bungled from the Union side, and in the battle of Pleasant Hill on April 9th Hans had been severely wounded. Nobody was quite sure how severely, but apparently

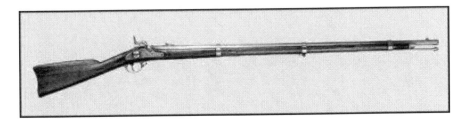

Caliber .58 model 1861 Springfield rifle-musket. Wikipedia.org.

he had taken a musket ball in the leg. Olaus shuddered. Amputation? He hated the thought – started cold sweating just thinking about it. If Hans lost a leg, his farming days were over before they had even begun. He could possibly make a living as a blacksmith, which was his trade, but with only one leg? Olaus pushed the horrifying thought to the back of his mind. He did not enjoy the rest of his furlough very much. He knew that Hans had been taken to hospital in Alexandria, Louisiana, and was not due to come north before he could be moved onto a steamer.

On April 25th the 12th Iowa reported back at Davenport. Leaving on the 28th by rail they reached Cairo the next day where they embarked on the steamer Luminary bound for Memphis. On May 2nd the regiment reported for duty and went into camp just outside the city limits. Olaus immediately inquired about Hans and was told that he had boarded the hospital steamer C.R. Wood in Alexandria on April 30th. The boat was making its way upriver towards Memphis. When it arrived – in about a week - Hans would be taken to the Adams U.S. Army General Hospital in the city.

Olaus started to prepare for upcoming campaigns. Arms and equipment were distributed to the 12th Iowa – 40 sergeants and 395 corporals and enlisted men. A requisition had been made for 435 Model 1861 Springfield rifled muskets, caliber .58. Olaus held the sleek gun in his hands - it always gave him a special feeling to handle a good gun. He pulled the hammer back to half-cocked and fully cocked positions a couple of times to feel how it worked and pulled at the trigger to test the tension in the spring. Then he shouldered the weapon and aimed at a crow on a tree top about 80 yards away. It was a beautiful gun falling naturally to his cheek and letting him easily see the bird on top of the bead without having to arch his neck. He nodded to himself as he put it down, butt first. He was already an excellent shot. With this gun, he would become even better.

On May 9th Hans was admitted to the army hospital in Memphis. Olaus did not let the grass grow under his feet, but was soon at the hospital. He was surprised to see

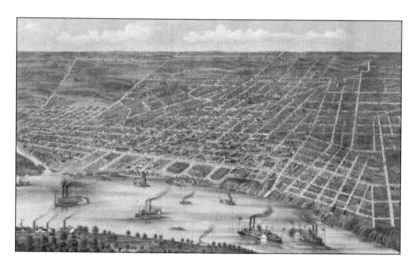

Memphis, Tennessee in 1870. The Library of Congress.

Hans sitting in a chair in the foyer with a pair of crutches across his legs – his two legs. He went over to the chair, grabbed Hans' hand and squeezed it. Hard.
"You're not in bed?"
"Nope." Hans grabbed his thigh. "I'm a lot better. Can limp around".
"Is your leg going to be OK?"
"So they say, these doctors, but they're not always to be trusted. They sort of treat you like a piece of meat, and make haphazard statements about the prognosis for recovery. I go by what I can see and feel. It's improving by the day. It's going to be fine".
Olaus felt relieved. He had been worried about Hans with a missing leg and what the future would have held for him. No he could wipe that out of his mind. The hospital visits were kept fairly short – he soon had to say good-bye to his brother and was ushered out by a nurse.

After a month of continuous camp duty Olaus and the veteran volunteers could finally welcome the non-veterans serving in the Red River Campaign back to Memphis on June the 10th. The next day the 12th and 35th Iowa, the 33rd Missouri and the 7th Minnesota were brigaded together as the 3rd Brigade, 1st Division of the 16th Army Corps. The very same day Olaus witnessed an execution of three soldiers in the 2nd New Jersey Cavalry sentenced by court martial to die in front of a firing squad. The army was drawn up in a hollow square on open ground outside fort Pickering. The convicted soldiers were marched around the square and then blindfolded. Seated on their coffins in the open part of the square they were shot dead. After the executions the army was marched past the coffins with the dead men slung across them. Olaus looked at the bullet riddled bodies. It was certainly no worse than what he had seen on the battlefield hundreds of times – it was just something odd about executions. It was cold blooded murder, whichever way you looked at it, deserved or not. On the battlefield you took your chances, fought, survived or died. In front of a firing squad - you just died.

General William T. Sherman had by this time maneuvered his army to the area outside Atlanta, Georgia. His entire line of supplies was dependent on one single railroad – the 473 mile track to Nashville, Tennessee. In early June Rebel General Nathan Bedford Forrest had massed his forces at Tupelo, Mississippi to harass the rear of General Sherman's army and cut his communication line. Eight thousand men under the command of Brigadier General Samuel D. Sturgis was sent out to break up the Rebel camp, but his force was defeated in detail by Forrest at Brice's Crossroad near Guntown. Subsequently Major General Andrew Jackson Smith was ordered to advance towards Tupelo with the 1st and 3rd Division of the 16th Corps, including eight companies of the 12th Iowa veteran volunteers. Companies A and F were on garrison duty at White River.

An army of 14 000 men left Memphis on June 18th, the 1st Division under the command of General "Wolf" Mower, Colonel Joseph J. Woods commanding the 3rd Brigade. Lieutenant Colonel John Stibbs was in charge of the 12th Iowa. Olaus found it a bit upsetting that the Hansen- and Steen brothers were breaking up – inevitably they were heading in different directions for different reasons. Only Olaus and Henry were marching with the 12th on the new campaign. Hans was in hospital, John was quartermaster sergeant in Memphis and Theodore was detached on recruiting service. Traveling in box cars they reached Colliersville in the afternoon where the railroad track had been torn up. The men were set to work building railroads and repairing bridges. The work was completed to LaGrange on June 24th where the army rested and waited for supplies to be brought up.

The cavalry scouted the surrounding country and provided protection for Sturgis' force making its way back to Tennessee. Black troops from Sturgis' army came out of the forest where they had been hiding out from fear of being captured. They told horror stories about soldiers from their regiment who had been taken by Forrest's men. Forrest – again. Olaus remembered Donelson, where he escaped. Shiloh. Vicksburg - Forrest, again and again. Rumors claimed he was an almost illiterate, extremely wealthy slave trader and a self-tutored military genius. He had

General Nathan Bedford Forrest, the Confederate States of America. Wikipedia.org.

been a thorn in the side of the Army of the Tennessee for a long time. Olaus would not mind drawing a bead on that Rebel general himself.

July 4th was celebrated by firing a hundred guns at midnight. The next morning the army marched southeast towards Pontotoc by way of Ripley and New Albany. After the slow camp duty Olaus was happy to be back on the road, although the conditions were very bad. Seven days of scorching July sun, all day every day, marching through deep dust - breathing dust – many of the men suffered sun stroke. It was the hottest march they had ever experienced. The difference between veteran regiments and new regiments quickly surfaced. Some of the newer regiments could not keep their organization and were allowed to fall out of rank and catch up when they could during the cooler part of the day.

The veterans were physically and mentally much better prepared for the arduous march. Olaus could feel his body working hard under the burning sun. After all the campaigning and the general lack of sufficient food for almost three years he was nothing but bones, muscles and a determined mind. He marched without letting his thoughts wander, just focused on putting one foot in front of the other, thousands upon thousands of times. His hat down in front of his eyes, a neckerchief covering his face against the dust, his blanket in a roll across his shoulder, his haversack, cartridge box and gun – he felt like he could march to the end of the world.

On July 12th the army rested at Pontotoc after skirmishing with the enemy along a mile long line of battle throughout all of the previous day on the approach to the town. At 4 am the next morning they were on the road heading towards Okolona. With the cavalry out on the road attracting attention the infantry suddenly turned east towards Tupelo. The rear guard consisting of the 59th, 61st and 68th U.S. Colored Infantry stood off harassment from Forrest's forces trying to push up to the Federals. At about 3 pm, when the army reached Bartram's Shop at Coonewar Creek ten miles from Pontotoc, Forrest had discovered the move and ordered an attack on the right of the train, guarded by the 12th Iowa. Edwin A. Buttolph and Harmon Grass were detailed as flankers, patrolling parallel to the train about 300 yards out. They were captured by the Rebel cavalry, but not before they had discharged their guns to warn the rest of the regiment. Lieutenant David Reed rode out to investigate and ran directly into the Rebel force, narrowly escaping down a path back to the train. Lieutenant Colonel Stibbs moved the regiment out from the train to a ravine, and ordered them to lie down. Olaus made sure nothing had gotten down the muzzle of his gun that could obstruct the ball, and cocked the hammer. Now he just had to wait. He looked at his hands. Not a shiver. His grey eyes squinted as he looked down the blued gun barrel, catching the shining bead at the front. He was ready. About six yards to his right he saw Henry Steen doing the last check on his gun, as calm as a quail hunter. There was not much left of the timid boy from the Montgomery prison – Henry was a battle hardened veteran, even if he was only 21 years old.

When Forrest's men discovered the Federal wagon train they came charging through the almost impenetrable thicket with a wild Rebel yell. The 12th Iowa rose like one man and poured a furious and completely unexpected volley into the faces of the surprised attackers from just twenty yards away. The regiment loaded with lightning speed and followed up with another volley – and another – and another. Within twenty minutes the Rebels still mounted were in headlong retreat. Almost instantly a call for help came from the 6th Indiana Battery on the left, which was in danger of being captured. As he turned to run Olaus saw the oldest Norwegian, Søren Sørensen, sitting on the ground clasping his leg, groaning loudly. He was trying to stop the blood pouring from a nasty looking wound – a ball had torn most of the tissue away and the bone was exposed. Olaus knew he could not stop to help him – together with the rest of the 12th he ran over to the battery on the double quick. Upon reaching the guns Olaus spotted a soldier who came racing across No Man's Land exposed to fire from both sides. In the confusion among the Rebels one of the flankers, Grass, had gotten away and ran for his life towards his own lines. He made it without being hit.

With the attack force driven away the Federals took time to unhitch the almost thirty dead or injured mules, shift the supplies to undamaged wagons and torch the wreckages. Nothing would be left for Forrest's men. Søren Sørensen was in agony and would not be fit for more fighting during the campaign. He was placed on a wagon and a doctor gave him Laudanum for his pains while dressing his wound.

As the train moved on, the 12th Iowa resumed its place at the right center of the column. Upon crossing a swamp on a corduroy road a Rebel battery on an elevated position outside the swamp opened fire directly across their path. The train was in a fatal dilemma – the battery was out of range for muskets, and because of the swamp, the train had nowhere to go but forward. The battery kept firing along the same trajectory, the shells shrieking overhead while the gunners were finding the distance. By following each shot Olaus could pretty accurately tell where the next one would hit. He did not like the projections he was making. Finally the gunners had zeroed in. The next shell ploughed straight through the ranks of the 12th Iowa, killing John Nichols from Cedar Rapids instantly. The train could do nothing but move on, until finally out of the swamp and out of sight of the battery.

About 8 pm the head of the column reached Tupelo. The 12th Iowa bivouacked in line of battle about two miles west of town, close to Harrisburg Post Office. The regiment was positioned at the extreme left of a crescent shaped Union line at the edge of a forest, across the road to Tupelo. A shallow bottom made up the rear. They were on the convex point closest to the enemy and Olaus did not have to use much imagination to realize that the brunt of the attack would fall on the 12th Iowa. During the oppressively hot and humid night they tore down a rail fence to build some slight protection from the Rebel bullets. On Thursday, July 14th at 3 am the regiment was in readiness for the expected attack. The Federal cavalry outposts were driven in and skirmishing started as soon as it was light enough to shoot.

About 6:45 the Rebel artillery opened up with a thundering barrage against the Union lines. Canister, grape and shell came like hail across the field, raining down on the men and forcing them to take cover behind the fence rails. Olaus lay behind a pile of rails covering his head. He knew that moving around to better positions was a useless waste of time. A shell would hit you – or not. After a short barrage the Confederates made a determined attack along the north side of the road and bore directly down on the 12th Iowa. The time was almost 7:30 am. Olaus could see long, double lines of gray he estimated to be about three brigades advancing towards them, and knew what was coming. The initial stand of the 300 men of the 12th could determine the outcome of the battle. Olaus felt calm – he looked at the advancing, grey army like it was something not quite real – something he was just giving time to get within firing range. He stroked the back of his head. No prickly feeling. He stroked his neck. Still no prickly feeling. The grey lines were closing in to about a hundred yards. Olaus took careful aim at the second coat button of one of the Rebels – or where he thought it might be. Better let every cartridge count.

"Ready! - Aim! – F......" Stibbs shout drowned in the firestorm from the infantry muskets. Massive clouds of gun powder drove like thunderclouds over the field in front of the Union line while the soldiers reloaded lightning swift to follow up on the first volley.

Zip! Zip! ZZZZip!
Olaus almost felt more than heard the bullets passing close to his head – instant death an inch or two away but yet so completely harmless, as he was not hit.
Zip. ZZZip!!

The last bullet hit somebody. From the corner of is eye Olaus saw a man spin around and roll down behind the fence rails. While tearing a paper cartridge open with his teeth and pulling the ramrod out he looked at the fallen soldier. 1st Sergeant Ralph M. Grimm of Company H had taken a musket ball in the shoulder. It did not look pretty, but Olaus could see it was probably not fatal. The Iowa veterans knew the law of war – you keep on shooting, no matter what happens. He ignored the sergeant and kept shooting and shooting until the Rebel force was checked at about sixty yards. There they took cover in ditches and behind a fence.

Olaus had seen a total collapse in the Rebel assault. The force had started out in three lines of battle, but as they came under fire the skirmishers, main line and reserve had become a jumbled mob of soldiers rushing towards the Union line yelling and howling until they were checked by canister from the 6th Indiana and the 2nd Iowa batteries. A few of them had gotten up to just thirty yards from the batteries. Through the clouds of gunpowder Olaus could see reinforcements being brought up, and a new assault followed immediately along a half a mile battle front. The Iowans gave them the same reception as the first wave of attackers and the assault stalled 150 yards from the Union line. The 12th kept up the intense fire and was suddenly supported by Battery G of the 2nd Illinois Artillery pouring enfilade crossfire all along the Confederate line from a hilltop on the left. Just like at Shiloh Olaus was positioned near a battery. He could feel the report in the

A charge of grape shot and a solid shot. Miller: The Photographic History of the Civil War.

ground every time the guns fired and timed his own shots accordingly to be able to take accurate aim.

1st Lieutenant Augustus A. Burdick from Olaus' company G - acting regimental quartermaster - had parked his train and returned to the front line bringing up ammunition. Olaus saw him standing behind a big tree holding his horse by the bridle watching the fight, when he was killed by a solid shot. The shot went straight through the tree, through Burdick – and his horse – and struck the ground a few feet away.

The time was about 9:30 and Olaus' musket was unserviceable. The barrel was choked up with gun powder preventing him from pushing the rod down - and his cartridge box was nearly empty. He looked over at Henry Steen who was wiping the sweat off his face with his neckerchief, pointed at his gun and gave him thumbs down. Henry nodded and drew his index finger across his throat. His musket was also useless. To keep up a steady fire the 7th Minnesota was ordered forward so the 12th Iowa could withdraw to clean the guns and replenish the ammunition. Company E and H had already been resupplied and stayed on the front line. Everywhere along the line Olaus could see wounded men being carried to the rear. One of the men had most of his abdomen shot away by a shell, his intestines exposed, another bled profusely from two wounds, in the shoulder and hip. A field hospital had been established on the east side of Old Town Creek, along the road where they marched to the battlefield. Members of the regimental bands were detailed to carry the wounded off the field during battle, but Olaus had rarely seen that happen. It was fellow soldiers who carried the wounded across the bridge to the hospital in rubber ponchos and on stretchers.

After forty five minutes the 12th returned to the front line just in time to repulse a third attack – volley after volley burst from muskets and cannons, and Olaus suddenly realized the advancing columns had stopped – and was in full retreat.

"Chaaaaaaaarge!!!"

He could hear the command from somewhere on his right and all the men in the brigade still able to leaped over the fence rails and stormed across the battlefield bayonets fixed, sweeping the enemy in front of them all the way to Harrisburg. The batteries continued to shell the Rebel forces until they disappeared into the woods.

Suddenly Olaus was ravenous with hunger although he had felt nothing at all in the excitement of the fight. He had not had anything to eat before the battle - spoiled bread had been issued at LaGrange, and the army was already on half rations. His lips were scorched by gun powder from biting and tearing open the paper cartridges and he took a handful of water rubbing it over his face and mouth. Walking back towards the Union line he could tell that he enemy's losses had been severe. Hundreds of Rebel soldiers were strewn dead or dying across the battlefield, many of them with officers' distinctions. At least five of them were colonels.

It had been one of the deadliest battles for the 12th Iowa. Olaus had seen 1st Lieutenant Burdick fall, and Francis Winter, George Holden, Philetus Butters, Robert Fowler, Jeremiah Myers, Philip Rutter - all dead. Olaus knew there were more than fifty men wounded, several of them seriously. Sergeant Valma V. Price was wounded in the leg and had to have it amputated and Corporal John F. Wilson was severely wounded in the thigh. Together with Søren Sørensen they would all die from their wounds.

During the night Company C stood picket duty along the battlefield. The next day Olaus spoke to William L. Henderson, one of the pickets. In the darkness he had not been able to distinguish between sleeping Federal soldiers and Rebel dead when we made his rounds to wake the next man for duty, and he almost touched one of the corpses before he discovered a ghastly looking face staring blindly at the moon.

On the morning of July 15th General Smith started to move his army away from Tupelo. The Rebel camp was broken up and the railway communication they had tried to reestablish between Mobile and Chattanooga was destroyed. About forty men were left behind as they were too seriously hurt to be moved. Hiram H. Andrews and Henry C. Winterstein volunteered to stay and take care of them, and go into captivity as nurses. Mower's division was deployed to cover the retreat while the four mile long train was moving back. Forrest's men were pressing all the way up to the Union lines – the Rebel general was aware that the army was pulling away, and wanted to strike detached parts of the Federal force. When the train was safe Mower assigned the 3rd Brigade as rear guard while moving the rest of his division across Old Town Creek.

The four regiments were drawn up in line across the Pontotoc Road behind temporary breastworks built from cotton bales. The order was to stay concealed and hold their fire until the enemy was within fifty yards. Olaus noticed that the regiment was visibly decimated – the 300 men from the first day had shrunk to 200. He wiped sweat out of his eyes with the back of his hand. The sun was scorching and he was out of water. He hoped the enemy would attack right away to get the fight over with. The Rebels advanced under heavy fire, but it soon became apparent they were not going to push all the way up to the Union line. Subsequently Colonel Joseph J. Woods ordered the whole brigade forward in a bayonet charge, driving the Confederates across the fields back to Harrisburg. During the charge many of the Iowans fell victim to sunstroke in the intense heat. Woods about faced his force and marched on the double quick back to Old Creek Town and crossed the bridge. This time the Rebels did not pursue. General Nathan Bedford Forrest had been wounded in the foot during the fight. It was one of the very few times he lost a battle with Federal forces, and it was the last time he engaged in pitched battle with Union infantry

As they came off the bridge Olaus could see the house which had been used as a field hospital during the battle. The operating table where arms and legs had been amputated was still standing, its end attached to a large tree outside the porch. He had heard horrible stories from men who had helped wounded to the rear during the battle. Arms and legs with gunshot– or shrapnel wounds where no remedy could help were sawed off and thrown aside. By the next morning a large pile of discarded extremities were all over the ground next to the table. Chloroform was administered to the patients during the operation, but a cavalryman whose leg was shattered above the knee had refused to be put to sleep. After some argument the surgeons went to work on his leg while he was sitting on the table gripping his thigh with both hands. With only a few groans he watched as they cut the flesh away and sawed through the bone, and then removed his whole leg from above the knee and threw it on the pile by the table. Olaus preferred not to think about it. He considered himself incredibly lucky to have been through all the battles without injury.

On the morning of July 16th the army returned via Elliston, New Albany and Ripley towards LaGrange, where they arrived four days later. After Olaus saw the field hospital and the operating table he had been watching the wounded soldiers on the wagons. The ones with amputations were terribly bothered by flies. There were always massive swarms of flies following the trains – nothing attracted them like the manure from several thousand horses and mules. The insects would lay eggs in the wounds, and within a short time they would fester with fly maggots. The only way to relieve the wounded was to remove the dressing, pick the maggots out of the wounds, cleanse them and dress them again with soaking wet bandages. Instantly the flies would be back, and the wounds had to be redressed several times a day

On July 21st the army entered a train with boxcars at LaGrange, bound for Memphis. The following night the men filed into their camp in the suburbs, anticipating a long rest and recovery. The next day Olaus went to the Army hospital to see how Hans was doing. The recovery was slow. Hans anticipated several more weeks before he was released. He was still stiff and sore, but could bend his knee and was definitely improving. He had been following the news about the battle of Tupelo coming in over the wire, and was happy Olaus had not been hurt. Olaus assured him that he would be back next week to check on him. That was not to be.

GENERAL SMITH'S
FOOT CAVALRY

The rest lasted exactly eight days. The next three and a half months would be spent constantly on the march due to countermanded orders from several generals who all wanted to utilize the fighting qualities of Smith's divisions. Sometimes it would be very frustrating, as the men did not know to where they were marching, or for what. They were just on the move in forced marches. At 11 pm on Saturday July 30th an order was issued to move out the next day at 8 am. After a short march to the railway depot they entered the cars and before night they landed at Davis Mills, six miles southeast of LaGrange. The next day they marched via Lamar to Coldwater River.

The 12th Iowa formed the advance guard as the army marched into Holly Springs, Mississippi at 11 am on Tuesday August the 2nd. The regiment was distributed throughout the town as provost guard. The townspeople – mostly women and children - were particularly worried about the black regiments. They thought some or their old servants may have enlisted and had come back to take revenge. Olaus found that the soldiers were treated well, however, and the officers were overrun with invitations for dinner.

On the evening of August 9th an order came to rejoin the brigade at the camp on the south side of Tallahatchie River. There they reported to Colonel Woods at 9 am on Wednesday, August 10th. After a skirmish with the enemy at Hurricane Creek on August 13th they built a bridge across and drove a small Rebel force out of Oxford, Mississippi. The brigade at last got the order it had been waiting for: General Smith was ordered to join General Sherman's army outside Atlanta, Georgia with his two divisions. Olaus and Henry were jubilant – at last they would be able to rejoin "Old Tecumseh" during his advance. However – strings were pulled at high levels, and the order was soon countermanded.

The army re-crossed the Tallahatchie River on August 24th, easily fighting off an attack on the rear guard and taking some prisoners. They went into camp at Waterford on the 25th and the next day again entered the town of Holly Springs.

Major General Andrew Jackson Smith. Wikipedia.org.

General Smith was met by a delegation of citizens requesting the 12th Iowa to be detailed as provost guard, as during the last visit. Smith bit off the end of his cigar, chewed it up and spat it out, and said to the delegation: "The 12th Iowa is one of my best fighting units. I think it's a doubtful compliment for you d----- rebels to want it to guard your d----- town, and an imposition on the regiment to ask them to do it, but if those boys are willing to stand guard, they may." Smith sent a message back through the column to move the 12th to the front. He ordered the regiment to march into town and take charge of all the private property, and to make sure they would have a good report on their conduct. The next day the 12th Iowa formed the rear guard as the army marched back to the camp at Davis Creek. On August 29th the command was back at LaGrange, and the next day it boarded a train for Memphis.

Hans had been discharged from the hospital on August 22nd and could move around on his leg without feeling much pain. However, he was still not fit for long marches and hard campaigning and was stationed at Fort Pickering. Theodore, John, Henry and Olaus enjoyed four days in camp where they were all present to share stories and news from their different exploits.

The stay at Memphis was very brief. Instead of packing up and leave for Atlanta, as they had expected, the 1st division was suddenly diverted to another field of operation. Confederate Major General Sterling Price with his Army of Missouri, consisting of 12 000 men and fourteen pieces of artillery, had embarked on a cavalry raid through Missouri and Kansas. The raid was an attempt to regain Missouri for the Confederacy and help turn northern opinion against Lincoln before the 1864 election. Missouri guerillas flocked to his banners and made up close to half of the army. According to intelligence, Price organized his forces at Little Rock, Arkansas. Smith's 1st Division was put into action to catch General Price and his mixture of regular soldiers, guerilla fighters and deserters who had been returned to duty.

On September 3rd a flotilla of steamers left Memphis with Smith's 1st Division under the command of Major General Joseph "Wolf" Mower, promoted after the battle of Tupelo. The 12th Iowa was on board the Mattie, entering the mouth of White River on the morning of August 4th. Due to demonstrations from the enemy the army was disembarked at St. Charles on the evening of the 5th. Three days later the whole force was put back on the steamers, proceeding to Devil's Bluff where they again disembarked.

On September 10th Olaus was on the road with the 12th Iowa marching towards Brownsville. They marched across a perfectly level prairie where no water could be found, relying entirely on the contents of their canteens. At night camp was established in a grove near a slough providing sufficient amounts of water. Upon reaching Brownsville the next day they found that Price had avoided Little Rock by crossing the river below and was already moving north to invade Missouri. It was decided that Mower's division together with a small cavalry force would pursue Price's mounted raiders - already several days in advance - on foot……..

Mower's command left Brownsville on September 17th with teams and wagons for the ammunition. Wagons for the rations were provided by the 9th Iowa Cavalry, accompanying the command to Red River where the rations would be transferred to the haversacks. One man from each company was detailed to bring in beef cattle from the country as they marched. On the evening of August 19th they crossed Little Red River at a ford about four feet deep and with a very swift stream. Many of the men took their clothes off and held them in bundles over their heads. However – the river bed was covered with slippery rocks, and after watching several of the men slip and stumble across the ford, falling down and losing clothes and other articles in the swift current – Olaus kept his gear on. He would be soaking wet, anyway, and that was not such a bad thing – it would cool him down during the march as it evaporated.

Day after day the command made forced marches trying to gain on General Price and his mounted raiders. The roads were rough – across the spurs of the Ozark

Mountains and along swampy margins of streams. After crossing White River they reached Black River about 8 pm on September 22nd. The bridge across the river had been burned, and since the approach had been along a corduroy road with a swamp on each side – no camp could be made. The order "in place rest" was issued, and the army went into night quarter strung out as during the march. Olaus threw himself on the ground and had some of the ration in his haversack – and fell asleep almost instantly. The pioneer corps was ordered to the front and crossed over to a small town called Elgin. They found a saw mill with planks for the bridge covering and tore down a cotton press for timber to the stringers. At 3 pm the next day the pioneers had a bridge completed, 320 feet long.

The command crossed the river and camped at Miller's Church. The march continued up the east bank of Black River, through Pocahontas, Arkansas and Poplar Bluff, Missouri. They marched through endless swamps and the rear guard often worked all night hauling the wagon train and artillery into camp. On September 30th Olaus had been on rear guard duty with the 12th Iowa, marching from Poplar Bluff to Chipman's Ford. They had been dragging the train out of mud holes all day and continued into the night by the light from candles and torches. Just as they managed to get the last wagon across the ford and into camp – reveille was sounded.

They reached Greenville on October 2nd and got intelligence that Price had an engagement with Union forces at Ironton, forty miles to the north, and then set out towards northwest. On October 4th the division made a forced march of thirty miles through pouring rain and over bad roads, camping at White Water Creek at 8 pm. They reached Cape Girardeau, Missouri on October 5th. When they approached the town the local militia was alarmed by the ragged look of the army, thinking it was a large band of Missouri guerillas. That night Olaus took a piece of paper out of his pocket which he had been making notes on during the march. In the spring of 1862 Confederate General "Stonewall" Jackson had made news headlines when his soldiers had been dubbed "Jackson's Foot Cavalry" because of their forced marches during the Valley Campaign. They had marched 646 miles in 48 days, crisscrossing the Shenandoah Valley. Olaus made a quick calculation. That was thirteen miles a day. He had been talking to some of the men in the pioneer corps to keep track of the distance the 1st Division had marched in the hunt for Price's raiders.

The last nineteen days they had covered 336 miles and forded seven rivers. Six days out of the nineteen, rain had been pouring all day. They had out-marched even the cavalry horses and mules. When they reached Cape Girardeau most of the horses were unserviceable and half of the mules had been left worn out along the road. The march had been accomplished with only 10 days' ration. Olaus jotted a few numbers on his paper. Almost eighteen miles a day – average. That certainly dwarfed Jackson's Rebels. He smiled to himself and showed it to Henry Steen. Smith's Foot Cavalry!

The march had taken its toll on men and equipment. Some of the roads had been full of flinty rocks which cut away the shoes. At Cape Girardeau 5 officers and 102 of the 250 men were barefooted......... Some had old coffee sacks wrapped around their feet to protect them from the sharp rocks. Olaus shoes were still hanging on his feet, but the soles were paper thin. Henry was barefooted.

The division remained at Cape Girardeau only one day. Price was in the vicinity of Ironton facing the 3rd Division – also recalled from its planned transfer to Atlanta and Sherman's army. General Mower was ordered to join the 3rd Division as soon as possible. About 2 am on October 7th Olaus was marching to the steamboat landing where Company G together with B and E embarked on the Argonaut. The rest of the regiment boarded the Armenia. As usual the lower decks were crowded with cavalry and artillery. They arrived in St Louis the same evening and spent two days drawing supplies and clothes.

On October 10th Olaus looked like a new recruit. Wearing a brand new uniform he was heading up the Missouri River on the steamer Empire with the 12th Iowa and the brigade headquarter. The infantry of Mower's division was ordered to report at Jefferson City as Price was marching in that direction. Mower himself was ordered on detached duty. Even if his division could not join Sherman at Atlanta – personally he could. On the 11th he left the division and Colonel Joseph J. Woods assumed command. The Empire faced the same problems as the Minnehaha did in March. It was too large for the Missouri River and during the eight day trip it was most of the time stuck on sand bars. The entire regiment was disembarked with hawsers four times to pull her off. On the night of October 13th, while pulling off one bar she ran into another. Not able to move off again and get into shore, she left the regiment stranded. They had to sleep on the shore without blankets, food or shelter.

Next morning Olaus woke up shivering cold. The ground was covered in white frost. He got up and started walking around to get blood circulation in his frozen limbs. The regiment got back on the steamer and finally reached Jefferson City on October 18th, only to find that Price had turned west before reaching the city. They boarded a train for Lamine River. The bridge was destroyed, so the 12th Iowa was on the road again, marching to Sedalia where they caught up with the rest of the division on October 19th. They continued to Rolettea and went into camp at 11:30 pm after marching thirty three miles. The forced marches continued on Price's trail – Independence, Blue River, Kansas City – almost all the time within hearing range of the skirmishing between the Union cavalry and Price's rear guard.

At Blue River, on October 23rd, Olaus could hear heavy fighting ahead and the infantry pushed on all day and into the night to join in the battle. After marching thirty seven miles in twenty four hours they reached the river – just to find that their prey had escaped. Within two days Union cavalry managed to engage Price's force near Lone Tree in a fight resulting in the capture of one of his commanders, General John S. Marmaduke, and about 1 000 of his men. Olaus got the news at Harrisonville, Missouri on October 26th. The pursuit of Price by infantry was abandoned. Lieutenant Colonel Stibbs escorted General Marmaduke to St. Louis, and Major Edward M. VanDuzee assumed command of the 12th Iowa. The regiment remained three days at Harrisonville. One night by the camp fire Olaus pulled out his piece of paper. They had marched 176 miles in eight consecutive days - 22 miles a day, average. He nodded to himself and gave the paper to Henry.

"Smith's Foot Cavalry." Henry smiled.
"Smith's Foot Cavalry." Olaus replied. "We marched almost twice as far as Jackson's boys, every day for weeks on end – with a train and artillery."

On October 30th the division was ready to return to St. Louis. Although trains were available, they were used to transport prisoners, cavalry horses, mules and artillery – and they had to march back to the city, 300 miles away. Olaus was not even disappointed. By now, being on the march was his normal way of life. They set out in the unstable winter weather. On November 3rd it snowed all day, sticky, wet snow covering everything and everybody. Olaus was soaking wet and cold, but marching was much better than standing still, and they reached Sedalia at night. When camp was made the men realized no fuel could be found for fires – no trees, no rails and no wood – nothing. They marched into the city where the officers obtained permission to use sheds and old stores as sleeping quarters. Scottish born Brigadier General John McArthur had been appointed to succeed "Wolf" Mower as commander of the 1st Division. He joined the division at Sedalia and assumed command. With new commanders followed changes. On November 4th, Olaus had a pleasant surprise. Somebody brought him a letter from Major VanDuzee, which said: "Olans Hanson, you are promoted to 4th Corporal in the 12th Iowa Veteran Volunteer Infantry Regiment………"

At California the next day they camped in snow ten inches deep. This time they had access to plenty of timber, and large fires were made melting the snow so the blankets could be spread out on dry ground. When Olaus woke up the following morning he had a four inch cover of snow on top of his blanket. On November 8th they left Jefferson City marching twenty six miles to the Osage River. The river was wide, waist deep, full of slush and ice – and there was no bridge. Olaus was mentally prepared for the experience – he had been in ice water countless times in Norway – but it did not make the crossing more pleasant. As he jumped in he quickly and uncontrollably drew his breath filling his lungs to the fullest extent – the body's automatic reaction to being submerged in freezing water. He knew only one way to cross a stream running at just above 32 degrees – as fast as possible. He forced his legs through the water with all the speed he could muster – within minutes his legs would cool down so much it would feel like they were squeezed in a vice, and they would be useless. He raced up on the opposite side rubbing his calves and thighs frantically. The experience had not improved a bit since his youth - it was just cold and unpleasant!

At 2 pm on November 15th the division filed into Benton Barracks in St. Louis after marching twenty two miles. As they huddled around the coal heaters in the barracks, the long, forced marches was suddenly something of the past, quickly forgotten about – but not quite. Olaus pulled out his piece of paper. Harrisonville to St. Louis – 303 miles in fifteen days, with only one day's rest, and three of the days marching through snow storms. Olaus jotted some numbers down on the paper. More than 20 miles a day – average.

Their camp still stood outside Memphis. In three and a half months they had travelled 770 miles by steamer, 50 miles by rail and marched 950 miles. Since June 16th they had fought two campaigns in Mississippi and been through five states – Tennessee, Mississippi, Arkansas, Missouri and Kansas. Olaus felt convinced they were some of the toughest campaigners on the American continent.

Colonel Joseph J. Woods was mustered out of the army during the stay in St. Louis, as were the non-veterans. Woods had served more than his three years and Lieutenant Colonel John H. Stibbs assumed command of the 12th Iowa. There would be no rest for the veterans. On November 24th the 12th left Benton Barracks and embarked on the steamer Silver Cloud bound for Nashville, Tennessee. Hans Hansen arrived from Fort Pickering and joined the regiment on the steamer. He had served his three years and would be mustered out at Nashville.

CLOSING DOWN
THE CONFEDERACY

After the capture of Atlanta, General William T. Sherman was preparing his "march to the sea". He would conduct a campaign throughout Georgia with the goal of reaching Savannah. Confederate General John Bell Hood set out to stop Sherman by severing his communication line from Chattanooga, Tennessee. After a brief pursuit of Hood, Sherman decided instead to cut his line of communication entirely and set out for Savannah while living off the land. He sent General George H. Thomas to Nashville to take charge of the defense of Tennessee. General A.J. Smith's division with the hardcore veteran fighters of the 12th Iowa would become a part of the force now massing at Nashville to defend the city against Hood.

After a predictable delay the steamers left St Louis on November 26th, heading down the Mississippi River. Turning up the Ohio they reached Smithland, Kentucky on the 28th. Here the men left at Memphis months ago rejoined the regiment, and they brought all the camp equipage the 12th had left behind when they went to Arkansas. The steamers continued up the Cumberland River escorted by a flotilla of tinclad and ironclad gun boats, reaching Nashville on December 1st. Olaus and Hans spent some time on the boat talking about the future. Hans was going to Decorah to pursue his plan to buy a farm. He had quite a lot of his bounty saved up and would be due another $100.00 at muster out. The 12th disembarked immediately upon arrival at Nashville. Olaus and Hans did not have much time to say good-bye. They shook hands, and Olaus could tell that Hans was worried about him – he of all people should know how easily his little brother could be killed in battle. Olaus had lived a charmed life so far during the war, but there was another big battle looming on the horizon, and it would not be the last one. Olaus turned and waived as the 12th Iowa proceeded to the front. It would be a long time before he saw Hans again.

The 16th Corps – during the campaign called "Detachment of the Army of the Tennessee" - fell into line of battle across Hardin Pike. The army was buzzing with news about the battle of Franklin, fought the previous day. General John McAllister Schofield had successfully fought off General John Bell Hood with a devastating loss of officers and men in the Confederate army. Schofield had merged his forces with General George H. Thomas at Nashville, and Hood was hot on the trail with the 30 000 men he had left. Thomas had more than 60 000 men. However - about 15 000 were detached as reserves and ordered to stay within the inner works and not to join the active force. This brought the effective fighting force down to about 45 000 men.

Nashville was built on irregular ground south of the Cumberland River, with elevations rising two- to three hundred feet. The surrounding country was cultural fields subdivided into small farms by stone walls. Good roads radiated from the city center – Granny White Pike running directly south with Franklin Pike immediately to the east. Along these two roads Hood's army approached on December 2nd. Olaus saw the Rebels coming, and he also noticed how they came to a halt when they discovered the seven mile semicircular defense line around the city, studded with forts, and the Union Army drawn up in line of battle.

Apparently the Confederates had in mind to entrench – they deployed in a line about four miles long and started throwing up breastworks. Artillery was posted on

The outer perimeter of the Union line at Nashville December 16th, 1864. Wikipedia.org.

top of the most prominent elevations, usually within the infantry lines. On the night of December 8th the temperature fell to almost 20 degrees below freezing. Cold rain quickly turned to sleet and snow in a bitter storm covering the country around Nashville in a sheet of ice. Although camp rumors had told Olaus a Federal assault was planned for December 10th, the ice put an end to both the plans for an attack and the work on the entrenchments.

The men huddled in the pup tents waiting out the storm. Olaus sat cross legged on a blanket smoking his pipe while he looked at the driving, fine grained snow. He had found that under circumstances like these it gave a certain amount of comfort to light a pipe and drink the ever present hot coffee. Henry Steen was writing a letter – there was not much else to do waiting for the weather to abate. Olaus let his thoughts drift. He found it interesting how – when he was off the front line – the war seemed unreal and infinitely far away, but when bullets began singing around his head, his adrenalin raced and he became a different person. He was focused and detached at the same time – focused on what he needed to do to survive, but detached from the dangers involved. He had changed during his time in the 12th Iowa – irreversibly changed – and he knew it. He was a solider. He was no longer just a man in a soldier's outfit – he was a soldier.

On December 13th warm rain melted the snow and ice, creating axle-deep mud and slush even on the best roads, stalling all transport of wagons and artillery. On the 14th the roads started to dry up, and an order was given for a general assault the next day. The men would be issued three days' ration and sixty rounds of ammunition, and the ordnance wagons were to be fully loaded and double teamed, ready to go at an instant. The 12th Iowa line extended from the right side of Hardin Pike to the Northwestern Railroad. An order was issued to the regiment that the attack would be coordinated as a left wheeling movement where General Smith's corps, after marching down Hardin Pike, would turn left and attack the entrenchments along Hillsboro pike.

The officer situation in the 12th Iowa on December 14th was indeed peculiar. When the regiment arrived at Nashville on December 1st, the mustering officer at the post told the officers that reenlistments of officers in veteran organizations were irregular. Officers who had served three years either had to re-muster, or muster out. All but five commissioned officers of the 12th Iowa mustered out. That left the regiment without one single commissioned line officer before the battle, and all companies would be commanded by ranking sergeants...........

The men of the 12th Iowa were awakened without drum beat at 4 am, one hour before dawn, on Thursday December 15th. Breakfast was prepared and eaten and the men were under arms at 6 am. Olaus could tell there would be delays. A heavy fog blanketed the landscape, preventing them from seeing the enemy's works. When the fog lifted a few minutes after 8 am the column moved out to the right of Hardin Pike, two hours behind schedule. The 12th Iowa, commanded by Lieutenant Colonel John Stibbs, was initially deployed as the right wing of the 3rd Brigade. Later it was ordered to move left – to the left side of the pike – and form as the brigade's left center. About 8:30 a large cavalry force came up to their rear finding both pikes blocked by the division. Sometime before 10 o'clock came the order to advance. Company B was sent out as skirmishers and quickly ran into enemy forces which they easily drove back. Smith's corps slowly wheeled left and the cavalry could pass, setting out for the right flank. Some of the men pointed to the rear and Olaus turned and saw the hills around the city crowded with spectators to the coming battle. A thought flashed through his head: "Bull Run". Here was another battle viewed as entertainment by the local citizens, but he knew that today the spectators were not supporters, as they had been at Bull Run. Nearly all of the almost 100 000 inhabitants of Nashville were sympathetic to the Confederacy.

The 12th advanced over rolling ground obstructed by ditches and fences for about two miles before they came to the crest of a hill. As they moved over the crest they saw a Rebel force camped in the valley below and a battery started to fire from a hill beyond the camp, about a thousand yards away. Olaus was hiding in a position where he could overlook the enemy's breastwork while Battery I of the 2nd Missouri Light Artillery was brought up and opened fire on the Rebels. The 12th were spectators for about an hour and a half, while shots and shells were screeching overhead. Olaus looked at Henry. He was sleeping. Olaus smiled and shook his head – it was incredible how anyone could sleep in the turmoil of everything that was happening around them. While the 2nd Missouri Artillery shelled the Confederate battery on the next hill the 2nd and 3rd Brigade captured the redoubts immediately in front of the 12th Iowa, called No. 4 and No. 5.

At about 4 pm the 3rd Brigade was ready to charge Redoubt No. 3. Colonel Sylvester G. Hill ordered the 12th Iowa's colors to lead the charge directly into the redoubt, and the other regiments to follow, but take distance to the left and right so not to not crowd while going over the works. Olaus did not look down at his hands. He knew they were not shaking. His eyes were fixed on the top of the redoubt waiting for the signal to charge. The bugle sounded. Olaus jumped to his

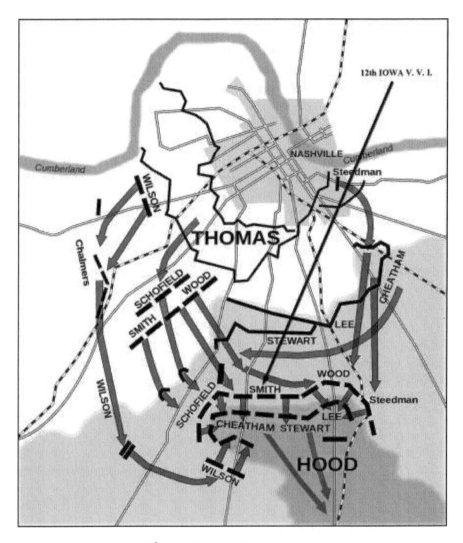

The deployment of the 12th Iowa Veteran Volunteer Infantry Regiment in Smith's division at the battle of Nashville, Tennessee December 15th, 1864. Map by Hal Jespersen www.posix.com/CW.

feet and stormed up the hill, bayonet fixed. He saw shadows moving on both sides of him, and knew they were 12th Iowa veterans racing towards the breast work trying to roll over the defenders before they could launch a destructive fire. Immediately in front of the work they came upon a deep ditch. Olaus held the musket in his hand, leaped across in one long jump and continued towards the breastwork. As he jumped he saw Color Sergeant Henry Grannis – with the flag – falling into the ditch and start crawling up on the other side. To help him Acting Adjutant David W. Reed grabbed the flag as he was climbing back up. Grannis would have nothing of it – nobody else could touch his colors. He grabbed Reed's hand, pulled himself out and stormed to the top of the parapet with the flag lifted high over his head.

The Rebels kept up a firestorm of musketry while they were wheeling the artillery to the rear and heavy clouds of gun powder drove from the redoubt. In the instant Grannis reached the top of the parapet a charge of grape shot from Redoubt No. 2 exploded directly in the fold of the flag, tearing it to shreds. Olaus heard a "thud" about ten feet away. Turning around he saw Colonel Hill reel in the saddle and topple to the ground. He had a gaping hole in the forehead from a Rebel musket ball and Olaus could tell there was nothing he could do for him.

The Confederate defenders withdrew to a breastwork about 300 yards to the rear and continued to shell the 3rd Brigade. While the brigade kept up a heavy fire on the breastwork it reformed the line which had gotten into considerable disorder during the charge – probably due to lack of commissioned line officers. Adjutant Reed and Colonel William R. Marshall from the 7th Minnesota with about 200 men in advance of the brigade wheeled left and charged directly towards a stone wall, capturing Redoubt No. 2. Olaus leaped onto the breastwork with the advance force and the Rebels instantly surrendered with three or four guns, several ammunition wagons and a large number of small arms.

Incredibly, the 12th Iowa had gotten away with only seven men wounded. Olaus found Peter Larson, a fellow Norwegian, sitting clasping his foot. Larson was a veteran and three years Olaus' senior. "Er det alvorlig?" (Is it serious?) Olaus asked. "Bare et kjøttsår. Kommer til å halte ei stund" (Just a flesh wound – I'll be limping for a while), Larson replied.

On the morning of December 16th Olaus was woken up before daybreak. He had breakfast in great haste when Colonel Stibbs ordered the 12th Iowa to fall into line of battle and move by the right flank about half a mile along Hillsboro Pike. In

Previous page: The 12th Iowa Veteran Volunteer Infantry Regiment with Corporal Olaus Hansen charging Redoubt No. 3 of General John Bell Hood's Army of Tennessee at the battle of Nashville, December 15th, 1864. Color Sergeant Henry Grannis' flag has just been torn to shreds by a charge of grape shot while Colonel Sylvester G. Hill (on horseback) is killed by a shot in the forehead from a Confederate sharp shooter in Redoubt No. 2. Wikipedia.org.

order to attack Hood's new line which had been formed overnight the three corps made a right wheel movement falling into line of battle across Granny White pike. The 16th Corps was at the center of the line with the 1st division deployed across Granny White Pike, the 12th regiment's right resting on the pike itself. The Rebel artillery opened up and the Federal infantry threw themselves on the ground watching the duel between the batteries. The position showed to be very exposed. Suddenly a musket ball whizzed through Company F. After almost hitting John Bremner it went through the blanket of one of the men and ended up knocking Russell Peasley on the head without killing him.

Compton's hill - or Shy's hill - about 1880, with one of the stone walls the soldiers had to scale. Battle of Nashville Preservation Society.

About 11 am it started raining – a pelting, chilling rain soaking everything and everybody, making it extremely unpleasant to lie on the ground. At 3:30 pm Olaus saw the 2nd Brigade charge up the right side of Compton's Hill - later to be named Shy's hill after the Confederate Colonel William Shy who died defending it. The colors fell to the ground three times before it finally floated over the enemy's works, and Olaus knew perfectly well what that meant. Three color bearers were either wounded, or died during the attack

"Forward!"

Olaus heard Colonel Stibbs' order and was on his feet in a moment. Finally the attack was on. The 12th Iowa charged full speed through canister- and musket fire across a corn field traversed by stone walls and ditches, towards the front of Compton's Hill. Due to the regiment's speed and the enemy's increasing panic they took few casualties during the first few minutes, but halfway across the field the Rebels had found the distance to the quickly approaching Iowans and the shots became deadly accurate. A few yards from Olaus Ole Tande Hansen fell down, holding his side. "Gå på!" (Carry on!) he shouted to Olaus. "Ikke bry deg om meg! Det går bra!" (Don't worry about me! It's OK!). Gustav Helgesen spun around and crashed to the ground, mortally wounded. Edward Wells took a ball through the knee – he would not be joining in the charge up the hill.

Suddenly a shell exploded in the fold of the colors – both the flag and the color guard were completely enveloped in gun smoke, and Olaus thought they were all dead. Color Sergeant Henry Grannis came storming out of the black cloud with the flag high above his head as if nothing had happened, jumped over a stone wall and raced up the hillside. Olaus watched in astonishment. That man had nine lives!

As Olaus started up the hill a man fell and came tumbling down, and in passing him he recognized eighteen year old James T. Loring of Company F. He was dead. Olaus kept his eyes on the colors, bullets whizzing around his head, and climbed the hillside as quickly as he could. As he came over the crest Grannis was already at the breastwork and the Rebels in full retreat. Olaus scaled the work – a heavy stone wall strengthen with earth and rails on the outside and a ditch on the inside. The 12th took the battery immediately inside the work and pursued the enemy to the hills at the rear of the line, capturing prisoners as they went. Olaus stopped – there was no point charging any further. The Rebels were either in full retreat out of range, or captured.

Darkness would soon be falling and the rain made the evening even darker. To follow on the trail of Hood's army would be futile. The regiment went into bivouac for the night on the front line. Olaus found Knud Iversen of Company B with a bandage on his hand. He waived the hand towards Olaus: "Blir ikke noe brevskriving på ei stund!" (No letters will be written for a while!). Olaus grinned. He would obviously survive. Henry Steen was sitting with his back against a tree. He lifted his pencil as a greeting to Olaus when he passed - he was doing just that: Writing a letter.

The rain which started to fall on December 16th continued almost incessantly until December 30th. The Union army followed on Hood's trail southwards over roads resembling quagmires, the men covered in mud from head to foot. The nights were usually cold enough for the surface of the mud to freeze, but not hard enough to carry a man. Every day when the march resumed the soldiers fell through, wading in icy slush. Smith's corps turned west at Pulaski and reached Clifton on the Tennessee River - via Lawrence and Waynesboro - on January 2nd, 1865. From Clifton they were transported on steamers to Eastport, Mississippi, a landing on the border between the two states. On the journey south they passed Pittsburg Landing, which did not rekindle any good memories about the events three years prior. However – he was alive, which was a lot more than could be said about thousands of other soldiers marching onto the battlefield on April 6th, 1862.

Upon reaching Eastport an order was issued to go into winter camp. All camp equipment was stored at Nashville, so the men immediately went about scouting the bleak, snow covered ridges for scrub pines and other small timber. They converted the trees to building materials and constructed shanties with bunks and fire places. The ordnance stores came by steamer in the middle of January, but the supply ship showed up with corn for mule feed instead of rations. By parching it, grinding it in coffee mills or beating it on rocks, the corn was their food supply for a week before another steamer arrived.

About the same time Lieutenant Colonel Stibbs was given leave of absence and went home. In Stibbs' absence newly promoted Major Samuel G. Knee assumed command of the 12th Iowa. Predictably, Eastport did not become the regiment's winter quarter. After just a month in camp they were again called to duty in another department of operation. Olaus started to realize that it carried a certain amount of responsibility to be well known veterans of many battles. They were trusted to do excellent service wherever and whenever called for, and there was never a lack of departments wanting to use General Smith's 1st Division as an "emergency corps". This time Olaus was to be member of a force of 16 000 veterans considered a "flying column of guerillas", handpicked by Ulysses S. Grant who was now the supreme commander of all Federal armies. The plan was to use this force to close out the war in the Deep South and put a permanent end to the Confederacy's last pockets of resistance.

On February 5th Olaus and the 12th Iowa vacated the shanties at Eastport. Heading south the regiment embarked on the steamer Magenta with the 3rd Brigade commanded by Colonel William R. Marshall. They passed Cairo on the 10th and arrived at Vicksburg on the 13th under orders to march overland for an attack on Mobile, Alabama. Olaus almost felt at home. The regiment camped in the same area at Walnut Hills for the third time during the war. The order to attack Mobile was soon countermanded by a new order to re-embark on the steamer on February 18th and go to New Orleans. Olaus and Henry were playing cards in the tent when the new order came. Henry looked at Olaus.
"Surprised?"
"Noooooooooot really......"
Olaus puffed on his pipe and beat Henry's two pairs with three jacks. He had taken to playing poker after a few months in the army. In Norway he had always thought playing cards was boring. In the army, it beat doing nothing during the evenings, and kept his mind off previous carnage and future battles.

After a three day trip downriver the 12th Iowa arrived at New Orleans on February 21st. They were now in the Military Division of the West Mississippi under the command of Major General Edward R.S. Canby. They disembarked from the Magenta on February 22nd and went into camp on the old Jackson battlefield from 1814. During the night the men were happy they could utilize some of the old earthworks to get upon higher ground. A torrential rainstorm practically washed the camp away leaving it under a foot of water. A high wind blew down the shelter tents and the whole command was completely unprotected from the elements. By morning muskets could be seen with bayonets sticking in the ground supporting blankets and haversacks hung to dry over the butts. Olaus was wading around in the water trying to find some of his supplies which had drifted away in the storm. Soon the water ran off and soaked into the ground. The shelter tents were reset and floors were laid by brush cut from nearby swamps.

The weather in Louisiana was a vast improvement over Cairo, Illinois. After leaving ice and snow behind they were greeted with warm sunshine and flowering orange trees. Olaus went into New Orleans and witnessed Mardi Gras, just revived from before the war. On Sunday, March 2nd the 12th Iowa marched six miles along Shell Road to Canal Street, about eight miles from Lakeport on Lake Pontchartrain. The steamer A.G. Brown made a four day trip via Lake Borgne across the Mississippi Sound bringing the regiment to Dauphine Island outside

Mobile Bay. On March 3rd – still on the boat – Olaus had an envelope handed to him by Major Knee. These envelopes started to look familiar. He opened it and found a document similar to the previous ones he had received – "Olans Hanson, you are promoted to 3rd corporal of the 12th Iowa Veteran Volunteer Infantry........." It was his third promotion in just over a year, his second in four months. Somebody had obviously taken notice of him at the battle of Nashville, where the 12th went into battle with no commissioned line officers.

They landed at Dauphine Island at 4 pm on March 6th. Located on the island was Fort Gaines, captured by the Federal fleet of Rear Admiral David G. Farragut the previous August. They quickly established a camp on the sands. Regiment by regiment the corps assembled on the island. Some of them came by the inner passage while others arrived by ocean steamer from the mouth of the Mississippi. Olaus felt like he had come to a tropical paradise - he had never seen anything comparable to Dauphine Island. Waves were slowly washing over the beaches and he had to squint his eyes against the bright sunlight reflecting from the sand and sea. The salt water breeze was flowing through his hair and flocks of pelicans and sea gulls were drifting across the water. Every day he was swimming in the crystal clear sea and outside the island were oyster beds so plentiful that six mule teams were filled up on low tide and hauled into camp. The oysters were shoveled out on the ground and eaten baked, stewed, roasted, fried..... or raw.

It was with great regrets Olaus left his tropical paradise on Saturday, March 19th. Gunboat No. 48 picked the regiment up from the beach and crossed the mouth of the bay to anchor up at Navy Cove above Fort Morgan – another fort captured by Farragut. No transportation was allowed – officers and men were issued five days rations in their haversacks and had to carry all equipment they were going to need. On the 20th the gunboat carrying the 12th Iowa crossed Mobile Bay in a flotilla with other gunboats and "mosquito" boats – small boats converted to gun boats. The flotilla ascended Fish River and continued about ten miles upwards to Dannelly's Mill, a place mainly consisting of two sawmills and extensive tar- and turpentine factories. The regiment disembarked and went into camp in heavy pine forest on top of a hill.

The order from General Canby was to throw up breastworks at every position along the march. The men cut pines more than two feet in diameter and forty to fifty feet long and braced them with eight foot long, notched poles. After piling the pine logs four feet high earth was shoveled on the outside until the breastwork was six feet thick at the bottom and four feet on top. Olaus took a look at the formidable fortification when it was done - not even shells from a field battery would make impact.

On Saturday, March 25th the army advanced northwest by north along the east side of Mobile Bay towards Spanish Fort, about twenty miles distant. Slogging through swamps and dense pine forests they skirmished with the enemy as they advanced. Every night they built strong breastworks, making the bivouacs into regular fortifications. After breaking camp on the 27th the column marched directly to Spanish fort, arriving within firing range of the fort's batteries about 9:30 am.

The 3rd Division of the 16th Corps deployed on the extreme right, the right flank resting on Minette Bay north of the fort. The 1st Division deployed next in line to the left and the 13th Corps extended the line all the way around the fort, resting its left on D'Olieve's Bay to the south. The 12th Iowa was situated at the extreme left of the 1st Division, next to the 13th Corps. Companies B and I were sent out as skirmishers, quickly driving the enemy's pickets inside the breastwork.

The fortifications were very strong with a deep ditch immediately outside the breastworks and a cleared space of a hundred yard in front. An abatiss of trees felled top outwards and wire stretched between the tree tops surrounded the fort. The 3rd Brigade with the 12th Iowa got into position out of musket range, and as the 13th Corps followed to get into line, an episode occurred which gave Olaus a flashback to the assault at Fort Donelson more than three years before. The 2nd Vermont Infantry opened fire on the Iowa skirmish line and Corporal Henry Fry went down with a scream, severely wounded in the foot. He was taken to the rear where the surgeon at field hospital decided it had to be amputated.

Olaus waited all afternoon for the order to attack, but a general shortage of ammunition stalled the advance and the ordnance train did not arrive before the night of the 29th. Gun boats had arrived the previous day, taking position on the left flank – one of them ran upon a torpedo and was blown up. The Federal batteries were slowly getting into position, pounding the Confederate works as they became ready. The Rebels were constantly shelling the Federal lines, and the men sometimes took too little notice of the shells flying over the camp. Two pieces of shrapnel from a 10 inch gun had already fallen down among the men without injuring anybody. On the night of the 29th Abner Dunham of Company F was playing ball with some of the men in the 12th when a shell exploded overhead, spreading shrapnel and parts of trees over the ball players. Nobody was hurt. Some of the men from the 29th Illinois were not so lucky – a shell fell among them when they were drawing rations. Four were killed and eight wounded. Olaus noticed that

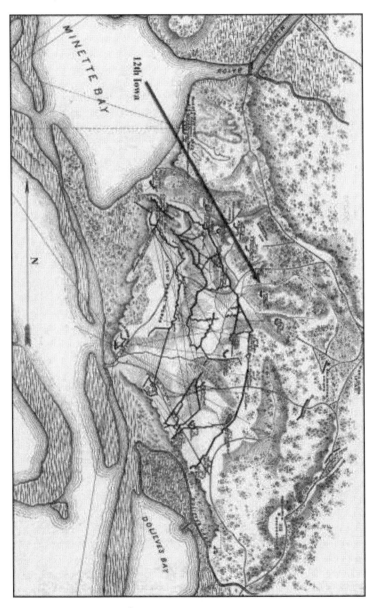

The position of the 12ᵗʰ Iowa Veteran Volunteer Infantry Regiment during the siege of Spanish Fort, Alabama. The Library of Congress.

some of the incoming fire was from two neighboring forts, Huger and Tracy, situated on islands above the Rebel entrenchment. He made sure to keep well protected on the side facing the forts, as he knew the batteries had already taken a fearful toll in the 3rd Division.

The 3rd Brigade was excused from picket duty as it was detailed to dig trenches. Olaus did not mind – it was hard work, but it beat being shot at. He realized that there would not be an immediate general assault – this work bore the hallmark of a siege operation. The first parallel of trenches were dug 400 yard from the enemy's breastwork, then approaches towards the work, and another parallel at about 200 yards. New approaches were dug from these trenches all the way up to 25 yards from the Rebel work.

On March 30th the 3rd Brigade was moved to the center of the 13th Corps to cover a temporary gap in the line. For five days every man in the 12th Iowa was held on continuous duty with three companies as pickets while the other companies dug trenches. Eight mortars were put in position next to their camp. The mortar shells went so slowly Olaus could actually follow their trajectory until they lit up inside the fort. The fort returned fire – the incoming shells exploded throughout the 12th Iowa camp. One shell exploded right next to John Coleman in Company F, completely burying him but leaving him unhurt, while a piece of shrapnel barely missed Sergeant John Bremner. On the morning of April 5th the whole line was moved up within musket range of the Rebel fortifications. The batteries had been drawn up in a semicircle approximately 800 yards from the Rebel works, while the trenches and approaches had reached the abatiss which was being cut away to make access for a general assault. The skirmishers were just fifty yards off the parapet.

The next day trenches were still being extended and improved. To venture out of the ditches meant immediate exposure to Rebel sniper fire. Abner Dunham was hard at work behind a pile of dirt when Marion Austin of Company I came to inquire if F had a spade not in use. Before Abner could answer, Marion spun around and fell to the ground with a musket ball through his leg. He was quickly carried away to the field hospital at the rear.

One night the regiment was much amused by an episode overheard by Sergeant Price. The Generals' headquarters were quite close to the 12th Iowa, and Price had spotted Canby ride up to A.J. Smith's tent, exchanging opinions on the progress of the siege. During the conversation Canby brought up the subject of some missing turkeys.

"General – I understand that your men sometimes take things that do not belong to them." Canby was heard saying.

"Yes, by G — d----", Smith replied. "We're going to take Mobile, and it don't belong to my men!"

"My cook procured half a dozen turkeys last night and put them in a coup by my tent. This morning I found that four of them had been taken."

"Couldn't have been my men – not my men." Smith replied, "They would have taken them all!"

On April 8th the 1st and the 3rd Division were ordered into the trenches and kept in readiness for a general assault. At 5:30 pm all batteries opened a terrific barrage on the Rebel fort, continuing until dark. Just as darkness was falling two companies of skirmishers from the 3rd Division pushed rapidly forward on the extreme right driving the Rebel pickets in headlong flight ahead of them. Olaus could see that the 12th Iowa would just be spectators to this drama when the 8th under Colonel Geddes together with the 124th Illinois made a dash for the fort and captured about 300 yards of the breastwork. The main attack was planned for the next morning,

Robert E. Lee (sitting, left) surrender to Ulysses S. Grant (sitting next to him) at the Wilmer McLean House, Appomattox Courthouse, Virginia, April 9th, 1865. Standing second from the left, facing the two is Major General George Armstrong Custer. Wikipedia.org.

but the 12th Iowa pickets soon discovered that the Rebel fort had been deserted under the cover of darkness. The 3rd Brigade was immediately ordered forward and the fort was occupied capturing 800 prisoners in the process. Early in the morning of April 9th Olaus was on the march north. Fort Blakely was situated a short distance from Spanish Fort and the 1st Division was ordered to support the 2nd Division already in the process of preparing an attack. Again Olaus would just be a spectator to a grand assault. When he arrived the 2nd Division made a charge and captured the fort. This left the road open to Mobile and a Federal force immediately advanced around the head of the bay to capture the city. The Rebel authorities made short work of Fort Eugene in the harbor, blowing it up and evacuating the city. On the same day Robert E. Lee surrendered to Ulysses S. Grant in Wilmer McLean's house at Appomattox Courthouse, Virginia. The Civil War was officially over. Present at the surrender was a commander Olaus would meet in person in Dakota Territory eleven years later – brevet Major General George Armstrong Custer.

On April 14th, after just a few days' rest, Olaus was on the march again. The 16th Corps set out for Montgomery, Alabama. He was wading through mosquito infested swamps, over beds of quick sand and through heavy forests of pitch pine where the only industry seemed to be pitch, turpentine and tar. Occasionally they would come upon an isolated log cabin with a small garden and a cotton patch. The corps covered fifty miles in three days, cutting a swath through the wilderness in the northwest corner of Florida crossing Perdido River and finally arriving at Escambia River. The next five days the Corps covered another seventy five miles on roads slightly more improved, arriving at Greenville, Alabama on April 21st.

On the 22nd General Benjamin H. Grierson arrived from Mobile with the confirmation of Lee's Surrender to Grant at Appomattox Courthouse. At 3 pm the 1st and 3rd Division batteries fired a 200 shot salute in celebration of the event accompanied by cheers from the whole army. Olaus was happy that the war was over, but could not help but harbor a feeling of uncertainty. He was a soldier now. He had been drilling, marching and shooting at human beings for three and a half years. He had seen the carnage of battle, men killed in front of his eyes - shot through the head, disfigured by musket balls, jaws shot off, noses shot off, men disemboweled by artillery shells, burned to death in brush fires or blown to pieces and scattered all over the ground. He had seen piles of amputated arms and legs outside field hospitals, smelt the stench from putrefying men and horses on the battlefield and dug burial trenches throwing unidentified Rebel soldiers in by the hundreds. The images on his mind from all the battles were not compatible with a normal, run of the mill day as a farmer in Iowa. He was not at all sure how he would be able to return to a path of land, walk behind a horse and watch the crops grow.

The 1st and 3rd Division continued forty miles to Montgomery, arriving at 1 pm on April 25th. Camp was made three mile east of the city and they soon had visits by paroled soldiers from Lee's army without food, clothes or money. The Federal soldiers shared some of their rations with the Confederate parolees before they continued on their way. Olaus went into Montgomery to see what kind of goods could be procured. It was a scant selection of supplies at incredibly inflated prices. Boots marked Confederate $ 250.00 could be had for $ 10.00 in U.S. money, or $ 7.00 in gold or silver. Flour had been selling for $ 500.00 a barrel and very little was available.

While in the city Olaus joined some of the men from the 12th walking down to the cotton shed where they were held prisoners, to try to find the graves of their diseased comrades. In a neglected corner of the cemetery they discovered a long trench, and in the records two words opposite the lot number: "Yankee prisoners"........

On April 29th Henry Steen came rushing over to Olaus with the same expression on his face as he had three years ago in the same city, when Bliss had been killed. His face had the color of white ashes, and Olaus knew something was seriously wrong. He did not ask – he knew Henry would get around to it.
"Lincoln er død! Skutt i et attentat!» (Lincoln is dead – assassinated!) Henry said.

Suddenly Olaus felt exhausted. He sat down on the ground with his back to a tree, pulling his knees all the way up to his chest. Slowly he took his pipe out, filled it with tobacco and lit a match. Almost four years for Lincoln. Four long years of carnage, death and destruction. Lincoln had personified the struggle. The thought of the Illinois lawyer with his stovepipe hat had made living in the twilight zone between life and death worthwhile, made Olaus see beyond the battlefield, made him able to turn his back on the horrifying face of war. And now he was dead. The brutality of the conflict had reached its hand all the way into the President's box at the Ford Theatre in Washington. From sunrise to sunset on May 1st guns were fired every half hour, and every minute between 12 and 1. All flags were draped and flown at half-staff.

On Wednesday, May 10th the brigade moved out of Montgomery heading towards Selma. To miles beyond the Alabama River - after crossing on a pontoon bridge - they were called back to embark on steamers. The 12th Iowa, 35th Iowa and 33rd

One Confederate dollar from Alabama. This bill had no value by the end of the Civil War. The author's collection.

Missouri crowded onto the Tarscon, reaching Selma at 1 o'clock in the morning. Disembarking at daylight they waited for a camp site for 24 hours, finally going into camp on May 12th.

Selma had been the center for production of weapons and ammunition before General James H. Wilson had raided the city with his cavalry, and the explosions from the torched factories had wrecked most of the business district. The 12th Iowa settled down to drill and guard duty. Some of the guard duty consisted of frequent trips into the country escorting agents of the Freedmen's Bureau when they adjusted differences between planters and freedmen. The Freedmen's Bureau – or the Bureau of Refugees, Freedmen and Abandoned Lands – had been created after initiative from President Abraham Lincoln and put into place by the Freedmen's Bureau Bill in March of 1865. The intention behind the bill was to encourage the plantation owners to rebuild their plantations at the same time as it urged freedmen (former slaves) to seek employment for the purpose of working with the planters as employers and employees rather than as masters and slaves. Last, but not least, it provided for a Freedmen's Bureau managed by the War Department through General Oliver O. Howard to keep an eye on the contracts between freedmen and planters. This was why Federal escorts were needed. With just 900 agents to cover the entire South and tensions running high between the plantation owners and the freedmen, the assignment as an agent of the Freedmen's Bureau was obviously associated with danger – hence the need for protection by detachments of soldiers.

About May 25th the tents and baggage left at New Orleans arrived at Selma, and a proper camp was established with awnings in front of the tents covered with brush to create shade against the burning sun. There was a simmering contention among

Work at the Freedmen's Bureau. Wikipedia.org.

the soldiers. They wanted to go home. The war was over, and they saw no reason to stay in the army. Olaus had no such feeling. He felt that he had nowhere to go, and another day in the army was another good day. He liked the drill, he liked the structured life style and he liked the danger associated with the trips into the country where – when it came right down to it - nothing or nobody ruled but the man with the gun. When a request came for volunteers to the Freedmen's Bureau at Selma, he was quick to put his name forward. Not only did he want to take on additional duty – the mission of the Freedmen's Bureau was something he could identify with from his native Norway: The protection of the underdogs of society, like the cotter class, where he came from. Subsequently, on June 1st, he was handed one of the now very familiar envelopes with his name on – for the 6th time. "Corporal Olans Hanson – you are promoted to 5th sergeant of the 12th Iowa Veteran Volunteer Infantry Regiment, assigned as an orderly sergeant to the Headquarter of the Freedmen's Bureau at Selma, Alabama". Accompanying the promotion was three sergeant's stripes and he also received the 5th installment of his bounty.

In the middle of July all the regiments of the 3rd Brigade were mustered out – except the 12th Iowa. Soldiers from regiments with a lot shorter time in the service were allowed to go home and together with continued poor rations, the simmering feeling of discontent among the soldiers of the 12th surfaced in open revolt. There was an agreement between many of the men – in two or three companies the entire company – not to answer roll call or do any kind of duty. Olaus kept well away from the instigators of the revolt, minding his job as a sergeant at the Freedmen's Bureau. Eventually they were arrested and sent to Montgomery to be tried by court martial. This course of action by the military authorities quickly changed the attitude of the leaders of the revolt, and they were sent back to Selma by request from Major Knee, who at the time was provost marshal of the city.

In August the provost marshal was Major J.P. Houston of the 5th Minnesota. He reported that the country was "emphatically in a condition of anarchy". Crime was rampant, life was insecure as well as property and the country was filled with desperadoes and bandits who robbed and plundered on every side. Murder was commonplace – Houston knew about at least twelve cases where blacks had gone missing or turned up dead at the hands of whites. After having been tortured for up to a week some of the blacks had eventually been killed in a most brutal manner - shot, dragged by the neck or drowned. Olaus learned that the task of protecting agents of the Freedmen's Bureau when they ventured out into the countryside was a matter of life or death.

On August 8th the 16th Corps was discontinued, after nearly all the regiments had been mustered out. With so many regiments gone, the remaining ones were required to spread out and cover more territory. Olaus' duty at the Freedmen's Bureau ended when the 12th Iowa was sent to Talladega to establish a new regimental headquarter on September 25th. By then, he had learnt a lot about the conditions between the planters and the former slaves in the South. Upon arrival at Talladega Company C was sent to Center, Company F to Ashville and Company I to Wedowee. Olaus experienced a life changing event. Company G was detailed as dispatch carriers between the four different posts, covering a large part of northeast Alabama. He was mounted. On a horse. He could not believe it. After several trips through the countryside carrying dispatches he knew he would never march again. The duties of the four companies consisted of adjusting the differences between planters and freedmen, administering the Oath of Allegiance by those who wanted to swear the oath to the United States and collect Government property previously owned by the Confederate States.

Olaus was riding dispatch duty until Christmas Day when the 12th Iowa received orders to abandon all outposts and report to the regimental headquarter at Talladega. Together with the 11th Missouri the regiment was under order to immediately proceed to Memphis, Tennessee, where a revolt was threatened by freedmen, and the citizens had asked for Federal protection. Due to bad railroad service the regiment did not arrive before January 2nd, 1866 via Selma, Meridian and Corinth. The first night in Memphis was spent on the platform at the railroad depot – the next day the regiment was distributed throughout the city, with five companies at the arsenal. After the 12th Iowa troops arrived no more indications were seen of a brewing revolt. Henry Steen had picked up a newspaper which he brought Olaus one evening they were patrolling.

"Here. Read this." Henry grinned. "It's great to know we're appreciated"

Olaus grabbed the newspaper. One of the columns read: "The 12th Iowa is one of the bravest, most orderly, best behaved regiments in the service. Its presence assures our people perfect security and protection." Olaus smiled.

"Certainly." He said. "I like this. Too bad there is no more to be done in the Army of the Tennessee. It's all winding down to the end. No way of telling what I'll do after muster out."

On January 20th the 12th Iowa Veteran Volunteer Infantry Regiment was ordered to muster out of service. The rolls were made out and all the Government property turned over. The regiment was directed to Davenport, Iowa for final pay and discharge. Olaus knew he had quite a bit of money coming – the rest of his bounty which was $ 140.00, and he was also due $ 55.55 on his clothing account. That amounted to almost $ 200.00.The Steen brothers were quite emotional when the four Norwegian comrades in arms, who had shared so much during the long conflict, stood together outside the recruitment office in Davenport after muster out on the 25th.

"Have you decided what to do?" John asked.

"Yes." Olaus replied. "I'm going to Norway."

"Norway?" Theodore looked at him.

"Yes. Norway. Your parents live in Glenwood. My parents live in Nannestad. Haven't seen them for almost five years. I have a bit of money and I can make the trip right now. No way of knowing when I can go next. I'm going to Norway."

"Are you going to visit your brothers?" Henry asked.

"I am." Olaus replied, "Haven't seen Ole for years, and I've got to say hello to Hans before I leave. They probably want me to bring letters to Norway."

The Steen brothers shook hands with Olaus, bid him good-bye and walked off down the street. Olaus watched their backs for a while, feeling almost abandoned.

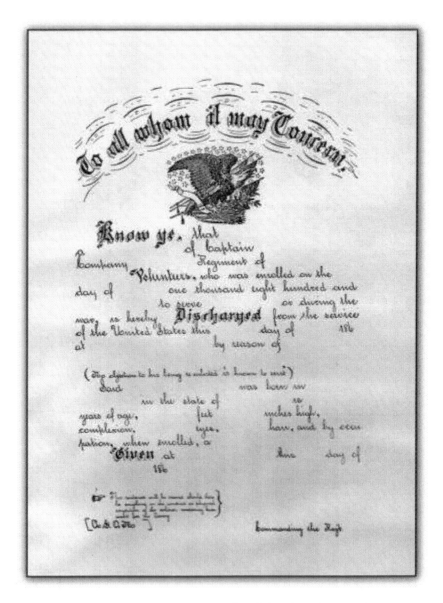

*Discharge paper. Since this document was handed to the soldier and no copy was
kept, they are very hard to find. From Carnahan: Manual of the
Civil War and Key to the Grand Army of the Republic and Kindred Societies.*

He had built strong ties to his comrades during the war, and it was hard to accept that they were being severed. He pulled out his pipe and lit a match. After puffing on it for a while he went into a shop and bought some tobacco. He felt strange and out of place in his citizen's suit – pants, jacket, shirt, socks, hat, belt – clothes he had not worn for years. He felt at home in a uniform. It would be strange not to have to sleep on the ground – but good not to have to wake up in sub-zero temperatures with a sheet of frozen snow on top of his blanket. He went down to the steam boat landing, boarded a steamer and bought a ticket for MacGregor. He was headed for Decorah. The Civil War was at an end.

NORWAY

Olaus stood on the deck of the large ocean steamer looking east, the wind blowing through his hair. No sail ship this time. He was heading for Liverpool, England to take a train to Hull, and from there sail to Christiania. He had spent a few days with Hans, and then Ole and Maren, before he left for New York to embark on the boat. He could tell that Hans was genuinely happy to see him - he was the only one who could really appreciate that Olaus had made it through the war without a scratch. 600 000 soldiers had not been equally lucky. The only man he could think of who had lived an even more charmed life throughout the whole war, was Henry Grannis. In spite of being the color sergeant of the 12th Iowa and a walking target for all the sharpshooters in the Confederate Army, he survived over a hundred hours of battle without being hit once.

Olaus already had flashbacks where he saw burial trenches he had dug on the battlefields in the Mississippi River Valley. Images of mangled bodies and faces - and puddles of blood - tended to pop up in his mind at the most inconvenient times. Especially at night. He could still smell the decomposing bodies - and he knew why. He was an idling soldier with no new battles to look forward to. No more action. Nothing would happen next to take his mind of what had happened already. No more hard marches, no more freezing temperatures, no more feeling of companionship and common purpose. Nothing. He was required to revert back to life as he knew it as a twenty year old innocent immigrant who just arrived in the United States. He did not think he could do it. It seemed like a life somebody else had lived - not him. He was not that young man anymore. Too much had happened, over too long time.

He felt relieved that he did not have to spend two months at sea, as he did when he crossed five years ago. The isolation would have been imposing. The steamer made excellent time to Europe – not more than about a week. He travelled light – with just a travel bag – and did not have to wait long to enter the train to Hull when he arrived in Liverpool. The train sped through the night and staring out into the darkness he felt the locomotive struggling uphill. It was climbing the Pennine Mountains. Olaus was not used to characterizing areas like the Pennines as mountains. To him mountains were rising out of the sea 2000 feet straight up – like in Newfoundland. In Norway the Pennines would have been called hills.

Arriving in Hull he immediately boarded a steamer for Norway. It was not due to leave for several hours, so he went to his cabin and made himself comfortable. It had been a long trip, and he was tired after the train journey. He took his boots off, stretched out on the bed – and fell asleep.

When he woke up it was dark and he heard the splashing from the side paddle wheels. He was starving. He lit his pipe and spent a few minutes on deck in the fresh sea breeze. It would not be too long before he could see the coast line of southern Norway. He went to the lounge for something to eat. After a quick look at the menu he knew exactly what he wanted. Fried herring and onions. He had not had herring since he left for America. It was a North Atlantic fish he would not find on the menus in the Mississippi River Valley. He had caught lots and lots of catfish during the campaigns. He found it tasteless compared to the herring unless it was heavily seasoned, but if he wanted fish - catfish was the only option.

He kept to himself for the rest of the journey. He did not find it easy to socialize at the level of the average citizen and stayed in his cabin except during meals. As the steamer stood into the Christiania Fjord next morning he recognized Ferder lighthouse, which he had seen on the way out with the Northern Light. In daylight he could not see all the small places he had noticed lit up in the darkness when he left. In late afternoon the waterfront of Christiania slowly grew on the horizon. The city looked bleak in early spring, none of the deciduous trees had leaved out yet, but the surrounding country was covered in a deep green color from the conifers – heavy forests of pine and spruce. The docks were crowded with people – a ship arriving with passengers from America was a big attraction. He puffed on his pipe as he gently showed and pushed his way down the landing. Heading for the railway station he came upon Karl Johan's Street, Christiania's main street. On a hill to the left the skyline was dominated by the Royal Castle. No king resided there. The Swedish King Carl IV, ruler of "the Brother Countries" spent most of his time in Stockholm. Walking up Karl Johan he passed the Parliament. Ground had been broken the year he left for America, now the building was occupied – he could see people running in and out of the doors.

Olaus made his way a short distance to the railway station and bought a ticket for Kløften on the trunk line to Eidsvold. Soon the steam engine locomotive pulled out of the station belching black smoke hundreds of feet in the air, leaving a long trail stretching far behind the train. The rocking motion and the monotonous clattering from the rails made Olaus sleepy. He realized he had shut his eyes when

Karl Johan's Street with the Royal Castle in 1866.

The Norwegian Parliament in 1866.

he heard the announcement: "Kløften!" He got up, grabbed his travel bag and was ready. With screeching brakes the train slowed down. Olaus was on the platform – the bag slung across his shoulder - before it came to a complete stop. Within minutes he was walking down the dirt road leading towards Ask. There he would hit the Nannestad road, which would take him directly home. It was late evening as he approached Nannestadteiet, and suddenly he found himself outside the small log cabin at the fork in the road. He opened the door without knocking and walked in, like he had done a thousand times before. Hans was sitting with his back to the door, looking into the fire place puffing on his tobacco pipe. Kari looked up as he stepped inside the door. Disbelief was written all over her face.

"Olaus!" she said.
Hans turned around. "Olaus?"
They both came over to him, grabbing and touching him like they had to make sure it was really him - that he was actually there with them, in the log cabin. He could not remember them looking so old when he left – but Hans was 75 years now, and Kari just about 68.
"Kommer du helt fra Amerika, Olaus?" (Are you coming all the way from America, Olaus?) Kari said, tears running down her face.
"Ja, mor – helt fra Amerika. Jeg kom til Christiania i dag." (Yes, mother – all the way from America. I came to Christiania today.)
"Og du overlevde krigen – jeg kan ikke tro det! Hans ble jo skutt!" (-And you survived the war - I can't believe it! Hans was shot!)
"Jeg overlevde krigen, mor. Uten en skramme! - Og Hans er helt i orden. Jeg har med meg brev fra både Hans og Ole." (I survived the war, mother – without a scratch! – and Hans is all right. I have brought letters from both Hans and Ole.)

His father pulled out a chair and brought it over to the fireplace. He started talking to Olaus about everything that had happened since he left. Things had not gotten any better. Norwegian agriculture was experiencing a crisis. He did the right thing to leave. His oldest sister, Anne Marie, was doing well, however – she owned the Nordeeg farm. Ingel Pedersen had died just about a month ago – on March 8th - and left everything to his wife. His sister, Karen, was still living at home with her parents - she had never married. She was at Nordeeg, helping Anne Marie. There was a lot to do when she had to run the farm all on her own.

"That's a big farm." Hans said. "Five horses, twenty two cows, twelve sheep, three pigs – she's got fields of wheat, rye, barley, oats and lots of potatoes, and she's got seven servants and farm hands, including your brother, Nils. She's doing well".

Olaus was overwhelmed. Anne Marie had forty two animals, large tracts of land and seven servants! His sister was in deed wealthy.

The next day he walked over to Nordeeg. His three siblings were very surprised and happy to see him. Anne Marie asked how long he would be staying, and he told her the truth – he did not have his return trip scheduled. He had some money saved, he would not be spending too much in Norway, he had not seen his family for a long time………..it could be a couple of months.
"You could work here, you know – if you wanted to." Anne Marie said.
"Naah – I'll be going back. - Kind of like it over there"
When he walked back to Smedstua he knew full well that the reason why he did not want to work for his sister was not at all that he liked it so much better in America. He just could not be a farmer. Manual labor tended to make his mind grind over and over again on the same subject - and he knew what that subject would be….and he feared what it would do to him.

Summer arrived with all the smells, sights and sounds he remembered from his youth. The community seemed somewhat empty – because it was. All the young people moved out, just like he had done. Some went to America, some to Christiania, some went to sea………..as a result the community lost its youth. Olaus helped Nils on the farm – getting the seed in the ground, the potatoes - there was always more to do. By the end of June he became restless. His mother could tell. One night she grabbed his arm.

"Skal du reise tilbake, Olaus?" (Are you going back, Olaus?), she said.
"Jeg tror jeg må dra, mor. Jeg må være tilbake før høsten setter inn." (I think I'll have to go, mother. I'll have to be back before fall), Olaus answered.

He got hold of a newspaper and checked departure dates. There was a ship leaving on July 17th. He had to be aboard when it left. He went by Nordeeg for the last time on the evening of the 16th. Early in the morning on the 17th he was ready. Darkness did not last very long during Norwegian July nights. It fell about 11 pm, and started to fade already after 1 am. By 3 am it was bright as day. As he left the log cabin his father shook his hand and his mother embraced him. Kari pulled the shawl around her shoulders and said:

"Farvel, Olaus, og på gjensyn" (Goodbye Olaus, until we meet again). As he started walking down the Nannestad Road, they all knew that would not come true. They would never meet again.

ST. LOUIS

Three weeks later Olaus was back in Iowa. He delivered letters from Norway to Ole and Hans and started to look for a job. What he found was what most soldiers discharged after the Civil War found: While they were away fighting for the Cause, new immigrants had taken the available land, and the available jobs. Many of the soldiers came back to nothing, and decided to go either east or west to seek their fortune. Olaus did not feel like doing either. Certainly not go east. May be out west. He boarded a steamer at MacGregor for his favorite city: St. Louis. He thought there had to be lots opportunities to get work in St. Louis – and he was right. As he spoke English fluently and could write well he soon managed to land a good job as a clerk. He knew he would be itching sitting behind a desk, but his bounty money was slowly running out, and he needed income. When he signed his labor contract he also manifested the significant change in his social status which occurred during his visit to Norway. He was no longer Olaus Hansen, the poor son of a cotter from Nannestadteiet. He was the brother of one of the wealthiest

St. Louis in 1873. The Library of Congress.

women in Nannestad. He was Olans H. Northeg.

Since the end of the Civil War Olaus had found the situation in the previous Confederate States somewhat peculiar. President Andrew Johnson had initially given the impression that he would put strict requirements on the southern states to let them return to the Union. However, already on May 29th, 1865 – eight months before Olaus was discharged from the Union Army - Johnson issued an amnesty proclamation to "- all persons who had directly or indirectly taken part in the rebellion and the restoration of all property except as to slaves......." Apart from certain exceptions including those who had left judicial positions and seats in congress, and those who owned property worth more than $ 20 000, Johnson would let the Rebels back into the Union with virtually no concessions made. He also urged each state to form new governments. Since Congress would not be in session until December 4th Andrew Johnson put the plan into action on his own initiative, later to be called Presidential Reconstruction. By the end of 1865 every Confederate state except Texas had re-established civil government.

The southern states held conventions that voided or repealed their ordinances of secession and ratified the Thirteenth Amendment, abolishing slavery. In spite of abolition of slavery, the control of whites over blacks was restored by enactment of the so called "Black Codes". The codes – an extension of the previous slave codes – included vagrancy laws targeting unemployed blacks, apprentice laws that made orphans and dependents available to hire for whites, excluded blacks from certain trades and businesses and restricted their ownership of property. In addition blacks were not allowed to vote, hold public office or receive any kind of public education.

During Sherman's "march to the sea" freed slaves had been following his army in ever increasing numbers. When they arrived at Savannah, Georgia, they had doubled the city's population. Eager to get them off his hands, Sherman issued Special Field Order No.15 on January 16th, 1865 appropriating 400 000 acres of abandoned lands in the coastal region of Georgia and South Carolina. He wanted the free slaves to establish their own homesteads and communities by claiming a parcel of forty acres as their own. In addition he would supply one of the army's discarded mules for each plot to work the land – hence the expression "Forty acres and a mule". By June, 10 000 freed slaves were settlers. As the plantation owners returned to their homes with deeds to the properties, Field Order No. 15 was repealed in the fall by President Andrew Johnson who issued a Federal decree returning the properties to their former owners.

To Olaus, this looked very much like the Confederate States of America were restored, and it sparked a question in his mind about the usefulness of a war that had lasted four years and claimed more than 600 000 lives. He was not alone in feeling that way. The general public in the North were enraged by events in the southern states, demanding action to be taken against the development in the former Confederacy. On July 30th, 1866, just before Olaus' return from Norway, an incident happened in Louisiana later to be known as "The New Orleans Massacre". The republican convention was attacked by an armed mob, killing at least 38 people and injuring 146. This thoroughly galvanized the opposition against President Johnson's lenient approach to the Rebel states and paved the way for Congressional Reconstruction when the second session of the 39th Congress convened in December. A more radical plan for reconstruction of the South would be enacted into a law directly influencing Olaus' future.

On March 2nd, 1867 the First Reconstruction Act was written into law - "An Act to provide for the more efficient Government of the Rebel States". It organized Virginia, North Carolina, South Carolina, Georgia, Mississippi, Alabama, Louisiana, Florida, Texas and Arkansas into five military districts, each commanded by a Union general, and soldiers would have to be recruited to fill the posts. This was a welcome opportunity for Olaus. He felt that he was done with the infantry, but after his service as a dispatch carrier in Alabama he found service in the cavalry very attractive.

On the afternoon of March 21st, 1867 Olaus walked into the hot, dusty recruiting office in St. Louis and was seated by an officer, who introduced himself as Captain Dwyer of the 5th U.S. Cavalry.
The Captain looked at him.
"Where are you from, Northeg? I can't place you're accent."
"Norway, sir."
"Do you have any military experience?"
Olaus pulled out his discharge paper from his pocket.
"Civil War, sir, November 1861 to January 1866", he replied.
Dwyer looked at the document. "Two enlistments, lasting nine months longer than the entire war?"
"Yes, sir"
"Were you ever wounded?"
"No, sir"
Dwyer leaned back in his chair.
"The 12th Iowa, in the Army of the Tennessee?"

Olaus Hansen's enlistment at St. Louis, Missouri March 21st, 1867. The National Archives.

"Yes, sir"

"I see you got promoted."

"Six times, sir."

"The Army of the Tennessee was never defeated, correct?"

"Never, sir", Olaus replied.

"Have you been around horses?"

"I grew up on a farm, sir, and rode dispatch in Alabama in -65."

"Since you were promoted to sergeant, I take it you can read and write?"

"Indeed, sir."

Dwyer stuck his pen in the inkwell, tapped it carefully against the edge of the well to wipe off excess ink, and started to write.

"I think that concludes the interview" he said. "Sergeants comprise the core of the fighting units in the regular army. If you were promoted to sergeant in the 12th Iowa during war time, you can have no better credentials. I will order you to Carlisle Barracks in Pennsylvania for initial cavalry training. We need men with experience from the war to train recruits - they are often Civil War veterans, and do not take orders well from officers who were not on the front line during the war. We are also in need of personnel who can write understandable reports. You will make yourself useful."

The recruits at Carlisle Barracks were indeed Civil War veterans – and rough ones. Just five days before Olaus' enlistment they had fought a virtual battle with the townspeople of Carlisle. Olaus got the details upon arriving in Pennsylvania. He came to think that Dwyer either had not received the report by March 21st, or he simply neglected to mention it, not to put doubt in Olaus' mind about enlisting.

There had been almost daily reports about insubordination, men who were absent without leave and even robberies at the barracks. However, the commander at the post, Brigadier General William N. Grier, was most concerned about soldiers stirring up riots with people in town. On March 16th, after several days of brawls, a group of soldiers marched into town and were met by a mob of roughs at the corner of Louther and Hanover streets. Gun shots were exchanged and several soldiers were seriously wounded. The police was without power to stop the riot and General Grier sent a detachment of the 6th Cavalry to arrest the soldiers. When the detachment arrived the town hoodlums fired into them, mortally wounding the sergeant in charge and wounding several others. Next General Grier sent an entire troop of cavalry to restore order. Closely confining the soldiers to the barracks prevented further trouble.

Barrack No. 2 at Carlisle with garrison soldiers, 1867. Photographic Collection, Cumberland County Historical Society.

Olaus boarded a train at St. Louis bound for Carlisle, connecting through Cincinnati, Ohio and Pittsburg, Pennsylvania. When he arrived he found it amusing to be treated like a raw recruit after more than four years on the front line. He was turned over to a first sergeant to be provided with equipment, uniform and sleeping quarters. Carlisle Barracks was in the process of being rebuilt after the post was burnt by Confederate cavalry in 1863. The hospital was makeshift, but one of the pavilions had been made into a theatre where the post's literary society arranged minstrel shows, short plays and dances, and the large library contained about nine hundred titles. Olaus found the most interesting structure to be a small kiosk outside the hospital with instruments for observations of weather conditions.

For eight weeks Olaus was put through intensive drill – some of it mounted – before he settled in to his new army life. He spent a lot of time on the shooting range. The single shot, muzzle loading Enfield- and Springfield muskets from the Civil War were hopelessly outdated, and he purchased a seven shot repeating Spencer carbine. The self-contained, powerful metallic cartridges could be loaded through the stock at the back end and fired in about fifteen seconds. It was an incredible improvement in fire power over his Civil War speed of four shots a minute including a nine step process to load each shot. For a side arm he chose the caliber .44 New Model 1861 Remington Army percussion revolver. He knew a lot of soldiers preferred the 1860 Army Colt in the same caliber, but he found that the

Remington felt very sturdy during shooting compared to the Colt, due to the top strap solid frame.

During his first summer at Carlisle Barracks he got a letter from Hans. He had been living in Decorah, Iowa for about three years after his discharge, but had moved to LaCrosse, Wisconsin. His childhood girlfriend, Petronelle Elisabeth Larson, had just come from Norway. They were going to be married on October 18th – would he like to come to the wedding? He asked for a leave of absence – but it was denied. He realized that his army life would eventually take him further and further away from normal family life and functions, but it was a commitment he had made, and chose to live with.

Because of his previous war experience and his ability to read and present a clear handwriting, he was put in charge of a recruiting office. Every week he saw a continuous flow of trained cavalry men depart from Carlisle Barracks for the West. He knew the Indians were troublesome for crews building the transatlantic railroads and protection by the army was needed. A string of forts had been built along the Bozeman Trail in the Powder River Country in northeast Wyoming to protect miners and settlers traveling to the gold fields in Montana and to Oregon. The forts had to be abandoned during Lakota Chief Red Cloud's war, a war that precipitated the Laramie Treaty of 1868. 525 troopers left Carlisle during October and November of 1869 and more continued to leave throughout the winter. The heavy demand for troops and horse replacement in the west raised the question if the Cavalry Depot had to be closer to the region where it was needed. The principal horse market was at St. Louis, Missouri, which was the gateway to the West.

On May 3[rd,] 1870 Olaus was kicked by a horse and had to pay a visit to the post hospital. He had a bad contusion and was off duty for five days. During sick leave he overheard several discussions about the possible move to St. Louis. It made sense to move the Cavalry Depot. Carlisle was about as far away as you could get when supplying the United States Cavalry with men and horses west of the Mississippi River. Seven months later, on December 15th, General Order No. 125 was issued by William Tecumseh Sherman, now General of the Army. The War Department transferred the Principal Depot and Station of the Superintendent of the Cavalry Recruiting Service to the St. Louis Arsenal. By February of 1871 the transfer had begun. Olaus left Carlisle Barracks on the afternoon of Wednesday 11th in a contingent led by Colonel Edward Hatch, commander of the 9th Cavalry. Hatch was a familiar name to Olaus – he had commanded the 5th Cavalry Division at the battle of Nashville in 1864. The contingent consisted of three 1st lieutenants, six sergeants, seven corporals, two trumpeters, one hundred and six privates and fifty recruits. Accompanying the contingent were two laundresses and eighty seven horses. They arrived at the St. Louis Arsenal late on Saturday, February 14th.

Colonel Hatch assumed command of the Cavalry Recruit Depot – officially named "the St. Louis Depot" - and Olaus was assigned to the garrison's Permanent Troop. Training of cavalry recruits started immediately. Already on March 6th, 1871 Adam Kramer - 1st Lieutenant, 6th Cavalry - led one hundred recruits, three recruits trained blacksmiths, four laundresses and one deserter to Galveston, Texas. 1st Lieutenant Moses Harris left for Louisville, Kentucky with one hundred recruits for the 7th Cavalry on April 5th. Harris left again on April 8th with one hundred more recruits for the 7th Cavalry.

Olaus had found his return to St. Louis rather disappointing. The Cavalry Depot had too many sergeants – six altogether - and their work assignments differed little from the enlisted privates. The tasks of the Permanent Troop at the Arsenal had taken on the shape of fatigue duty, far removed from the cavalry service he had

St. Louis Arsenal in 1876. Fortwiki.

envisioned after his dispatch rides in Alabama. The Arsenal served as a major demobilization point for the armies of the West, and it also received captured Confederate ordnance stores. The enlisted men had to prepare and move ammunition from the St. Louis Arsenal to Jefferson Barracks for storage. For 1872 the plan was to break up 27 000 rifle projectiles, 200 000 rounds of fixed ammunition and six million small arms cartridges. Then they had to separate the material according to kind and quality, weigh and sell the scrap metal and sift and pack powder. They had to skid cannons, pile and arrange shot beds and fix drawers and shelving for storage. The post - like most garrisons – was overrun by pests. Rats and mice followed the stores unloaded from the steamers for the Arsenal – food for the men and feed for the horses - roaches had taken over the kitchen and the barracks had bedbugs. In the summer the heat and humidity was oppressive and swarms of mosquitos made life miserable, winters were cold and blustery. Floundering in the backwaters at the St. Louis Arsenal he watched hundreds and hundreds of raw recruits mount horses and go south to do Reconstruction duty, or west, to Frontier forts.

Soldiers returning from the South passed through St. Louis, telling stories about dangerous details and how politics and general lawlessness in the previous Confederate States went hand in hand – a volatile mixture often exploding in armed conflicts along party lines, racial barriers and northern and southern sympathies. In addition, northern "carpetbaggers" went south to make their fortunes and regular criminals like Jesse and Frank James - who had fought under the infamous Missouri guerrilla Bloody Bill Anderson during the Civil War - went on robbing sprees under the thin guise of still fighting the United States. To Olaus the whole situation sounded almost like a state of anarchy.

On Christmas Eve 1865 an organization had been founded in Pulaski, Giles County, Tennessee which would eventually become a target for the U.S. Cavalry. Six college students and veteran officers of the Confederate Army came together to create the Ku Klux Klan, initially a social club for veterans which quickly developed into a tool of violence in opposition to the new social order. At a meeting in April of 1867 former Confederate General Nathan Bedford Forrest was elected the first Grand Wizard of the Klan. Olaus recognized the name of the cavalry leader from several battles against the Army of the Tennessee. This man certainly knew how to keep himself at the violent center of southern struggle.

In the mix of Indian fighting and southern reconstruction one Army unit's name surfaced over and over again – that of the 7th United States Cavalry. It had been organized by Colonel Andrew J. Smith on July 20th, 1866 - the very same A.J.

Smith who had been Olaus' Corps Commander in the Army of the Tennessee. Colonel Samuel D. Sturgis became the commander of the regiment on May 6ᵗʰ, 1869 – the very same Samuel Sturgis who had been routed by Nathan Bedford Forrest at Brice's Crossroads before the 12ᵗʰ Iowa and A.J. Smith's army launched the campaign leading up to the battle of Tupelo, and Forrest's defeat. The present field commander of the regiment was Lieutenant Colonel George Armstrong Custer. Olaus knew he had made a name for himself during the Civil War – the youngest brevet Major General ever appointed in the U.S. Army, and a participant of crucial battles in the Eastern Theatre. From 1866 to 1871 he had been stationed at Fort Riley on the Kansas plains where he became famous – or infamous – for the defeat of Cheyenne Chief Black Kettle's winter camp on the Washita River on November 27ᵗʰ, 1868. On April 3ʳᵈ, 1871 Custer was transferred from Indian fighting on the plains to Elisabeth town, Kentucky with two companies of the 7ᵗʰ. The intent was to control the Ku Klux Klan and the carpetbaggers, and break up illicit distilleries.

Despite his apprehension about the work at the Cavalry Depot, Olaus reenlisted on March 21ˢᵗ, 1872 and was sworn in by 1ˢᵗ Lieutenant Peter D. Vroom, 3ʳᵈ Cavalry, later to become a brigadier general and Inspector General of the U.S. Army. During the winter of 1872, when Olaus returned to the barracks after days of heavy work with the ordnance stores, he noticed that his joints swelled and hurt. His shoulders, hips and knees were painful and stiff when he woke up in the morning. At first he took it as an indication of too heavy work the previous day – he had probably pulled a muscle or a tendon. When it developed into a persistent pain around his joints, he went to see the post surgeon. After stretching, bending and squeezing his joints, looking at his tongue and peering into his eyes the surgeon sat back in his chair.

"What were you doing prior to your service in the cavalry, Northeg?"
"12ᵗʰ Iowa Volunteer Infantry, four and a half years, sir." Olaus replied.
"Marching." The surgeons stated it as a fact.
"Yes, sir."
"Thousands of miles through swamps, forests and over prairies, twenty miles a day on half rations – or no rations - spending the nights under a frozen blanket on wet, cold or frozen ground, waking up in a pile of snow or under a sheet of ice", the surgeon continued.
"Yes, sir."
"That kind of abuse of the body can't be done without repercussions, Northeg. Your joints are in a progressive state of aging. You have acute rheumatism."

Acute rheumatism. The surgeon's words slowly sank in. When he arrived in the United States he thought it was an old man's disease, but he had seen soldiers not more than thirty years of age virtually debilitated already at Camp Union in 1861. Now he was himself a victim – he was thirty one. There was no cure, just rest and medication – and no particularly good medication at that. The surgeon prescribed medicinal whiskey to be taken as necessary when the pain became unbearable.

Drinking whiskey was nothing new in Olaus' daily routine. Most of the soldiers drank – many of them to excess – and there were as many reasons for drinking as there were soldiers in the Army. Commonly soldiers drank because of boredom and inactivity in camp, because they were far away from civilization and what they saw as a normal life or to release nervous tension stemming from dangerous and life threatening situations in skirmishes and battles. Many of them became alcoholics – and many more probably never realized or cared if they were alcoholics, because they never tried to stop drinking. Alcohol – or rather whiskey - was heavily endorsed by doctors for use both internally and externally as a painkiller, sedative, digestive aid, antiseptic and anesthetic. It was also thought to be beneficial in treating influenza, cold and other illnesses, and was mixed with quinine for the prevention of malaria. You could not go wrong by drinking whiskey.

Olaus had already noticed that whiskey eased the pain. Although there was no way for him to know in 1872, alcohol as a pain killer was three times as effective as Aspirin, the future synthesized salicylic acid sold from 1897 and hailed as a new, non-dependency miracle drug against pain. The problem with alcohol was – when he had consumed enough whiskey to dull the pain in his joints – he was drunk.

Olaus continued the monotonous service at the Arsenal, watching cavalry recruits go south and west. He felt comfortable in St. Louis – he had friends, and lived a settled life. When his rheumatism bothered him he could slow down in his work, and still be on active duty. However – he could never dismiss the constant feeling of wanting to break out, do more exiting duty, be exposed to danger, involved where things happened – just like during the Civil War. He was itching for action, and hanging around the barracks or bars in St. Louis drinking whiskey could not stem the feeling - it actually gave it a boost.

During the summer of 1873 he read in the newspapers about Custer and the 7th Cavalry's Yellowstone expedition. Ten of the regiment's twelve companies were part of a detachment of 1500 men, 250 teamsters, 40 scouts, 250 wagons, 800 horses and 600 head of cattle providing protection for the surveyors establishing a

Hans Hansen's blacksmith shop in Lake Park, Becker, Minnesota. From an old postcard in the author's collection.

route for the Northern Pacific Railroad. As it was – the track would not be immediately constructed. An economic panic struck the United States the same year, and the financial backer of the pacific railroad, Jay Cook & Company in Philadelphia, Pennsylvania, went bankrupt. The track stopped at Bismarck, Dakota Territory, and 1500 workers were laid off.

That autumn he received a letter from Hans. He had been one of the pioneer settlers in Lake Park, Becker, Minnesota – in 1871, Olaus thought – and had just opened the first blacksmith shop in town. He would be doing well for himself – the blacksmith was an absolutely indispensable element in a settler community, creating or repairing the tools needed for farming and everyday life. He knew Hans was good at it – his apprenticeship had been a long one, in the shop of his father, Hans Henriksen.

On July 2nd, 1874 Custer again led an expedition west, this time with 1000 men and 110 wagons, into the sacred country of the Lakota Sioux – the Black Hills of Dakota. It appeared to be a thinly disguised expedition to look for gold, although

Captain "Holy Owen" Hale, 7ᵗʰ Cavalry. Wikipedia.org.

the official order was to find a suitable place for a fort and a route to the southwest. With the economical panic of the previous year Olaus knew that when the newspaper headlines in the East read "Gold!" and the text continued to describe a country where you could just turn the sod over and gold hung on to the grass roots – a stampede westwards was impending.

On Friday September 18ᵗʰ, 1874 a new superintendent arrived to take charge of the General Mounted Recruiting Service. It was Samuel D. Sturgis – the officer from the battle of Brice Crossroads, now technically in command of the 7ᵗʰ Cavalry. He brought Captain Owen Hale and put him in charge of the recruiting office. Hale also assumed command of the Permanent Troop at St. Louis Arsenal. Owen Hale was a career officer with thirteen years in the army. He enlisted in the Civil War from Troy, New York, served from 1861 to 1865 and was brevetted captain of volunteers on March 13ᵗʰ, 1865 for gallant service during the war. He was appointed 1ˢᵗ lieutenant, 7ᵗʰ Cavalry on December 4ᵗʰ, 1866 and commanded a company during the action against the Cheyenne camp on the Washita River in Kansas in 1868.

The following day, Saturday 19th, Olaus suffered badly from rheumatism. It was a chilly, damp day by the Mississippi River - not at all a condition conducive for improvement in the pain radiating from his shoulders, hips and knees. He was off duty and settled down in the barracks with the only pain reliever available – whiskey. After several drinks he lost track of time and place, but he could still feel the pain. The last thing he remembered was opening bottle number two. It was late Sunday afternoon when he woke up - in the post hospital. The alcohol still numbed his body from the rheumatic pain, but his head suffered severely from the same "medicine". He got out of bed, discharged himself from the hospital and walked over to the barracks.

At Christmas something peculiar happened – a strange mix of events turning Olaus' world around and launching him unexpectedly onto a completely new path – directly down the road he had been looking to go – and it all came during an incident similar to the one on September 19th.

On the second day of Christmas – a celebrated holiday in Norway - Olaus was drinking. As the Irish did on St. Patrick's Day, the Norwegians drank on the 1st and 2nd day of Christmas, which in 1874 happened to fall conveniently on Friday and Saturday. Olaus "cheered the Christmas in" - as the saying went in Norway - with 1st Sergeant Peter Jacobs. Again the whiskey served the beneficial purpose of easing his rheumatic pain, which had become increasingly bad from the cold winter weather. Captain Hale had issued a permit of absence for several of the men at the arsenal until 12 pm on Sunday the 27th. Olaus, knowing he would not be in very good shape early that morning, simply added the names of Jacobs and Northeg to the permit.

When called for by Captain Hale on Monday morning Olaus sent words back that he was sick, and could not report for duty. The Captain took it upon himself to investigate the situation, and quickly established the truth behind the story. Inevitably a court martial followed, already on Thursday, December 30th. The prosecution, represented by Assistant Surgeon J.B. Hamilton, produced four witnesses – Captain Hale, hospital steward Francis W. Fitzgerald, Corporal (Acting 1st Sergeant) Charles Clifton and Corporal (Acting 1st Sergeant, select recruits) W. William G. Chapman. Olaus declined to cross examine the witnesses, but 1st Sergeant William Sigismund – who Olaus had known since the fall of 1868 - testified as a character witness on his behalf.

The sentence was a foregone conclusion. Olaus and Peter Jacobs lost their sergeant's stripes and were reduced to the rank of privates, and Olaus had to pay a fine of $ 10.00 a month for three months. The chain of events precipitated by the court martial, however, was totally unexpected. To prepare for the case, Captain Owen Hale had reviewed Olaus' file, and after the court martial summoned him to his office.

"Northeg", Hale said. "I have reviewed your file."

"Sir", Olaus replied.

"You were in the 12th Iowa, one of the best fighting units in the Army of The Tennessee, during the entire Civil War. You were at the Freedmen's Bureau at Selma, Alabama. You rode dispatch carrier through some of the most dangerous territory in the Deep South. You ran a recruiting office for the Mounted Service. You are a trained cavalry trooper. You are a marksman shot. You have been in the army for almost twelve years." Hale stopped to look at him.

"Yes, sir", Olaus replied.

"Then what in the D----- name are you doing in this Godforsaken H---hole??"

Owen Hale had not earned his sobriquet "Holy Owen" for nothing. He was famous for being the most profane soldier in the 7th Cavalry – may be with the exception of 1st Lieutenant Edward "Bible Thumper" Mathey.

"We could use you where the action is", he continued. "We've got some pretty bad places down south where cool and experienced men are needed. Have you ever heard about Caddo parish?"

Bloody Caddo, Louisiana. Olaus had indeed heard about Caddo parish. It was situated in the northwest corner of the state, and the capital was Shreveport, which also served as the capital of Confederate Louisiana after the fall of Baton Rouge. The city suffered very little during the Civil War and the end of hostilities certainly did not bring peace to Caddo. On the contrary - in a parish considered one of the most violent in the state already before the war, the violence reached unprecedented highs during the post war years, a period of almost complete lawlessness. Most of the violence was based on racial tensions and had its origin in the outcome of the Civil War and the black population's struggle for equal rights aided by northern republicans. This was vehemently opposed both politically and through violence by hooded night riders like the White League, The Knights of the White Camelia and the Ku Klux Klan.

"From the end of the war until last year we had almost 3500 murders in Louisiana", Hale continued, "432 of them in Caddo alone. This year we have experienced a wave of violence in the parish, not seen since 1868. No less than thirty murders were committed in July and August. The coroner preferred to resign rather than go out into the countryside to carry out his duties. He was afraid he would be killed. I could tell you horror stories you would not believe. Earlier this year a black man by the name of Jack McCready was suspected of killing a white man – a rare occurrence indeed if it was true. He was taken by a group of armed white men and turpentine was poured on him. After having shot him several times, the men cut his throat before they set him on fire. A Spaniard, Manuel Nunez, was brutally murdered in July just because he taught in a black school. The Governor of Louisiana, William Pitt Kellogg asked President Ulysses S. Grant to send Federal troops to northwest Louisiana because the White League had taken control of the district. Grant sent the 7th Cavalry."

Hale paused and lit a cigar.
"I want you to transfer to Company G of the 7th and go to Caddo parish", he said. "Report to 1st Lieutenant Donald McIntosh and 2nd Lieutenant George Wallace. Company G has been stationed there since October 6th, together with Company B, to suppress the violence and support the U.S. Marshal. It's extremely dangerous along the Red River. We need men who can look the White Leaguers in the eye without flinching. You have the experience, and judging from your file it appears you have the courage. Will you do it?"
"When do I leave, sir?" Olaus replied.
Hale took the cigar out of his mouth and blew a large smoke ring. He looked down at the documents on the desk in front of him.
"You have to be there by February 10th", he said. "I'll prepare the paper work."
Olaus rose to attention, saluted and walked out of the office. He was a soldier in the 7th Cavalry, the most famous fighting unit in the United States Army.

THE 7TH CAVALRY

Olaus boarded a train at St. Louis, heading south. During the meeting with Captain Hale he had realized that there was an added benefit to the transfer. He would be stationed in Louisiana – far to the south. His rheumatism was aggravated by the cold winter weather in St. Louis and Shreveport had a much more pleasant climate. However, there were other maladies to worry about in Louisiana besides violence - a severe epidemic of yellow fever broke out in Caddo parish in 1873 – people collapsed and died in public on Texas Street in Shreveport. The death toll had eventually reached 759. The outbreak had ceased with the onset of fall, and no cases had been reported in 1874.

Olaus would be attached to the Military District of the Upper Red River, commanded by Major Lewis Merrill of the 7th Cavalry. Merrill was an experienced fighter of white terrorism – he had been instrumental in breaking up the Ku Klux Klan in the Piedmont region of South Carolina in 1871-72. In October of 1874 Merrill submitted a report to the Adjutant General of the United States Army in Washington from the headquarter of the Red River District stating: "No civil authority or machinery of any kind has for a long time existed here, and the community was fast drifting into a state where any uncontrolled lunatic could set a match to the mine. My action was to set civil function going and to restore respect for civil law, to remind community that this was not a state of war. My name was appended to the affidavit, because anyone else who signed it would have been killed........"

Upon arrival in Shreveport Olaus reported to 1st Lieutenant Donald McIntosh, Company G. He soon learned that McIntosh – like Merrill – had experience with white terror. He had been stationed in Spartanburg, South Carolina in 1872 fighting the Ku Klux Klan together with another officer at the post, Benjamin Hodgson. McIntosh was one of the few officers in the Army with Indian heritage. His mother was Charlotte Robinson, a direct descendant of Red Jacket, a Seneca chief of the Wolf Clan. From troopers already stationed at the post Olaus learned more about the difficult situation in the Red River District. Clearly, Governor William Pitt Kellogg's republican government in New Orleans was only - literally - kept alive by intervention from Washington. It was claimed that the state government could not maintain itself in power for a single hour without the protection of Federal troops. The White League had been established as a powerful faction in the spring of 1874. It emerged into public view by a newspaper published in Alexandria on March 28th called "The Caucasian", and by June the League had reached New Orleans.

On October 19th Lieutenant Benjamin Hodgson had led a detachment of fourteen troopers in support of U.S. Marshal Seelye who set out to serve arrest warrants to four men wanted for murder. After picking up three of them – one of whom was the mayor of the town they visited - they continued to Vienna to pick up the fourth suspect, whereupon they proceeded to Monroe. A few days later an armed posse of several hundred men appeared on horseback, claiming they had a warrant for Hodgson's and Seeley's arrests. The leaders of the posse said that the two had failed to comply with the order of a local judge to have the prisoners appear before him. Hodgson and Seelye had to return to Vienna where they were put in arrest. Only by heavy involvement from Colonel Merrill and by dispatching another cavalry detachment commanded by 1st Lieutenant James M. Bell were they able to be extricated from the situation. A lawyer friendly to the White League was conducting the negotiations between Merrill and the local authorities. He made it plain that upon release, Hodgson and Seelye would be wise in leaving town at the first opportunity.

Company G under the command of 1st Lieutenant McIntosh had been on a similar mission. They returned in November after a month in the field as a posse for the deputy U. S. Marshal to serve arrest warrants in Coushatta and Natchitoches. In Coushatta they had ridden to a site where six republican office holders had been murdered in August. The six were the sheriff in town, Frank Edgerton, Homer Twitchell, Clark Holland, Henry Scott, W.R. Howell and Justice of the Peace M.C. Willis. Homer Twitchell was the brother of Marshall Twitchell, a Freedmen's Bureau agent turned politician and married into a southern family. Clark and Holland were the Twitchells' brothers in law, and together they formed a nucleus of northern political power in the Red River parish. The "Twitchell Clan" had been ordered by the White League to leave the parish, and while riding for Texas they were overtaken by a force of thirty to forty armed men and gunned down. They were buried in two shallow graves about two miles apart, and the posse dug the bodies back up. In Natchitoches the editor of a local newspaper threw a chaw of tobacco in the deputy marshal's face and made loud threats to Lieutenant McIntosh. "The Coushatta Massacre" created a national scandal and paved the way for wholesale arrests of White Leaguers in parishes along the Red River.

Three members of the Ku Klux Klan
arrested in Mississippi in September
of 1871. Wikipedia.org.

Olaus advanced quickly. Due to his extensive experience from the Civil War and his administrative skills he was promoted to corporal on May 17th, and on July 27th he regained his sergeant's stripes. Reconstruction duty was dangerous service, but the danger was different from what he had been used to during the Civil War. He realized that this was just a different kind of war – even if it was peace. Federal troops held Louisiana under an iron fist to enforce Radical Reconstruction. However, with the intense political and social resistance from white democrats backed by the armed force of the White League, the Government could only sustain the military victory from the war, not make Louisiana society conform to a new structure.

The duty in Louisiana was destined to be short. The economic panic of 1873 had made the public in the North lose sight of Reconstruction. Nine years had passed since the Civil War and thousands of businesses went bankrupt, millions of people were out of work. The social and political situation of the disenfranchised southern blacks was no longer at the forefront of the northerners' mind – but westward expansion was. After Custer's Black Hills Expedition in 1874 the Newton-Jenney

Sitting Bull (Thathanka Iyotake), Hunkpapa
Lakota. Wikipedia.org.

Expedition was undertaken the following year, confirming the presence of valuable minerals in the country the Lakota Sioux regarded as their spiritual home. The Black Hills were protected by the Laramie Treaty of 1868, as was the rest of the Great Sioux Reservation covering the southwestern part of Dakota Territory. When the news of gold broke in eastern newspapers, prospectors poured into the Black Hills. Soon there were 15 000 miners in the region and the stage was set for confrontation between Indian preservation and white encroachment.

Initially the Army made a token gesture to keep the miners out of the Hills. However, white Americans believed that they had a "Manifest Destiny" to settle the country from the Atlantic to the Pacific Ocean, and the Indian tribes in between would inevitably have to give way, as they had done since the first Europeans set foot on American soil. The relationship between the Sioux tribes and the Indian agents had always been tense – the Indians were discontent with the reservations and the agents could not keep them contained in the summer time. They would go off roaming and hunting and return for handouts during winter time. There were Sioux Indians who did not even acknowledge that there was a treaty in effect, and they had no intention of ever signing one. Two of the most prominent leaders of these factions were Sitting Bull of the Hunkpapa band and Crazy Horse of the Oglala. They were leaders of roaming bands who refused to live a life on the reservation and preferred to stay in the Powder River country in northern Wyoming and Montana. This territory was in the treaty designated as "unceded", which meant that the Indians could hunt there as long as the buffalo existed – but they could not "occupy permanently the territory outside the reservation".

Sitting Bull's band had not signed the treaty, and saw no reason to remain neither on the reservation nor in the designated hunting area. They roamed into the Yellowstone Basin and created trouble for the first surveyors of the Northern Pacific Railroad in 1871 and 1872. This had prompted the Yellowstone Expedition of 1873. In the autumn of 1873 large numbers of Sitting Bull's band arrived at the agencies complaining of surveyors and troops in their hunting grounds. Hostilities escalated and in February of 1874 the Indians killed an agency clerk, and then two soldiers outside Fort Laramie. General Philip H. Sheridan, commander of the U.S. Cavalry insisted that the Army needed a more strategically located post to discourage the violence. This had prompted the Black Hills Expedition of 1874.

The Grant administration realized that it would become politically and physically impossible to keep miners and settler out of the Black Hills. In September of 1875 the Allison Commission, named after its chairman Senator W.B. Allison, met in a council with 15000 Indians at a site eight miles east of Red Cloud Agency. The Northern Cheyenne, Arapaho and all the Sioux tribes including the Hunkpapa and Oglala sent representatives – except the bands of Sitting Bull and Crazy Horse. The council ended in a riot where the Sioux internal police had to restrain some of the young warriors from killing the Government's representatives.

On December 3rd President Grant met with his cabinet and General Sheridan to discuss the situation. Two decisions were made: The order barring the miners from entering the Black Hills would remain in effect, but the Army would not make any move to stop the trespassers, and – the hostile band of Sitting Bull had to settle on the reservation. On December 6th, Grant issued an order for all Indians to move onto the reservation and report to an agency before January 31st, 1876. If they did not, they would be considered hostile, and an enemy of the United States. Even if the order had reached all the bands in the unceded territory, they would probably not have made it onto the reservation in time in the severe winter weather. As it was, Sitting Bull and Crazy Horse had no intention of coming in anyway, under any circumstance.

On February 1st Secretary of the Interior, Zachary Chandler, informed Secretary of War, William W. Belknap that "Sitting Bull refused to comply......" Two days later Belknap notified Chandler that the Army had received orders "to take immediate measures to compel the Indians to remain upon the reservation". For the first time since its organization in 1866, the 7th Cavalry would be assembled into a full regiment with all twelve companies present for duty. Orders went out to the detachments stationed in Louisiana, Kentucky and at forts in Dakota Territory to report to Fort Abraham Lincoln at Bismarck. The United States had declared war on the Sioux- and Cheyenne Indians. Lieutenant Colonel George Armstrong Custer and the 7th Cavalry would be in the thick of the fight – and so would Olaus Hansen.

TO THE LITTLE BIGHORN

By April 11th, 1876 there were rumors about a transfer at the post in Shreveport, but orders were not issued from Washington before April 15th. Company B and G were moving to Dakota Territory to campaign against the hostile Lakota and Cheyenne. The assignment was not at the top of Olaus' list of preferred deployments. Indians, hooded night riders or Rebel soldiers – to him it made no difference which of them he fought, but his plans had been to stay as far south as possible to reduce the suffering from his rheumatic pain. Dakota Territory with its freezing cold and stormy winters was at the complete opposite end of the scale. To his understanding the Army's intention had been to launch a winter campaign, and that would have been a miserable trek to make – from Shreveport to Bismarck in February.

Early in the morning of Wednesday, April 19th Olaus was on a northbound train speeding towards Bismarck. Passing through Texarkana, Texas and Poplar Grove the train reached St. Louis on Friday April 21st at 8:30 pm. At noon the next day it left St. Louis, arriving at Ottumwa, Iowa on Sunday April 24th. As they were pushing on through the night of the 24th Olaus was woken up twice from the train stopping. It stood still on the track for several hours. Men were moving up and down along the track with lights and equipment, and he heard somebody yell that a stock car had run off the track and the tender had broken down. They finally arrived at Austin, Minnesota at 11 pm on April the 25th.

During the short stay Olaus noticed an altercation between the commander of the detachment, 1st Lieutenant McIntosh, and 2nd Lieutenant Benjamin Hodgson. Rather improperly, Olaus thought, Hodgson displayed insubordination in front of the whole detachment and McIntosh had to put him under arrest. Hodgson appeared volatile, and McIntosh had reportedly intervened at Shreveport when Hodgson wanted to shoot one of the enlisted men. Three and a half hour later the train continued towards St. Paul. After an overnight stay from the 26th to the 27th the train set out from St. Paul on the last leg of the journey, arriving at Bismarck on May 1st. There the two companies were ferried across the Missouri River to Fort Abraham Lincoln.

Fort Abraham Lincoln, Dakota Territory. Fortwiki.

Fort Lincoln was the largest fort Olaus had seen. It was sprawled out over an area of one mile north-south and half a mile east-west. The fort had existed as a small infantry post callèd Fort McKeen. Due to the increasing problems with hostile Indians and the trouble caused by the building of the Northern Pacific Railroad, congress authorized the addition of a cavalry post in March of 1873. In the fall of that year Custer arrived with units of the 7th Cavalry and took command of the post. In May of 1876 it was the scene of preparation for the upcoming campaign against the hostile Plains Indians.

The weather had been brutal in Dakota Territory during the winter of 1876, and no provisions had gotten through to the fort before the middle of April. Three soldiers had frozen to death at Fort Totten during Christmas, after they wandered off from the fort to buy some whiskey. They were found by a six man patrol sent out to look for them. By March 5th it was still twenty degrees below zero at Totten. Predictably, coming from the sunny south switching to Dakota weather in just ten days, Olaus rheumatism returned with a vengeance. The day after he arrived he was admitted to the hospital, where he spent the next two weeks. He could barely move around due to the pain radiating from his shoulders, hips and knees.

On May 5th Company M arrived from Fort Rice. Their reputation as a wild bunch had preceded them. They were known to be heavy drinkers getting involved in shoot-outs over poker games. They visited "hog ranches" with prostitutes where they came down with venereal diseases. Just a couple of months before the campaign some of them had gotten into a flying fistfight with two of the sergeants. Two troopers had even managed to pick a fight with James Butler "Wild Bill" Hickok, spy for the Union Army during the Civil War and arguably the fastest gun fighter on the American Frontier. In short – they probably behaved like a lot of soldiers did at Frontier forts.

As they rode into Fort Lincoln, Olaus noticed a man of impressive frame towering over the other enlisted men in the company. Everybody called him "Big Fritz". A German? His horse acted up and the trooper jumped from the saddle. With an apparent long experience with horses he held the bridle with his right hand as he would have held the muzzle of a big dog, keeping the horse from rearing.
"Faens hæst!" he shouted.
Olaus grinned. In cursing at the horse the trooper had just revealed his nationality. He was Norwegian. Blacksmith. The word struck him as he looked at the soldier's hands. He had seen those kinds of hands before, having three blacksmiths in his family. He walked over to the tall private and stopped six feet away. Olaus did not usually have to look up when he addressed somebody. Now he did. He fixed his grey eyes on the troopers face. The man stood at attention, staring back at him. His blue eyes showed no emotions - fear, animosity, respect, submission or otherwise. They just stared.

"Er du norsk?" (Are you Norwegian?) Olaus asked.
"Ja, æ e' da de' da, sju'!» (Yes, I am indeed!), the trooper said, surprised. "John Sivertsen".
Olaus smiled. He could hear from the trooper's dialect he was from the Trøndelag counties outside of the city of Trondheim in middle Norway.
"Trønder." Olaus stated it as a fact.
"Fannrem, Orkdal" (Fannrem, Orkdal Valley) Sivertsen confirmed.
"Olaus Nordeeg, Nannestad", Olaus said. "How did you end up in the wildeness?"
"I was working for the Northern Pacific in -73", Sivertsen said. "They went bankrupt in June, right here at Bismarck. I enlisted at Fort Rice. Nothing else to do unless I wanted to go back East. Didn't feel like doing that."
"John – got to go back to the hospital", Olaus said, "bad case of rheumatism. We'll talk more".
Sivertsen saluted and took his horse towards the stables.

Olaus had never seen Custer, he only knew him by reputation. The Lieutenant Colonel had still not shown up in camp and the 7th was scheduled to march against the Indians in just ten days. Olaus would have no way of knowing exactly how Custer had managed to get himself entangled in a political web in Washington. On March 29th and April 4th he testified in front of a congressional committee led by democrat Hiester Clymer, looking into a graft scandal involving the army post traders and Secretary of War William W. Belknap. By hearsay testimony Custer

Private John Sivertsen from Fannrem, Orkdal, Norway –
Company M, 7th U.S. Cavalry. Harold B. Lee Library,
Brigham Young University, Provo, Utah.

involved President Grant's brother, Orville in the scheme. A furious Grant relieved Custer of duty from the 7th Cavalry and on April 29th ordered Brigadier General Alfred Howe Terry to command the combined force of infantry and cavalry from Fort A. Lincoln. Terry – knowing full well that Custer was a far more experienced Indian fighter - endorsed a letter from Custer to Grant pleading to regain command. Custer was given command over the 7th Cavalry only – Terry would stay the overall commander.

On May 10th Terry and Custer arrived at Fort Abraham Lincoln and on the 11th they came to the camp. Olaus was somewhat surprised when he saw Custer. By every account he was a tall, blonde man with long, golden hair, but that was a description of the "Boy General" from the Civil War ten years ago. Custer had cropped his hair short, and it was more ginger from what Olaus could determine.

Lieutenant Colonel (Brevet Major General)
George Armstrong Custer, 7ᵗʰ U.S. Cavalry.
Wikipedia.org.

He was about 5' 11", wiry and seemed to have a nervous intensity about him making him appear very energetic.

The regiment was scheduled to depart on May 15ᵗʰ, but a heavy rainstorm on the 14ᵗʰ with lightning and thunder delayed the march for two days. Olaus could barely move because of his pain, but he did not want to be left behind like a few of the other soldiers. Charles Hood was still in hospital when the column left and Patrick McCann and Charles Avery would miss the campaign because they were in confinement. James Abos and Andrew Lieberman made absolutely sure they would miss it - they deserted in March and May.

On May 14th Olaus moved out of the hospital and into a hospital tent, to be ready when the regiment left. He was the only patient. The bout he had with rheumatism was the toughest he had ever experienced. Medicinal whiskey – or "stimulant whiskey", as Acting Assistant Surgeon James DeWolf preferred to call it - was unequal to the task of dulling the pain. After moving out of the hospital he suffered even more. On May 17th, when the regiment finally moved out, it had been raining the night before and a cold, heavy fog enveloped the valley. When reveille sounded at 4 am Olaus rose from a wet ground and there was no dry wood to light fires. Breakfast consisted of hardtack washed down with muddy water, as no coffee could be made. The situation gave him a perfect flashback – it was like he was back in the Civil War, fifteen years earlier.

The sun rose at 5:05 and by 6 am the train was on the march – approximately 650 men, 31 officers, more than 40 scouts - and one journalist, although Custer was under strict order not to bring any newspaper man. The train consisted of 752 mules, 695 Government horses, 32 quartermaster horses, 95 private horses, 26 battery horses, 74 hired horses, 77 head of cattle, 114 large wagons and a number of smaller wagons. In spite of all the horses they were still short, and 78 cavalry recruits had to start the march on foot. Olaus rode in an ambulance wagon and he anticipated a long campaign – the latest intelligence from the scouts was that Sitting Bull was camped along the Little Missouri River about 150 miles to the west with 3000 warriors. That would have been a short campaign. The Sioux and Cheyenne were actually 200 miles further west.

About 2:30 pm the regiment established camp at the Little Heart River. Before tents could be pitched the campground had to be cleared for prairie rattlesnakes, a very abundant rattler on the Great Plains. The method was a tried and proven one for the troopers – they formed a skirmish line equal to the width of the camp and moved across the site, slashing the grass with sticks and sabers and firing into the ground with their revolvers until they had killed all the snakes they could find. Then a sufficient amount of wood was gathered for the camp – none of which would burn.

The first night out of the fort the men got paid. Both Custer and Terry knew that it would have been impossible to pay the men at Fort Lincoln the day before a campaign. That would inevitably have sent all the troopers to Bismarck, spending their money on whiskey, women and cards and the campaign would have been delayed for at least another day. Some of them may not even have made it back, but simply deserted.

It was a sleepless night. A Prairie fire started near the camp and the men spent two hours battling the flames before they could go back to bed – and be woken up by reveille at 2:40 am. After about ten hours of marching they camped on Sweet Briar Creek where a heavy rainstorm struck at 3 pm, washing away most hopes of kindling fires. Dinner for some of the men was hardtack and raw bacon – a very familiar Civil War diet for Olaus. About noon on May 19th a heavy hailstorm struck. Hailstones as large as hickory nuts were bouncing off the canvas on the wagons and the backs of the animals putting the beef cattle into a headlong stampede. Infantry soldiers sought shelter under the wagons while cavalry troopers pulled their horses up along the wagons for protection.

One more night of chilly rain and damp, cold blankets made sure there was no improvement in Olaus' rheumatism. On May 20th he was still confined to the field hospital. As the surgeon checked him that morning Olaus patience was wearing thin.

Laudanum – 10% opium dissolved
in alcohol. The author's collection.

"I need something to get me on my horse" he said, massaging his knees. "I have been incapacitated for twenty days - I can't remain an invalid. I have to be in fighting condition – soon!"

Without a word the surgeon reached into his voluminous medical bag and pulled out a bottle containing a reddish-brown liquid. Olaus recognized the label instantly. He had seen it on an emigrant ship fifteen years earlier, administered to a poor little boy who ended up as food for sharks. LAUDANUM. The surgeon carefully measured twenty five drops in a spoon.

"Take this", he said, "You'll be on your horse tomorrow".

The compound tasted extremely bitter, and the surgeon gave him a whiskey chaser to wash it down. The effect was incredible. Within less than two hours it was like a wind had swept his pain away. He fell into a deep sleep, lasting all night. The next morning the surgeon gave him another twenty five drops. He checked himself out of the field hospital, found his horse and saddled up. It was an intense relief not to feel the effect of the rheumatism. He could focus on the campaign and resume his duties as a non-commissioned officer.

Company G set out with two commissioned officers, four sergeants, four corporals and thirty five privates. The four corporals, Akers, Hagemann, Hammon and Martin were in charge of the four squads. Consedine and Hansen, the two new sergeants recruited to Louisiana, were in charge of the sections with two squads in each. Edward Botzer and Alexander Brown were the sergeants with longest service in Company G. Botzer, who joined in 1866 was Acting 1st Sergeant, and Brown, who joined in 1867 was assigned to the pack train. With all the new recruits, an experienced sergeant with the vulnerable pack train was an absolute necessity.

The weather turned nice on the 21st and the men gathered "buffalo chips" – dried manure – for firewood. When the command established camp the troopers could finally have a hot meal and coffee. Olaus saw scouts leave and return at all times of night and day. The Arikara Indians – or Rees – camped close to Custer's tent to be available for instant missions. Olaus knew that Custer's favorite scout was a half-breed Arikara and Sioux called Bloody Knife who wore white-man shirt and pants and had three feathers rising from a piece of flannel holding his loose hair down. He grew up in a Sioux camp and was mercilessly taunted by one of the future war chiefs, Gall, and had his own, personal reasons for retribution. Bloody Knife had accompanied Custer on the Yellowstone – and Black Hills Expeditions, and was a trusted ally of the Lieutenant Colonel.

Bloody Knife and Custer. Wikipedia.org.

The blistering hot sun was burning Olaus' ears the next three days, and the regimental band played a tune he found very fitting – The Mosquitoes of Dakota Waltz. The stinging insects were a persistent menace, just like he was used to from the coniferous forests of Nannestad. On May 27th they reached the Little Missouri Badlands and camped at Davis Creek at 2:15 pm. The horses were being badly stuck up from cacti and the cavalry troopers had a hard time controlling them. The available water was most often alkaline and gave the troopers diarrhea, a condition known as "The Dakota Quick Step". On May 28th a man was bitten by a prairie rattler and Surgeon James M. DeWolf performed the only possible treatment – he cauterized the wound, put on a bandage and gave the trooper "stimulant whiskey" to dull his pains. The man said he felt fine and that whiskey was "a big thing". Olaus was detailed together with John Sivertsen and companies G, M and K to bridge two crossings for the train. Finally in camp at the Little Missouri on May 29th Olaus occupied himself with a pastime from the Civil War – removing graybacks from his clothes before he had a bath in the river. After the weather turned hot he noticed less and less of his pain, and was doing well without Laudanum.

The briefing of the non-commissioned officers in regards to the plan for the campaign had not been very extensive, but Olaus had gathered that he plan was to strike against the Indians via a three pronged attack executed by three columns of

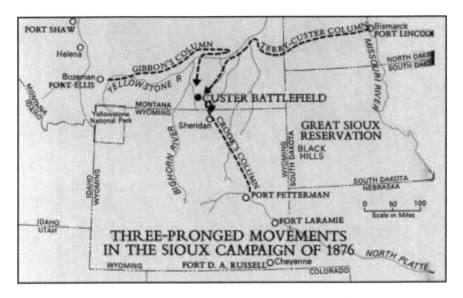

The movements of the three columns during the Sioux Campaign of 1876.
Wikipedia.org.

cavalry and infantry. One column under the command of General George R. Crook would move north from Fort Fetterman and one would strike southeast from Fort Ellis under Colonel John Gibbon. The third would approach from the east, from Fort Abraham Lincoln, under General Alfred Terry and Lieutenant Colonel George A. Custer. The main strategy behind the campaign was to "catch" the Indians, who had always shown a propensity for protecting the camps with a screen of mounted warriors while escaping from the cavalry's grasp.

Unbeknownst to the Army, the camp on the plains by the Little Bighorn River was immense. The Sioux and Cheyenne had no intentions of escaping..........

At 5 am on May 30th Custer took a few Arikara scouts, five pack mules and companies C, D, F and M for a reconnaissance to the south to look for Lakota locations. As they rode out John Sivertsen saluted Olaus, who tipped his hat, in his mind wishing him good luck. They were in dangerous territory, and nobody knew when a Sioux war party could rush from ambush, even if Arikara and Crow scouts were crisscrossing the terrain miles ahead. Custer's Crows had their own agenda in the war with the Sioux. In historic times they had lived in the Yellowstone River

Custer's Crow scouts revisiting the Little Bighorn battlefield more than thirty years later. From left White-Man-Runs-Him, Goes Ahead, Curly and Hairy Moccasin. Wikipedia.org.

Valley, but had been pushed out by the Lakota and forever remained their bitter enemies.

In camp at Anders Creek on June 1st, snow and sleet started falling. It turned into a blizzard continuing into June 2nd. That day Olaus was doing stable duty, moving around with aching joints and puffing on his pipe. It had been so cold the previous night the water had frozen in his canteen. The pipe was now the cheapest way to smoke – the one-cent cigars he had enjoyed coming to Iowa fifteen years ago were in Dakota ten cents apiece. On June 3rd – after a cold breakfast - the column mounted and continued the march. Before he saddled up, Olaus had to stick the bridle bit in warm water to prevent it from freezing in the horses' mouth. The sunshine was bright, reflecting from the snow covered hillsides and the wind was cold, but in the afternoon the temperature quickly rose and the burning heat returned.

On June 7th the column reached the Powder River after a march of about 300 miles. From then precautions were taken no to be spotted by the Indians. The band did not play at night and the men were careful with the fires, extinguishing them quickly after coffee was made so no smoke could be seen. Olaus was again detailed to stable duty. The regiment had its first casualty the previous day – David McWilliams, a Scot from Edinburgh, accidentally shoot himself in the calf with his revolver while mounting. At 3:30 pm on the 10th the regiment's second in command, Major Marcus Albert Reno, took six companies with a Gatling gun, seventy pack mules and twelve days' rations for a scout. They were going from Powder River across the Little Powder, the Mizpah, the Pumpkin and the Tongue to the Tongue's confluence with the Yellowstone. Olaus knew Reno by reputation. He was a West Pointer who had been brevetted Brigadier General during the Civil War and served at the Freedmen's Bureau in New Orleans in 1866.

From the Powder River the regimental band and all the wagons were sent back. The sabers were loaded onto the wagons, as they were considered useless in a hand to hand fight with Indians using lances. From then on rations, ammunition and supplies would be carried on a mule pack train. General Terry had ordered the steamers Far West and Josephine to the confluence of the Yellowstone and the Powder with supplies. A large camp was set up when the column arrived in the afternoon of June 11th, dry and dusty after a march of about twenty miles. Olaus was assigned to stable duty.

The next day the traders were doing brisk business out of two large tents. One of the tents had an improvised bar, crowded with soldiers. Partitions of canned goods separated the men from the officers. Olaus shouldered his way into the tent together with John Sivertsen. Along the back wall they could see forty-five gallon barrels of liquor – some of the finer brands came in casks. Sivertsen was not a big drinker – he had seen firsthand in Norway what excessive drinking could lead to, and had from a young age taken notice of what not to do. He preferred a bottle of beer after a long, hot day while Olaus stuck to his "medicinal whiskey". The rheumatism was bothering him, but the blistering hot weather helped to make him function.

At 6 am on June 15th the column marched for the mouth of the Tongue River under the command of Captain Frederick Benteen. Olaus was very familiar with Benteen. The captain had been in the 10th Missouri Cavalry during the Civil War. When Olaus fought at Tupelo Benteen had been there, too, and also at the siege of Vicksburg. He became most famous for his action at Mine Creek in 1864, when his 10th Missouri halted its charge against a Rebel stronghold of about 7500 men just a hundred yards from their line of artillery. Benteen rode back and forth across the front of the regiment yelling for them to continue the charge, but nothing could make them move. Olaus knew Benteen's courage was unequalled.

The next day, as they were getting close to the Tongue River, they came upon an old Sioux camp where a number of dead Indians had been placed on burial scaffolds. Some of the troopers from Company G unceremoniously tore them down, took the trinkets for souvenirs and threw the bones in the Yellowstone River. Olaus thought it was an unnecessary desecration of a burial place, but it was not much he could do to stop them.

They reached the Tongue on June 17th, and Olaus was again detailed to stable duty. The 7th stayed at the river for two days, the men bathing and fishing when they were off duty. Major Reno returned from his scout on the 19th. He had not encountered Indians but had seen abandoned camp sites at Rosebud Creek. By June 21st the 7th Cavalry was reunited under Custer and not hampered by wagon train or infantry. They rendezvoused with General Gibbon's force at the mouth of the Rosebud, where the traders' tents were already waiting. The men swarmed to the tents, and Bloody Knife purchased more than his fair share of whiskey. Olaus noticed that he was not at his usual place when the 7th set out at noon the next day.
"Bloody Knife?" he asked as John Sivertsen was passing, riding towards the rear.
John shook his head and showed thumbs down.
"Hors de combat", he replied.
The Arikara scout caught up with the column late that night.

On June 24th the regiment set out a 5 am. Within an hour the Crow scouts came in and reported signs of Indians. Custer took the lead with two companies, the regiment following about half a mile back. At 1 pm a halt was ordered to make coffee and wait for new information from the scouts. It was a very hot day and Olaus was sitting with his back against a large rock talking to John Sivertsen when the scouts came in at 4 pm. It felt good when the heat from the sun baked rock warmed his back and shoulders. Sivertsen went over to catch the news. He came back with the cup still in his hand, trying not to spill the coffee.
"Crows say less than thirty miles", he said.

At 5 pm the regiment moved out along the west bank of the Rosebud, passing through several large, abandoned camps. The poles were still standing for the lodges where the Indians had their sun dance and they found a fresh scalp from a white man. The whole valley was scratched up from trailing lodge poles. At about 7:45 pm the regiment halted and a little more than an hour later the Crow scouts came in and reported to Custer. They had followed a Sioux trail up the Rosebud which had abruptly turned west and continued across the divide, into the Little Bighorn Valley. Custer decided to march through the night across the divide to the valley of the Little Bighorn and conceal the command the next day. Then he would have the scouts pinpoint the exact location of the camp for an attack at dawn on the 26th.

The column marched at 11 pm. The only sound penetrating the total darkness making Olaus able to navigate was that of tin cups or frying pans being pounded against the saddles of the men in front of him. The progress was extremely slow and when the first daylight started to peer through at about 2:45, Custer ordered a halt. Olaus was bone tired and threw himself on the ground without unsaddling his horse. He fell asleep instantly with the reins wrapped around his arm. About 4:15 – at sunrise - he had some hardtack, raw bacon and cold water, and fell asleep again. When he woke up a short while later he saw Bloody Knife and the Arikaras together with Custer and a half-breed interpreter squatting in a circle on the ground. Bloody Knife was agitated and Olaus found out that the Rees had told Custer there were so many Indians in the valley they would be fighting for days. Custer initially dismissed the information.

His chief of scouts, 2nd Lieutenant Charles A. Varnum was in the Wolf Mountains, further ahead on the divide between the Rosebud and the Little Bighorn valleys. About 2:30 in the morning two of Varnum's Crow scouts had climbed a promontory known as the Crow's Nest and studied the valley floor along the Little Bighorn. They spotted the enormous camp. Varnum dispatched two Rees – Forked Horn and Red Star – to alert Custer. Custer jumped on his horse and rode bareback out of camp, ordering the regiment to move out at 8 am. He took the interpreter, Frank Girard and Bloody Knife, Red Star, Little Brave and Bob Tailed Bull back to the Crow's Nest.

By now reports came in that the Sioux had spotted the regiment. The advantage of a surprise attack appeared to have been lost. The Crow scout White-Man-Runs-Him insisted on an instant daylight raid to capture the pony herd, leaving the Sioux afoot and unable to make a rapid escape – or an attack. Custer consented. The 7th Cavalry with Captain Benteen and Company H in the lead continued across the divide and started the descent into the Little Bighorn Valley. It was just after 12 pm on June 25th, 1876.

RENO'S FIGHT

After marching about eight miles Custer halted the regiment by one of the tributaries to the Little Bighorn River and gave his last orders to his officers face to face. From now on couriers had to carry dispatches. No matter what the orders were, Olaus knew one thing for sure – this would not be a frontal assault against an entrenched enemy behind earthen breastworks, shooting four shots a minute. This was his first battle against Plains Indians, but in no way did he underestimate the new enemy. He knew they were excellent horsemen – superior to anybody in the 7th Cavalry – and they were Government supplied with repeating rifles and ammunition for hunting. Their 15-shot Winchesters and 16-shot Henrys in caliber .44 gave the Indians an immense firepower. Even if just a portion of the warriors in the large village owned a repeater and the remainder would fight with single shots, muskets and bows and arrows, the ones with the repeaters would probably be able to suppress the cavalry without help. It would be a hard fight.

Olaus was puzzled by the Army's choice of the single shot, breach loading Springfield carbine as the standard arm for the cavalry. He had seen what the troopers could do on the shooting range, and was not very impressed. Even if they would have done well against a fixed target which did not shoot back, it could not be repeated from a bucking horse against an Indian charging at them with a spewing Henry. His best guess was that they would be able to get off one round – and that would probably miss if it was not fired at close range. Reloading would be out of the question. He was happy he had his seven-shot Spencer in the saddle scabbard. He had switched his Remington revolver for the Army standard, an 1873 Colt Single Action Army – "the Peacemaker" - in caliber .45. It was an extremely powerful gun for close combat.

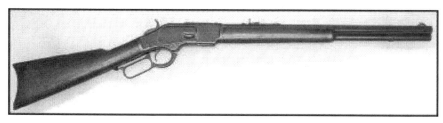

1873 Winchester lever action repeating rifle caliber .44-40. Wikipedia.org.

Upon approaching the creek Olaus had seen about fifty Indians take off in front of the regiment while some of the troopers gave them a parting volley. Obviously – wherever the camp was, the attack would not come as a surprise. The Ree scouts were gathered with Custer's staff together with the white scouts "Lonesome" Charley Reynolds and George Herendeen, the half breed Sioux Mitch Bouyer and the black interpreter Isaiah Dorman. Finally they moved out. Olaus saw three companies – D, H and K – "the Dude Company" - move off to the left under the command of Captain Benteen. The Dudes in K had gotten their nickname by the tailor remaking their white canvas trouser for stable duty into tight fitting cavalry breeches.

Acting 1st Sergeant Edward Botzer repeated the orders to Company G in his heavy German accent. Benteen was to scout along the bluffs to the south, making sure no Indians escaped during the attack. Reno would proceed in column of twos down along the bank of the creek with companies A, G, M and all scouts except Mitch Bouyer and six Crows. He was then to cross the Little Bighorn River and execute the main thrust of the battle, charging down the valley towards the Sioux- and Cheyenne village about 2 ½ miles distant. Custer would follow in support. The two Norwegians in the 7th Cavalry had been deployed together in the attack on the largest Indian encampment ever assembled on the North American continent.

It was about 2:15 in the afternoon when the detachment reached the Little Bighorn

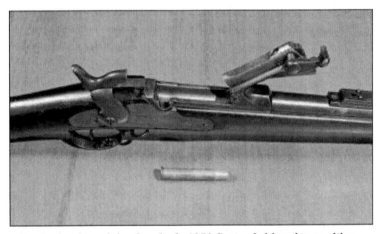

Single shot breach loading lock, 1873 Springfield carbine caliber .45/55. Wikipedia.org.

Major Marcus A. Reno, 7th Cavalry. Wikipedia.org.

River, under a burning hot sun. Custer and companies C, E, F, I and L could still be seen on the bluffs to the right. The river was belly deep where Reno with company M, A and G splashed across. Some of the troopers let their horses drink while crossing although Miles O'Hara, sergeant of Company M, was detailed in the river to make sure they did not. On a knoll next to the river Ree scouts were shouting that the Sioux were not running away, as Custer was convinced they would do - they were going to fight. One of the scouts kept gathering grass in his hand and dropping it, indicating that the Sioux were as thick as grass. Once the companies were across Reno ordered them into a stand of cottonwood to reorganize. After deploying A and M as left and right wings and G to bring up the rear, the whole detachment swung out on the valley floor. As they did, Chief of scouts Charles A. Varnum rode ahead of the battalion and waved his hat while he shouted:

"Thirty days' furlough to the man who gets the first scalp!"

Reno ordered "Left into gallop - forward, guide, center!" and the detachment charged ahead. They had still not seen the camp.

Second Lieutenant Luther Hare with a few Arikara- and Crow scouts was in the lead as the battalion started towards the village. Varnum and other Arikara scouts moved along the left flank - the Rees' target was the immense Sioux pony herd. Varnum followed the bench land veering to the left pulling Company A with him, and as Captain Thomas French followed the forest line by the river with the right flank of M, a gap opened between them. Reno ordered Company G to increase speed and advance to the center to shore up the gap. Olaus sped up and made sure his section fell into line as ordered. All the way over by the forest he could see John Sivertsen standing in the stirrups, trying to get a glimpse of the village.

"Chaaaaaaaaarge!!!"

Reno's order rang out and everybody put the spurs to their horses, thundering down the valley in a headlong charge towards the camp about a mile away. Mounted Sioux warriors crossed back and forth in front of the teepees throwing up enormous clouds of dust, obscuring the view of the camp itself. Olaus crouched down over the horse's neck, the Spencer in his right hand and the reins in his left. The big sorrel shot like an arrow across the grassy plain – he was surprised the horse could muster that much speed after the 350 miles from Fort Lincoln.

"Zip!" "Zip!Zip!" "Zip!"

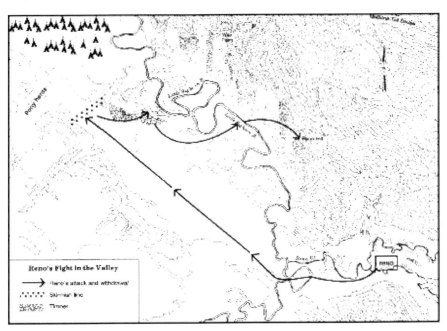

Major Marcus Reno's charge, skirmish line and retreat with companies A, G and M in the valley of the Little Bighorn June 25th, 1876. Wikipedia.org.

Olaus heard bullets fly past his head, but could hear very few reports from guns, let alone see who was doing the shooting. It did not make much difference to him – he felt the same excitement as during the Civil War when he charged an enemy stronghold at full speed, only on horseback the speed was infinitely higher. Suddenly several events happened in quick succession. About two hundred warriors came charging from the front left along a hidden creek bed whooping war cries and shooting at the same time as a ravine cutting across the valley floor came into sight in front of the mounted soldiers. Reno halted the charge. For George E. Smith and James Turley of Company M the order to halt came too late. They were unable to control their frightened and unruly horses, charged directly into the Indian village and were not seen again alive. John "Snopsy" Meyer also charged pell-mell through the Indian line, but did not share the two other privates' fate. To everybody's amazement he managed to wheel his horse around and shoot his way out with his .45.

"Fight on foot!"

Olaus heard Reno's order to dismount and form a skirmish line across the valley floor and quickly gave his horse to "number four". "Four" was the horse holder who would keep the horses of three soldiers together on a "skirmish link" with snap hooks on their bridle straps and lead them to cover. The cover was a horseshoe shaped patch of cottonwood with heavy underbrush interspersed with rose bushes on the right flank next to the river. Olaus could not fathom how Reno intended to charge the village on foot with such a small detachment, or even shoot accurately at it. It was more than half a mile away and the scouts had said the Indians were in the thousands. In a few minutes they would be mounted and on their way out. He pulled the carbine out of the scabbard and threw the sling across his shoulder while he tightened his cartridge belt. The belt had one full row of hoops for the .56/50 Spencer cartridges and two additional rows for the Colt .45s. The soldiers around him stared at the Spencer and his belt.
"Something you needed for the Ku Klux Klan, Sarge'?"
"Nope", Olaus replied. "You can never have too much firepower".

Olaus paced the distance between each trooper for his section and made sure they all had ammunition and the carbines were loaded and ready. He ordered everybody to spin the cylinder of their Colt and make sure every chamber was loaded. There was no requirement for safety by leaving the hammer on an empty chamber when

The skirmish line. Charles Schreyvogel 1912. The National Cowboy
& Western Heritage Museum, Oklahoma City.

Gall (Pizi), Hunkpapa Lakota war chief. Wikipedia.org.

facing an oncoming assault by mounted Sioux warriors. As the skirmish line was formed the companies were realigned. Company M - on the right flank during the mounted attack - had come closest to the village and it was moved back across the front of the two other companies, becoming the new left flank. Company A moved to the left behind G and occupied the new center. This made G's position the extreme right and Olaus' company was now closest to the river – and the forest. When John Sivertsen passed him on his way to the left flank he drew his index finger across his throat – Indian sign language for Sioux – Cutthroats. Too many Cutthroats. Olaus nodded and looked along the skirmish line. May be a hundred soldiers. May be. Definitely too many Cutthroats.

The skirmish line moved slowly forward about a hundred yards, the men shooting as they went. The new recruits fired more or less at random, and even worse – they fired as quickly as they could and expended all their ammunition in a short time. Some took careful and deliberate aim, but as the mounted Sioux warriors came pouring out of the village yelling and screaming like a horde of demons, holding a steady aim with rattled nerves proved difficult.

Nobody on either side knew who they were fighting that day. The Indians had no knowledge of Custer's presence at the Little Bighorn, although they knew perfectly well who he was. They thought they were attacked by the force of General George Crook, who they had defeated on the Rosebud on the 17th. When the mounted Sioux warriors came like a human tidal wave out of the enormous Indian camp, nobody on the skirmish line knew they were facing Gall, one of the most famous war chiefs in the Hunkpapa band, who were camped closest to the attacking soldiers. His two wives and three of his children were among the first to be killed when the troopers fired into the camp, hitting the teepees. Sitting Bull was still in the camp and would not join in the fight, while Crazy Horse was busy going through his pre-battle ritual, putting on war-paint and sacred amulets. He would emerge with his followers about fifteen minutes later.

Quite a few warriors were not mounted and moved through the forest to the right of the battalion. Olaus focused his fire on the warriors on foot. They were easier targets and posed a real threat if they were to infiltrate the timber were the horses were kept. He was watching how the skirmish line was quickly enveloped on three sides. Reno gave order to fire from a lying position and most of the men lay down, but Olaus kept firing at the Sioux in the forest from a kneeling position.

"Zip! – Zip!Zip!.

Bullets were flying thick and fast around him as the fire from the Indians intensified. He saw a few Sioux ponies roaming around without riders, but discounted that as having impact on the enemy's strength. Reno and French were still on their feet, Reno directing the fire and French practicing long range, accurate target shooting with his long gun. Olaus section was running out of ammunition and he ordered one of the troopers to give his remaining ammunition to the trooper next to him and run to the horses for more.

Olaus turned and looked to his rear. Painted warriors were sweeping - whooping and yelling - around the left flank of the skirmish line.....and fast. They fought Indian style, hanging hidden on the sides of the ponies for protection while shooting across their necks. Soon they would roll up the flank and get into the battalion's rear, and the fight would be over. "Over" in the Indian sense of the word did not mean the troopers would become prisoners of war. The Sioux and Cheyenne only took torture victims. Olaus was aware that if he was on the brink of falling into their hands, he better be sure to get killed – or kill himself. Company M was still far out on the plain anchored on Bloody Knife and the Ree scouts on the extreme left. John Sivertsen's position grew increasingly perilous.

Suddenly he saw officers from A and G companies retreating into the forest. He knew what was coming – the situation grew very bad, very quickly. He looked at his time piece. Almost twenty minutes since he dismounted. The man dispatched to bring ammunition did not return. His men started to break for the forest and the line lost any semblance of cohesion. He could not have kept them back any longer with verbal orders - the whooping warriors had unnerved the troopers completely. Olaus loaded the Spencer lying down before he started to retreat. He knew he would need those seven shots – and may be the six in his Colt - to cover the distance. As he walked backwards shooting at any approaching Indian he realized that Company M was getting detached from the line. Across the plain he could see some of the men starting to run headlong towards the forest. Captain French and 1st Sergeant John Ryan managed to stem the wave, ordered the men back to the line and wheeled the company to the left rear, facing the Sioux as they retreated. They had almost made it to the timber when Miles O'Hara threw up his arms and fell flat on his back.
"Bullet in the chest."
The thought flashed through Olaus' head. His experience from the Civil War left him in no doubt as to where O'Hara was hit. He knew there was probably little to be done for the sergeant.

The troopers withdrew to an open patch in the center of the forest where the horse holders kept the animals and got the remaining fifty rounds of ammunition from their saddle bags. When he came in among the trees Olaus realized the forest was part of an old riverbed with an embankment of about four feet offering excellent cover. He could see warriors in their rear on the other side of the river. The Indians had them surrounded and he heard the signals from their bone whistles from all directions. Most of the warriors were dressed only in breech-clouts and had a few feathers in their hair, but at the edge of the forest Olaus could see an Indian – obviously a war chief – with a magnificent bonnet of eagle feathers hanging down his back and extending down the sides of his pony. At the speed he was moving and through the dense underbrush, Olaus could not get a shot at him. He grabbed his reins from "number four", put his carbine in the scabbard and mounted. By now the din of battle was deafening. Mounted warriors were circling the detachment dashing to and from in waves of attacks, pouring rifle fire into the three companies. The troopers fired back, albeit at a slower pace, having to load the Springfields at each shot.

Olaus tried to organize his section but the troopers were scattered throughout the timber firing at will. He could sense a complete inactivity and breakdown in command which cascaded the detachment into disaster at a rapid rate. He looked at Reno who sat mounted with Bloody Knife about forty yards away. A red mist suddenly appeared around Bloody Knife's head enveloping Reno's chest and face. Olaus failed to comprehend what had happened before he saw Bloody Knife crash to the ground. The red mist was a gush of blood and brains from the Arikara's head blown open by an Indian bullet. Reno jumped to the ground – and then jumped back on the horse in one fleeting movement. He said something, swung around and started riding out of the timber. While he was trying to find out what was happening Olaus followed at a walk loading his Spencer. Troopers ran through the underbrush grabbing hold of any horse they could find. 2nd Lieutenant Wallace appeared with a few troopers from Company G, and Olaus rode up to join them. As they came out of the timber he saw Companies A and M in column-of-fours moving off at a gallop.

At the time Olaus came in from the skirmish line they had still not taken any casualties except Miles O'Hara, but in the unorganized mad dash out of the forest men started to fall. Private Lorenz took a rifle bullet in the neck which exited through his mouth and toppled him out of the saddle. Although the surgeon, Dr. Henry Porter tried to treat him, he was mortally wounded. After the surgeon gave him a dose of Laudanum he was left to die. A sudden volley hit three soldiers simultaneously – Dan Newell, Frank Braun and Henry Klotzbucher. Klotzbucher was just mounting his horse when he was shot in the stomach and fell back on the ground. He was mortally wounded, and he knew it. Privates William Slaper and Francis Neely jumped off their horses and dragged Klotzbucher into some dense underbrush where the Sioux would not find him. They gave him a canteen of water and raced out of the timber to catch up with the fleeing column.

As 2nd Lieutenant Wallace took the remnants of Company G out they set off at a gallop to connect with the rear of the two companies already on the plain. The Sioux- and Cheyenne warriors seemed somewhat taken aback at the approach of three companies charging at them, but when they realized it was an attempt to escape they started yelling and whooping, hanging onto the right flank and rear, pouring rifle fire into the troopers. Some of them held their repeaters across the saddle and without aiming fired into the column. The soldiers soon emptied their revolvers and there was no time to reload. It was a race for their lives. The warriors knew they were chasing unarmed cavalry. They were riding along the column about fifty yards away, waiting for injured soldiers to slow down or horses to fall and throw their riders. As they were galloping across a prairie dog town and the plain was covered in holes, there was an imminent danger of the horses breaking their legs. To show their bravery some of the warriors rode all the way up to the soldiers and tried to pull them from the saddle or shoot them at close range.

As he rode out of the forest Olaus saw the scout, "Lonesome" Charlie Reynolds down on one knee deliberately aiming and firing at the Indians. His horse was shot and he expended his last bullets at the approaching warriors. Private Henry Cody's horse was also shot from under him. He got up and retrieved his carbine from the saddle looking for somebody to pick him up on the back of the horse. Nobody did. Olaus had been puzzled by 1st Lieutenant McIntosh's absence from the company when Wallace took them out of the timber. He suddenly saw the reason why. McIntosh's horse was injured and could not get up speed. The Lieutenant was mounted at the edge of the forest, calmly shooting his handgun at about thirty approaching warriors. As the column raced past Olaus saw the Indians pulling him off the horse.

In about seventeen minutes the fleeing cavalry was at the Little Bighorn River. There was no ford across the fifty feet wide stream and the water reached almost to the backs of the horses. The river bank on the side they approached was steep and about six feet high, the opposite side eight. The troopers forced their mounts into the river by jumping off the bank, falling off and splashing around as they hit the water. The river was a struggling mass of men and horses trying to get away from the Indian warriors close on their heels. Some of the men managed to stay mounted while others waded across hanging on to the horses. Lieutenant Benny Hodgson – the officer detained by an armed mob of White Leaguers in Louisiana eighteen months before – was hit and fell off his mount just before reaching the river. As he fell Private James Darcy's horse stumbled over him and went headlong over the bank into the stream. Darcy managed to hang on to the saddle and the horse carried him across. It appeared that Hodgson was shot in the legs and could not move. He was waist deep in water when he grabbed hold of a passing trooper's stirrup and was dragged across the stream, just to be hit again and killed upon reaching the other side.

Olaus saw the melee in the river as he reined his horse in at the edge of the bank. Wheeling left he rode along the stream about fifty yards where he found a spot to jump in. He splashed across while he held the Spencer over his head and forced the sorrel up on the opposite bank. Within a few seconds he was back where the men crawled up from the river, some of them hanging on to their horses' tails. The Sioux and Cheyenne in pursuit had reached the river and started to fire into the struggling troopers. The Indians he had seen across the river while in the timber had swung around to the left and come up to cut the troopers off. They were firing from the bluffs in front when the men started their ascent from the river.

Olaus knew he could not be staying where he was for very long. The fleeing soldiers had found a narrow ravine running up the hill towards the top, but it was only passable for one horse at the time. While he was waiting to get into the ravine he picked out several of the most active Indian snipers. With four shots he toppled as many warriors off their horses - it was hard to miss at that distance. The Indians paid little or no attention to his shooting – they were consumed by firing at the troopers in the water. Within minutes Olaus was on his way up the ravine. The hillside was steep and he jumped off the horse and pulled it by the reins. Some distance up the trail he stumbled across the body of "Tinker" Bill Meyer. He was shot through the head by a bullet entering his eye socket.

He pulled his horse across the hilltop to safety. A lot of questions were swirling around in his mind. Why did his ammunition carrier not return? Why did Reno not sound any orders via a bugler to the troopers scattered throughout the forest? Why did he not have a rear guard when they left the timber? Why did he not have a rear guard at the river crossing? Where was Custer? Where was the rest of Company G? - And last, but not least – where was John Sivertsen? He looked at his time piece. It showed 4:10 pm.

Suddenly the firing died down. He peeked over the crest of the hill down on the crossing he just passed. The horde of warriors turned and melted away. What was happening? Within a few seconds he knew the answer. Captain Frederick Benteen appeared on the hill with his three companies, guns drawn and ready to fight and a little later, volleys of fire downstream the Little Bighorn River answered the question about Custer's position. The Lieutenant Colonel had engaged the hostiles, and Reno's opponents had gone in support of Custer's combatants. Olaus looked back down at the crossing. The dead soldiers in the creek looked like massive, white fishes floating belly up. He knew that Acting 1st Sergeant Edward Botzer was one of them. He had seen the German down by the crossing, but he was not on the hilltop.

Captain Frederick Benteen, 7ᵗʰ Cavalry. Wikipedia.org.

He looked at Reno who was having an exited conversation with Benteen, Captain Moylan of Company A, Lieutenant Godfrey of Company K, Chief of scouts Varnum and young Lieutenant Luther Hare. Moylan was sobbing, tears running down his cheeks, Varnum was crying and swearing, shooting haphazardly at the vanishing Indians – the only part of the conversation he could hear was Luther Hare's loud exclamation:
"We had a big fight in the bottom and got whipped like Hell!"
Reno and Varnum had apparently lost their hats and had bandanas tied around their heads and Reno still had particles of Bloody Knife's blood and brain on his face. Olaus hesitated to think that they would be able to impose a feeling of confident military command on the troopers wearing that kind of headgear.

The disappearance of the hostile Indians gave the detachment a welcome break to arrange a defensive position on the hilltop. Benteen threw his three companies out in a skirmish line along the crest facing the river. The men were digging rifle pits with the tools they had – which were not many: Three shovels, hunting knives, canteens and boards from broken boxes of hardtack. The ground was hard and the rifle pits shallow. The men piled up breastworks of saddle bags and boxes of hardtack. With Benteen present and the pack train soon to come up the question was raised if they should go to Custer's support. Olaus had a strong feeling about the disappearance of the hostiles downriver and the subsequent intense volleys of rifle fire. He thought Custer was engaged in battle with an overwhelming force of

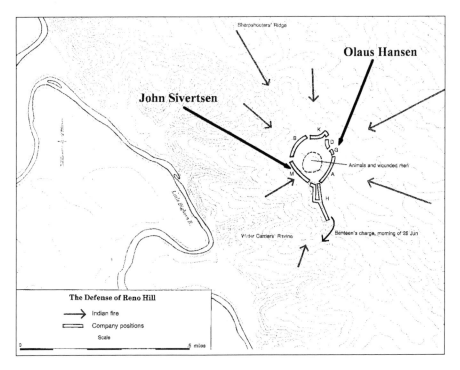

Olaus Hansen's and John Sivertsen's positions during the defense of Reno Hill June 25th and 26th, 1876. Wikipedia.org.

Indian warriors. However, Benteen clearly had no intention of leaving the hilltop for a while. He had unsaddled his horse immediately upon arrival, and anybody with knowledge about horses – which Benteen indeed had – knew that it would be impossible to saddle up again within at least half an hour. If he did, the horse would suffer burns on the back under the saddle and become unserviceable.

Olaus made a roster of Company G troopers he could not account for. Sergeants Botzer and Considine, corporals Hagemann and Martin, privates Wells, Lattman, McCormick, McGonigle, O'Neill, Petring, Weiss, Moore, Rapp, Rogers, Saefferman and Stanley. Sixteen missing – 35% casualties. He reported the ones he could account for and the ones missing to Lieutenant Wallace. Wallace took the list, looked at it, shook his head and walked away.

Olaus was starving and got some food scrap out of his saddlebag. He still had water in his canteen. The heat was oppressive and the wounded were already asking for water, and with the hostiles gone troopers were sent to the river as water carriers. About 5:30 he heard exited shouts from the crest of the hill. The survivors had discovered a column of men ascending the trail from the river. One of them towered over the others and was easily recognizable – John Sivertsen. Olaus shook his hand when he arrived on the hilltop.

"Thought you were done for, John! How did you get away?"

"Couldn't find my horse", Sivertsen said. "Hid in the bushes for a while – heard shots downriver and suddenly all the warriors took off. Stumbled into some other survivors and here we are".

In the group of newcomers were several of the missing troopers from Company G. Olaus crossed them off his list of casualties. Suddenly he saw Captain Weir of Company D move out with an orderly immediately followed by his company under 2nd Lieutenant Winfield Edgerly. Weir was eager to find out what was happening to his close friend George Custer – he had fought under the brevet Major General in the 3rd Michigan Cavalry during the Civil War. Wallace ordered the few G troopers to mount and Reno led a detachment out, consisting of Company M, H and K. Company A under Captain Moylan was still in camp. Olaus was not quite sure what the orders were – the detachment was strung out, and it looked like even the pack train was about to move out with the wounded. It came to an abrupt end, however, as Indians returned in force from downriver. The column started to retreat - Weir's company D crossed through French's company M deployed as rear guard, and soon they were both in full retreat with warriors close on their heels. Farrier Vincent Charley was abandoned after he was shot through the hips and tried to crawl towards the rear. He was helped into hiding with a promise that somebody would be back for him, a promise which became impossible to keep. He was later found dead with a stick rammed down his throat.

Back on the hill the soldiers prepared for a siege. The companies were spread out in a circle as well as circumstances allowed, Olaus with his small contingent from Company G on the east side, Sivertsen's Company M on the west side. The position did not offer much protection when the Indian warriors started to pour enfilade fire into the camp from surrounding elevations. When the men initially put up boxes for breastworks, a trooper had thrown himself behind one of them for cover. Within seconds and Indian bullet came crashing through the box and hit him the head, killing him. Olaus observed the most peculiar reaction among everybody watching the incident, and attributed it to extreme excitement among the troopers – they all burst out laughing.

Clouds of gun smoke from rifle fire could be seen up to 900 yards away. Private Charles Windolph took pot shots at an Indian shooting from a remote position, appearing to rest his gun on a bleached buffalo skull. The bullets from his Springfield struck the ground short of the Indian. Most of the sniping was done from about 200 to 500 yards. Sometimes the warriors crawled up so close they were just a stone throw away. Olaus looked for puffs of gun smoke about 150 – 250 yards out. He carefully examined the area when the cloud drifted away to distinguish the shooter. Sometimes he could only see the head, and he held his fire. A head shot at 200 yards would be impossible, even for a marksman. At 100 yards, he gave it a try. At 200 he would shoot at a torso. He reloaded the carbine from a ten-tube Blakeslee cartridge box he kept in one of his saddle bags. Throughout the afternoon he took out several Indian snipers, but only by shooting at the torso. Every headshot was a miss.

A hospital had been established in a depression at the center of the camp, covered by a fly tent, and the horses and mules were also concentrated in that area. A few of the Sioux warriors had found a clear view into the hospital and continued to fire at the horses. The bullets were ripping through the fly tent. The animals became frightened by the intense rifle fire - private Henry Voight was in the process of untangling some horses when he got struck in the head by an Indian bullet. Forty six horse and mules would eventually be killed on the hilltop.

It was not difficult for Olaus to recognize which of the troopers were raw recruits, did not know much about firing their rifles and had never been under fire or seen an assaulting enemy close up. Many of them broke - some of them were crying, some trembling, some were faking illness to retreat to the hospital and some were skulking as far away from the Indian fire as possible. Not even all the officers were up to the task. Captain Moylan of Company A spent a lot of time dug in behind a mule pack, earning him the nickname "Aparejo Mickie", the Spanish name for "pack". First Lieutenant Frank Gibson was lying on the ground without getting up during most of the battle, and Reno spent his daylight hours in a rifle pit together with a bottle of whiskey, only to come out at night. With Captain Benteen - as Olaus knew from the Civil War – it was quite a different story. He walked along the lines all day and all night, making sure the sentinels kept awake, reorganizing the defense perimeter and gathering troopers for counter charges when the Indians got too close with their rifle fire. He had the heel shot off his boot by a sniper bullet without giving it any heed. If anybody urged him to take cover, his comment was:
"If they are going to get you they will get you somewhere else if not here."

That evening the sun went down like a ball of fire and the blistering daytime heat quickly turned into a high plains chill. It was a moonless night, very much appreciated by the troopers since the Sioux and Cheyenne could not keep up their long distance sniping. By 10 o'clock the Indian fire had ceased completely. Down in the valley they could see large campfires and hear the steady beat of drums interrupted by loud whoops from the dancing Indians and the firing of guns. The question of Custer's whereabouts surfaced over and over again – why did he not come to their rescue? Benteen was convinced he had left them to their fate, just like he did Major Joel Elliott and a detachment of nineteen troopers at the battle of Washita. They were later found butchered by the Cheyenne. Captain Weir was of the opinion that Custer had a big fight on his hands where the previous volleys were heard further down the valley, and he was unsure of the result. It did not look promising.

Olaus was suffering badly from thirst, but he knew the situation was a whole lot worse for the wounded. After he had his last hard tacks the feeling of hunger had just become a dull pain. While he was waiting for a renewal of hostilities he remembered June 26th fifteen years earlier. Back then he could never have imagined that he would be celebrating his 20th birthday on an emigrant ship across the Atlantic Ocean. Even more unfathomable would have been that he would sit on a hilltop in Montana under siege by Sioux and Cheyenne Indians on his 35th. The eastern sky became grey from the dawning day at about 3:00 am. Two shots rang out from the Indians – they had returned to pick up where they left off the previous day. The sun rose at 4:22 and Captain Benteen ordered the bugler to sound reveille. The troopers dragged dead horses to some of the firing positions for breastworks. Olaus saw John Sivertsen hard at work with his butcher knife – it looked almost ridiculous to see the big blacksmith dig a shallow rifle pit behind some sagebrush not two feet high. The protection the sagebrush provided was a lot more perception than it was reality.

About 9 am the warriors started to press heavily against Benteen's company on the south side of the makeshift fortifications. He requested assistance from Reno and was given permission to take Sivertsen's Company M and charge the Indians. Olaus could not see the detachment, but he could hear them as they tore out of the hilltop and down the gullies almost a hundred yards, screaming, yelling and shooting. The Indians were taken by total surprise and scrambled to safety while the troopers retreated to the hilltop. One man was killed halfway down the hillside while James Tanner of Company M was shot through the lung. The reorganization of troops had shifted the pressure from the Indians to Reno's front, and about 10 am Benteen found Reno's in his pit and recommended a new charge. There was a large group of Indians a few hundred yards away gathering for an attack. Benteen took companies B, D, K and Olaus' G, and as they moved out Reno got to his feet and led the charge. They advanced only about fifty yards - Olaus firing at any Indian he could see with his Spencer, drawing his Colt when the carbine was empty – but it was enough to disperse the Indians and prevent the assault. During the charge one of the troopers had been left inside the defense perimeter, lying in a rifle pit crying like a child. Ironically - a while after they returned, he was shot in the head by an Indian sniper.

Some of the troopers exposed themselves unnecessarily as they continued shooting at the Indians. Civilian packer Frank Mann was firing over a breast work when he went quiet for about twenty minutes in an aiming position. Closer examination showed that he was dead, hit by a bullet. Private Herod Liddie fired at potential targets pointed out by Benteen, talking as he did so - but suddenly he went quiet. The men next to him noticed blood running down from the rim of his hat. He was dead. Private Andrew Moore drew fire when - in spite of warnings - he rose every time he shot, instead of kneeling down. Soon an Indian sniper drew a bead on him, fatally shooting him through the stomach.

By noon the temperature had risen to a hundred degrees and Doctor Porter informed Reno that without fluid, some of the wounded would soon die. The men were chewing on grass to exercise their saliva glands and one private – Cornelius Cowley – went insane from thirst and had to be tied up to keep him restrained. Several water carrier details were formed by volunteers. Every run to the river took about ninety minutes and passed through a long ravine exposed to heavy Indian fire. Captain Benteen asked for volunteers from Company H to a detachment of sharp shooters. They were to suppress the Indians by raking the bushes where the warriors hid with rifle fire during the water carriers' advance and retreat. Five Germans came forward – Sergeant Henry Fehler, Charles Windolph, Otto Voit, George Geiger and Henry Mechling. Several carriers were injured – James Darcy was wounded in the left leg, Michael Madden's leg was broken and one trooper was killed - but they managed to secure a few containers of water for the hospital. Madden's leg was amputated the next day. When one of the water details came across the hilltop heading for the hospital, they were hailed by Captain Myles Moylan requesting a drink. Private James Weeks threw all military etiquette aside: "You go to Hell and get your own water. This is for the wounded!"

About 2 pm the intensity of the Indian fire reached a peak and then began to slacken. Within an hour they appeared to withdraw. Olaus could see large clouds of smoke billowing up from the valley floor. The Indians had put the grass on fire.

This was a tactic used to mask large movements – the Sioux, Cheyenne and their allies were about to leave. About 7 pm the soldiers on the hilltop watched some 7 000 Indians move out of the Little Bighorn valley – on foot, on horseback, with their dogs, pack animals and travois - and driving a herd of 20 000 ponies. Olaus estimated the column to be about three miles long and half a mile wide. It took several hours before the last Indians were gone. John Sivertsen came over, puffing on his pipe. As they watched the tail of the immense column disappear, Sivertsen knocked the pipe against the heel of his boot to clean it out and shook his head. "Definitely too many Cutthroats", he said.

AFTERMATH

On the morning of June 27th the sun rose at 4:22 am – and Private James Tanner died from his wounds. After burying the dead in the shallow rifle pits Reno ordered the camp moved to the south, closer to the river, to get away from the overwhelming stench from dead animals. Olaus ate his first meal in thirty six hours - coffee, soaked hardtack and bacon. Water for the wounded was no longer a problem and the horses and mules plunged their heads up to their eyes in the stream to drink. Sometime between 8 and 9 am a cloud of dust was seen rising downriver in the Little Bighorn valley. A detachment dispatched from Reno's camp found that it was Lieutenant James H. Bradley, chief of scouts for Gibbon's 7th Infantry.

About an hour later General Alfred Terry arrived with four troops of the 2nd Cavalry and six companies of the 7th Infantry. Olaus watched Terry as he passed – tears were running down his cheeks. The question was on everybody's mind:
"Where is Custer?"
"To the best of my knowledge and belief" Olaus heard him say, "- he lies on a ridge about four miles below here – with all his command killed."
Olaus was not completely surprised – a nagging suspicion had grown in him over the last two days. The force of thousands of warriors, their disappearance from the river crossing where Reno's detachment escaped, the firefight downriver to the north abruptly ending, the victory dance in the camp on the 25th – putting it all together, in all its horror it made sense.
"I can hardly believe it", Benteen said. "I think he is somewhere down the Bighorn grazing his horses. At the battle of the Washita he went off and left a part of his command and I' think he'll do it again."
Terry looked at him. "I think you are mistaken, Benteen, and you will take your command and go down where the dead are lying and investigate for yourself."

The wounded from Reno's hilltop position was moved to General Terry's camp and Captain Benteen with fourteen troopers from Company H rode to the Custer battlefield. Details were made to bury the dead from the skirmish line and in the timber from the first day's fight – McIntosh, Reynolds, Bloody Knife, Bobtail bull and the enlisted men. The valley floor was black from burnt grass and shrubs, still smoldering. The bodies were a gruesome sight – Olaus had never seen such mutilation of human beings, and he started to fully realize the saying that the Sioux and Cheyenne did not take prisoners of war. The scout Charlie Reynolds' head was severed from the trunk. Lieutenant McIntosh's head was beaten to pulp with stone hammers and he could only be identified by a button next to his body. The black interpreter Isaiah Dorman had been shot repeatedly in the legs below his knees with a small pistol, apparently when he was still alive. A horse's picket pin was driven through his scrotum, his penis was cut off and stuck in his mouth and his head crushed. An unidentified soldier had strips of skin cut out of his body, probably when he was still alive. Henry Cody, the corporal who had his horse shot from under him and tried to get somebody to pick him up in the mad dash to the creek, was horribly mutilated.

When they later passed through the abandoned Indian camp Olaus could barely imagine what had taken place on the night of the 25th when they were listening to the Indian drums and whoops from the valley. There were remnants of human bodies scattered across the village. He saw what appeared to be bones and parts of blue uniforms where men had been tied to stakes and trees. From a lodge pole hung three heads which had been tied together with a string and burnt. A man's heart was found with a lariat tied to it. A dead cavalry horse had been cut open and a naked soldier forced head first into the horse's belly. Private James Turley, who was one of the two soldiers the horses took into the camp during Reno's charge, was found with his hunting knife driven to the hilt in one eye. John McGinnis' head was found on a pole. For Olaus the most shocking discovery came when Private John Foley lifted an overturned camp kettle from the ground. Under the kettle was the head of one of his corporals from Company G. He had seen a lot of horrific sights during the Civil War, but nothing compared to the butchery in the Indian village.

The next morning Olaus was detailed with Lieutenant Wallace to go to the Custer battlefield to bury the dead. It was a sobering experience. The troopers were marched onto the battlefield in column-of-fours, dismounted and started to dig graves. 204 bodies were scattered across the hillside and in ravines, all naked and horribly mutilated. It was the third day the bodies were exposed to the burning Montana sun and the skin started to turn black on the bloated, festering corpses. Green bottle and blue bottle blowflies were covering the bodies, laying eggs in noses, eyes, open mouths and other cavities. Fly maggots by the thousands were crawling around in the wounds. The bodies had been cut open, intestines were protruding, hands, feet and legs cut off and thighs slashed. One of the men was scalped down to the ears, the crown of his head chopped off and his cap forced into the hole. Up to thirty arrows had been shot into some of the corpses. Troopers were found with their scrotums removed – the squaws used them for tobacco pouches. The bodies were in an advanced stage of decomposition, and seventy rotting cavalry horses added to the intense, repugnant stench across the battlefield. When Olaus grabbed hold of a body's wrists the skin would sometime come off, or the shoulders would become dislocated. No efforts were made to identify the enlisted men. All the bodies were put in shallow graves – some barely covered with a layer of dirt – and a few were simply covered with branches of sagebrush.

Of the fifty four wounded men from the hilltop many had to be carried. When the column moved out on the evening of the 28th this showed to be an insurmountable task and they halted after only four miles. On the 29th the litters were redone and rigged between two mules in tandem, and this worked so well that after starting at 6 pm Terry kept the column going all night. Captain Grant Marsh had managed to maneuver the steamboat Far West all the way up to the confluence of the Little Bighorn and the Bighorn rivers, and they reached the boat at about 6 am on June 30th. The wounded were placed on mats of newly cut grass on the deck of the steamer, which started on the 710 mile journey to Fort Abraham Lincoln.

General John Gibbon had established a camp – Fort Pease - at the confluence of the Bighorn and Yellowstone rivers. Terry's column arrived on July 2nd and was ferried across to the north side and went into camp. Olaus settled in to rest, but through the grapevine he had already heard that the Sioux campaign of 1876 was far from at an end, despite the loss of five companies of the 7th Cavalry. On July 6th the steamer Josephine arrived with supplies for the trader, and the men flocked to the tents. On July 14th myriads of grasshoppers suddenly swarmed all over the area, follow by a violent thunder storm after midnight of the 17th. At 5 am Olaus was woken up by another thunderstorm, this time with heavy showers of hail, and water was rising to an uncomfortable level in the tent.

While in camp, one of the non-commissioned officers initiated a campaign to have Reno and Benteen promoted to lieutenant colonel and major of the 7th Cavalry. A petition was circulated to be signed in support of the proposition. Olaus signed it and eventually it gathered 235 names. He had no wish to keep Reno as the lieutenant colonel of the 7th. However, he did want to retain Benteen, and he knew there was no way he would get Benteen without taking Reno. He expected Reno to be phased out because of his behavior at the Little Bighorn, and that would leave the way open for Benteen – or at least that was how it would have worked in the volunteer army of the Civil War. The petition was denied by General Sherman who pointed out that promotions went strictly by seniority and these particular promotions had already been made by the President and approved by the Senate. As the petition was making its way through camp, Major Reno was put under arrest by the commander of the camp, Colonel John Gibbon - Olaus could never make out the reason why.

The soldiers remained at the Bighorn for a month, moving to a new camp at the confluence of the Yellowstone and the Rosebud Rivers on July 30th. Steamers came up with reinforcements for the new campaign. On August 1st six companies of the 22nd Infantry arrived, the next day another six companies of the 5th Infantry and 150 new recruits and 70 horses for the 7th Cavalry. A battery of artillery was also unloaded. Supplies were provided from the trader, and the aftermath of the horrific battle five weeks earlier started to show. Many of the survivors from the hilltop drank heavily. Reno purchased almost as much whiskey as everybody else put together - on August 1st the trader sold him three gallons.

On August 8th the 7th set out along the Rosebud with 400 men as part of a large force trying to catch up with the Sioux. 1st Lieutenant Francis Gibson was in charge of Company G, an arrangement less than ideal in Olaus' mind after Gibson's sorry performance on the Hilltop. He did not feel in competent hands with a commander who spent most of the battle flat on his belly. On August 10th he saw a cloud of dust on the horizon and suspected in could be a force of Sioux Indians. However, a lone rider approached way ahead of the cloud who was clearly a white man. When he came up to the column Olaus recognized him. It was William F. Cody, who was assigned as a scout to General George Crook. Cody had served in the Civil War and was chief of scouts for the 3rd Cavalry. In 1867 and 1868 he worked for the Kansas-Pacific Railroad, supplying meat for the railroad workers. In eighteen months he shot 4 280 buffaloes with his Springfield trapdoor .50/70 rifle "Lucretia Borgia", earning him the sobriquet "Buffalo Bill".

Crook and Terry joined forces until they went into Camp Supply at Powder River for a week, whereupon Crook left. Reno continued to purchase whiskey – six gallons on August 19th, one gallon on the 21st and one gallon on the 22nd. During his stay in camp Olaus heard astonishing news about "Wild Bill" Hickok. The Prince of Pistoleers had left his newly wed wife back east to come to Deadwood in the Black Hills to prospect for gold. He was a national celebrity, having served as marshal in some of the most lawless cow towns in the West – Hays City in 1869 - 70 and Abilene in 1871. He was also the one who got into a bar brawl with two troopers from Company M, 7th Cavalry in Hays on July 17th, 1870 where he shot John Kyle dead and wounded Jeremiah Lonergan in the knee. The news was he had been assassinated at the Number 10 saloon in Deadwood – a man by the name

William "Buffalo Bill" Cody. Wikipedia.org.

of Jack McCall had shot him in the head from behind.

After a march up the Rosebud and back to the Yellowstone the column spent several days scouring the countryside before going back into camp at the Yellowstone on September 3rd. No Indians had been seen. Life in camp became tedious. Olaus watched the horse races arranged on a course behind the camp, and played cards and baseball. The troopers from the Little Bighorn battle continued to drink – they were still at a loss as to how to cope with the sudden deaths of their flamboyant Lieutenant Colonel and more than 200 of their fellow troopers at the hands of the Sioux and Cheyenne. It had been a life changing event, and even if Olaus had seen far more casualties during the Civil War, the images of the horrifying mutilations stayed with him. Three times officers of the day reported drunk on duty, and were taken under arrest to their tents. A court martial was convened where Captain Weir was appointed president of the court. He held the proceedings under a cottonwood tree with a two-gallon demi john of whiskey between his knees, drinking from it at regular intervals.

On September 9th the 7th was again ordered out, this time down the Yellowstone with ten days' ration. The next day a report came in about Indians crossing the Missouri at Wolf Point. They marched ninety miles in four days without encountering any hostiles. Eventually the 7th was ferried across the Missouri, given three days' ration and ordered to go to Fort Buford. After a march of another ninety miles they reached Buford on September 18th at 10 am where they halted for only two hours and continued towards Fort Lincoln. On September 26th Olaus rode into the fort, more than four months after the Indian campaign of 1876 had begun. He noticed that the officers' quarters occupied by the ones who fell at the Little Bighorn were already abandoned, and the doors and windows painted black. Army wives had only thirty days to vacate their homes when their husbands were killed in battle.

On October 19th Colonel Samuel Sturgis led twelve companies of the 7th Cavalry from Fort Lincoln to the Standing Rock and Cheyenne River agencies. There they dismounted and disarmed the Sioux completely, putting an end to any immediate danger of attacks. General Gorge Crook got intelligence about a Northern Cheyenne war party in Wyoming Territory and ordered Colonel Ranald McKenzie with his 4th Cavalry to investigate. McKenzie brought about 1 000 soldiers from the 2nd, 3rd, 4th and 5th Cavalry. At dawn on November 25th - in blistering cold weather - he attacked Cheyenne Chief Dull Knife's village of 173 lodges and about 400 warriors at Bates Creek. He used Shoshone- and Pawnee warriors as scouts, longtime enemies of the Northern Cheyenne – the Cheyenne were in fact having a celebration because of a recent victory over the Shoshone.

McKenzie moved quickly in behind his Indians scouts and captured the village, driving the Cheyenne half naked out into the snow. Most of the Cheyenne later surrendered, but some of them joined Crazy Horse at his Oglala Lakota camp. First Sergeant James H. Turpin of Company L, 5th Cavalry was one of the troopers going through the lodges. He found a lot of trophies from the Custer battle at the Little Bighorn. Among the trophies were a guidon, overcoats, a buckskin jacket, saddles, canteens – and Company G's Acting 1st sergeant Edward Botzer's roster book. Botzer had been killed at the crossing of the Little Bighorn River during the retreat from the timber, and his book was picked up by a Cheyenne warrior by the name of High Bull. It was used by the Cheyenne to depict victories in battle. The troopers also found more gruesome trophies – the scalps of two young girls, one white and one Shoshone, a buckskin bag containing the right hands of twelve Shoshone babies and a necklace of human fingers. McKenzie's attack on Dull Knife's village effectively ended any remnant of Cheyenne resistance.

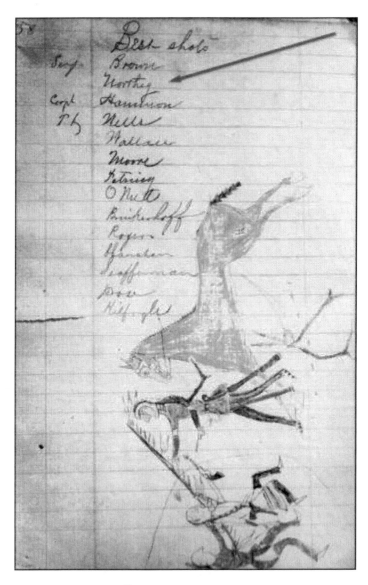

High Bull's Victory Roster - 1ˢᵗ Sgt. Edward Botzer's roster book found in Chief Dull Knife's Cheyenne village on November 25ᵗʰ, 1876. Olaus Hansen's name is second from top as a marksman in Company G, 7ᵗʰ Cavalry. Photo: The author. The Smithsonian Institution, National Museum of the American Indian # 108725.

THE NEZ PERCE

Olaus settled down to camp life at Fort Abraham Lincoln. Everything taken into consideration – his move to Dakota had not been very successful. Apart from the disastrous Sioux campaign, the weather in Dakota was a catalyst for deteriorating health. A snow storm with cold temperatures occurred on November 12th, and on November 17th another snow storm covered the area around Lincoln. As if the cold was not enough, the wood supplied to the fort was of inferior quality. It was cottonwood just cut from the stump which would not burn in the stoves by itself, and when green it was completely useless. He was used to extreme temperatures from Norway, but at least there he had wood to fight the cold with – dry pine and spruce burning like gun powder and the hardwood birch. If he filled the stove with birch at night and reduced the air flow to a minimum, it would still be embers the next morning.

In November Olaus was detailed to daily duty as acting sergeant major of the 7th Cavalry, an assignment he certainly saw as an honor. The sergeant major was to the sergeants and corporals what the major was to the commissioned line officers and he was expected to conduct both practical and theoretical instruction for the non-commissioned officers. The sergeant major was also responsible for transmitting orders through the first sergeants, and they would be obeyed as if they came from the adjutant. On November 28th there was a suicide at the fort – if it was accidental or premeditated, nobody could tell, and the coroner would not draw that distinction. It appeared that a long time soldier in the 7th Cavalry by the name of John Steintker from Hanover, Germany had taken his own life by an overdose of Laudanum. A vial was fund in his pocket and it was common knowledge that he had been drinking heavily for about two weeks prior to his death.

Captain Thomas Weir of Company D - who almost set out to join Custer from the besieged hilltop when Indians drove them back - had been detached to New York on September 30th to do recruiting. Sometime before Christmas Olaus learned that he had been found dead on December 9th. The medical examiner's report stated "congestion of the brain". Olaus thought the alcohol had gotten the better of him in the end, or at least helped to finish him off. He was 38 years old.

Olaus did not ponder Steintker's and Weir's deaths for very long – everybody had their own reasons for what they did on the Frontier – drinking themselves to death, using opium, shooting themselves - you could never tell who was going to be next, how or why. It was a tough life, and the troopers took one day at the time, enjoying the time they had. If they did not enjoy it, they simply disappeared, never to be seen again. Bonner, Littlefield and Williamson had deserted on July 7th, after the battle. They were caught near Fort Lincoln on July 13th, starving, and again escaped from confinement on September 6th. William Channel deserted on July 26th, Louis DeTorreil on September 30th, Patrick Connelly on October 2nd, Sergeant John Thomas Easley on October 17th, William Chapman on October 15th and Thomas Conlan on December 21st. Clearly these men were not interested in meeting Sioux, Cheyenne or other Indians under any circumstance.

From February 20th to March 7th 1877 Olaus was detailed as the regimental standard bearer. He was discharged on March 21st, and thought long and hard about what to do next. He did not like Dakota – it was much too cold. His rheumatism was rapidly getting worse. The 7th Cavalry was a new and recreated regiment. There were 30 new officers and 500 new recruits, and many, many of his old comrades were gone. However – he was a professional soldier, and there were no wars going on in the United States. The fights – if there were any left – would be on the Northern Plains, against Indians. The Sioux were suppressed, although he was in no doubt they would rise again. May be the Cheyenne, too. The soldiering was here, if anywhere. He also realized that the freedom he felt living on the Frontier would be quickly strangled in the Victorian society back East – and so would he. The glory days from the Civil War were gone and it was hard to find work in a society where the attitude to soldiers was that they were useless for anything but soldiering. If they were not – why had they not found a "normal" job like everybody else, settled down and raised a family? Three days later he reenlisted in the 7th Cavalry for another five years. There were still Indians to fight, and within a couple of weeks he would find out which ones.

It had been a long and very cold winter when the sun finally started to thaw the snow along the south walls of the fort. During the first ten days of March the temperatures hovered between 10 and 35 degrees below zero. The sleeping quarters at Fort Lincoln left a lot to be desired - iron bunks with bed sacks filled with twelve pounds of straw called "prairie feathers", which was changed once a month. Four or five blankets which was never enough. Olaus was always cold, not to say he froze. The rheumatism had been ravaging his body all winter. He drank his medicinal whiskey – and got drunk. Whiskey was not sold on the grounds of the fort, but he could go to the trader's store north of the post, closer to the river.

THE UNITED STATES OF AMERICA.

OATH OF ENLISTMENT AND ALLEGIANCE.

State of _____

Town of _____

I, _____, born in _____, in the State of _____, and by occupation a _____, DO HEREBY ACKNOWLEDGE to have voluntarily re-enlisted this _____ day of _____, 1877, as a SOLDIER in the ARMY OF THE UNITED STATES OF AMERICA, for the period of FIVE YEARS, unless sooner discharged by proper authority: And do also agree to accept from the United States such bounty, pay, rations, and clothing as are or may be established by law. And I do solemnly swear, that I am _____ years and _____ months of age, and know of no impediment to my serving honestly and faithfully as a soldier for five years under this enlistment contract with the United States. And I, _____ do also solemnly swear, that I will bear true faith and allegiance to the UNITED STATES OF AMERICA, and that I will serve them honestly and faithfully against all their enemies or opposers whomsoever; and that I will observe and obey the orders of the President of the United States, and the orders of the officers appointed over me, according to the Rules and Articles of War.

Subscribed and duly sworn to before me, this _____ day of _____ A.D. 1877.

[A. G. O. No. 71.]

Olaus Hansen's reenlistment at Fort Abraham Lincoln March 24th, 1877. The National Archives.

Sometimes the alcohol had good effect, but other times there was no stopping the pain. When it became unbearable he went to the dispensary to get Laudanum. That produced an instant relief which was hard to imagine when his joints were aching at their worst.

Many troopers decided to tell the Army good-bye during the winter and spring. George Henderson deserted in January, John W. Franklin on February 2nd, Harry Criswell on March 25th, James Barsantee and Jesse Kuehl on March 27th, Frank Clark on March 29th, Alonzo Jennys on April 18th, William Caldwell on April 22nd, Charles Aller on April 24th and Milton DeLacey on May 9th. Olaus had a feeling that many of the deserters were "snowbirds", men who enlisted in the army to have a place to eat and sleep during the winter and deserted in the spring.

On April 30th eleven companies of the 7th Cavalry reunited a short distance below Bismarck. Three days later the regiment took the field heading towards Fort Buford under the command of Colonel Samuel Sturgis on a summer campaign to round up non-reservation Sioux and Cheyenne. Lieutenant George Wallace was in charge of Company G. They reached the fort without incident on May 16th. It quickly became apparent that they would not have to look for Crazy Horse. He had surrendered with his Oglala band at Red Cloud Agency by Fort Robinson, Nebraska on May 5th. Neither would they have to look for Sitting Bull. He escaped with his Hunkpapas to Canada the same week.

The companies were ferried across the Yellowstone on May 23rd and started to patrol the north bank. Six days later the regiment went into camp on Cedar Creek and was ordered to remain there by Colonel Nelson A. Miles. During the stay on Cedar Creek Olaus was ordered out on small patrols commanded by 2nd Lieutenants, but they showed to be futile exercises. The regiment moved twice more in June, then stayed in camp until the middle of August. Captain Thomas French of Company M appeared to be losing the battle with alcohol, and alcohol was not his only problem. On one occasion he stole some opium from the farrier and while turning blue in the face fell unconscious to the ground outside Luther Hare's tent. The doctor had to come to his rescue.

Even if there were no Sioux to fight, trouble was brewing among the Nez Perce Indians for the same reasons as it had been brewing among the Sioux and Cheyenne – non-treaty Indians refusing to move onto reservations and friction between white prospectors and settlers leading to murders on both sides.

Chief Joseph (Hin-mah-too-yah-lat-kekt)
of the Nez Perce. Wikipedia.org.

Throughout 1877 tensions grew – in June the Nez Perce were ordered onto the reservation within thirty days or face the consequences. They complied and came in from their homeland in Wallowa Valley, northeast Oregon to Fort Lapwai, Idaho Territory. By June 14th, 600 Nez Perce had gathered on the Camas Prairie when three warriors attacked four settlers and killed them in revenge for previous personal   disputes. After the incident Chief Joseph of the Nez Perce saw peace talks with the U.S. Army as futile, and General Oliver O. Howard – from the Civil War Freedmen's Bureau - had already sent a military force to deal with the hostilities and force the Nez Perce onto the reservation. When the army detachment arrived it was defeated by the Indians at the battle of White Bird Canyon, and the Nez Perce set out on a 1170 mile trek – later to become famous - towards freedom in Canada.

Soon the news broke in Dakota about the Nez Perce and action was taken to prevent Sitting Bull from returning from Canada to unite with them, and to catch the escaping Indians. On August 12th Olaus Hansen and John Sivertsen were marching up the Yellowstone with companies F, G, H, I, L and M heading west to Pompey's Pillar and then north to Musselshell River and Judith Gap. Judith Gap was a strategic pass which the Nez Perce was thought to come through. Sturgis received several dispatches throughout the rest of August about the Indians' whereabouts, marching to the Crow Agency and then to Clark's Fork Canyon. The six companies went into camp about thirty five miles north of the canyon on September 1st. From there they marched to Heart Mountain on September 7th where Sturgis dispatched two miners up Stinkingwater River to see if they could locate the Nez Perce. They did not return. While the troopers – constantly running low on food – were fishing trout in a nearby river, Sturgis sent out two scouting parties. One party found the miners, one living and one dead, the other found the Nez Perce slipping away with a large pony herd towards the headwater of the Stinkingwater. By trying to anticipate the Nez Perce's route through the mountains Sturgis led the 7th on an arduous march which eventually threw the regiment off the Indians' trail and gave them two days' head start.

Sturgis decided to catch up with the Nez Perce via forced marches. At 5 am on Wednesday, September 12th he set out with the regiment and covered forty eight miles in eighteen hours before he went into camp about eight miles above Clark's Fork's confluence with the Yellowstone. Somebody found a fallen tree to use for firewood and soon they had a large fire burning. Olaus stood with his back to the fire, letting his clothes dry while puffing on his pipe. John Sivertsen came over.
"I don't think we stand a chance to catch up to the Indians." John said.
"Of course not" Olaus agreed. "They can run circles around us, even with a pony herd in tow. You know it, I know it - but Colonel Sturgis can't allow himself to know it. We'll be chasing those elusive ghosts around the mountains for a while until our horses are worn out. Then we can go home and the Nez Perce will continue to Canada."

Next morning, September 13th, the Nez Perce went foraging for supplies down the Yellowstone Valley, killing settlers and burning haystacks and buildings as they went. Sturgis' cavalry had crossed Clark's Fork and turned north when a Crow scout came galloping saying that the Nez Perce were just a few miles ahead. They could actually see the smoke from the burning hay stacks. Companies F, I and L were sent forward under the command of Major Merrill – the Major Merrill from reconstruction duty in South Carolina and Louisiana – while Captain Benteen with Olaus' company G, John's Company M and Company H were held in reserve waiting for the pack mules. Major Merrill caught up with the Nez Perce as they were passing across his front about five miles ahead, but instead of charging them he decided to make a dismounted charge on foot from fear of sniper fire from Indian sharp shooters.

Olaus and John were still waiting for the pack mules. The country was wet from the previous day's rain and a gale force wind was blowing through the mountains.

Upon learning that Merrill was not going to be able to cut the Nez Perce off with his slow foot-charge Sturgis left Company H to guard the pack train and took Olaus' and John's G and M forward across an open plateau towards the escaping Nez Perce. Benteen charged the Indians with his two-company detachment expecting support from Major Merrill by Merrill flanking the rear of Benteens troopers and cover them from Indian snipers. The support never materialized. Olaus pushed his sorrel all the way in among the trailing animals of the Nez Perce pony herd, reins in his left hand and Spencer carbine in his right. He could already see they were not going to be able to stop the Indians. The pony herd ran like a large wave of animals through a pass up ahead and the Nez Perce quickly deployed snipers on top of the cliffs on both sides of the canyon to act as rear guards.

"Zip! Zip!Zip!..........Zip!"

The familiar sound of bullets flying by his head made Olaus rein his horse in and take cover behind some boulders on the side of the entrance to the pass. He knew it was suicide to charge into the canyon – for the Indians it would be like shooting fish in a barrel.

Just after 4 pm Merrill finally linked up with Benteen. Company H and I charged the snipers on the cliffs to the north and south and Sturgis again deployed G and M companies to charge towards the canyon. They were all pinned down by a galling, accurate Indian fire. Darkness was falling and Sturgis pulled his whole force off the cliff faces and went into camp. The Indians had escaped and the horses were worn out. His losses were three men killed and eleven wounded.

The next morning Crow scouts explored the canyon while the 7th Cavalry remained in camp. By midday the regiment was in cautious pursuit of the Nez Perce. They passed Judith Gap and reached the Musselshell River on September 19th. There they waited for General Howard and Lieutenant Varnum's supply train coming from the Crow Agency until they caught up on the 22nd. On October 2nd they got news of a battle between another detachment of the 7th Cavalry under Colonel Miles and the Nez Perce in the Bear Paw Mountains. Two officers had been killed – one of them was Olaus' recruiting officer from Jefferson barracks, Captain "Holy Owen" Hale. He had taken a shot in the neck. Howard's and Sturgis' combined force set out for the Bear Paws but on the 7th of October they turned back. The Nez Perce had surrendered to Nelson Miles.

Olaus Hansen and John Sivertsen remained with the 7th Cavalry at the Missouri River under the command of Major Merrill. Merrill got permission from Miles to take the wounded back to Dakota Territory, leaving Benteen in charge of nine companies of the 7th. Miles had notions of another winter campaign. Olaus was not in favor of that – it was already starting to get cold in Dakota and he had been sleeping on the ground all summer. On October 28th they marched to Fort Buford where they went into camp on November 9th. Winter had arrived in full force with cold temperatures and high winds. Since they were not a part of the regular force at Buford they had to endure the inclement weather outdoors in tents or other shelters they managed to construct. Five of the seven companies of the 7th were detailed to escort Cheyenne prisoners from Fort Buford to the rail head at Bismarck where they would be transported to Indian Territory. By Christmas they arrived at Fort Stevenson, upriver from Fort Lincoln. After marching nearly 230 miles through snow drifts and bitter cold weather they arrived at Fort Lincoln on December 30th – just to find that the stables had burnt down the previous night.

A cavalry detachment on the march in Dakota winter weather. The Library of Congress.

When Olaus finally walked into the barracks at the fort the day before New Year's Eve of 1877, rheumatism had been tearing at his joints for weeks.

THE COURT MARTIAL

On July 16th, 1877 a particularly brutal Indian attack took place north of Bear Butte, on the plains near the Black Hills. In spite of warnings three Norwegian immigrants – Frank Wagnes, his twenty year old pregnant wife and her brother – were travelling alone home to Moorehead, Minnesota. They had been putting up hay in the valleys around Deadwood over the summer, and were going to Moorehead for Mrs. Wagnes to have her baby. The Indians overtook them by Bear Butte, killed them all and mutilated Mrs. Wagnes' body.

This incident, together with other Indian depredations in and around the Black Hills, prompted the construction of a fort at Bear Butte Creek. On July 18th, 1878 Olaus reached the camp site at Spring Creek about two miles west of Bear Butte, after a twelve day march from Fort Lincoln together with Companies A, C, D, E, G, I and K. Companies H and L were left at Fort Lincoln under Captain Benteen to guard Cheyenne prisoners captured the previous year. Whiskey peddlers and prostitutes from Deadwood descended on the new camp, and the newspapers reported that drunken soldiers were "lying around over the prairies and in the western woods between Crook and their camp thick as hair on a dog's back". On August 8th Companies H and L arrived in camp with the Cheyenne prisoners – numbering several hundred - marching under military escort to Indian Territory.

On September 26th the camp was moved about five miles to a new site in Bear Butte Valley, which would become the permanent site of the fort. Fort Meade was named after Major General George Gordon Meade of Gettysburg and Civil War fame. The place was selected by General Philip Henry Sheridan, who had come out west to survey the site in person. On October 6th camp was broken and Olaus was on the march again with the 7th Cavalry, hurrying to detain Cheyenne bands under Dull Knife and Little Wolf. They had refused to stay on the reservation in Indian Territory and were on their way back to their northern homeland. The Cheyenne were chased from Oklahoma through Kansas and into Nebraska by a large force of soldiers. In early October Olaus moved out with seven companies from the 7th Cavalry, riding east to the area around Wounded Knee Creek to intercept the Cheyenne. On October 23rd Dull Knife's band was found on the Dakota – Nebraska border by the 3rd Cavalry. After having been detained for about

Fort Meade, Dakota Territory with Bear Butte in the background. Wikipedia.org.

ten days they again refused to go to Indian Territory and started to dig rifle pits. Olaus with Company G and C from the 7th went out to reinforce the 3rd Cavalry, and seeing the increasing number of soldiers the Cheyenne surrendered. The prisoners were escorted to Fort Robinson, Nebraska. On November 13th the 7th Cavalry set out towards Fort Lincoln where they arrived seven days later and went into winter quarter.

The harsh Dakota winters, outdoor life, cold sleeping quarters and inferior army food started to take a severe toll on Olaus' health. In the spring of 1879 he was almost 38 years old, at a time when average life expectancy in the United States was 43. His rheumatism grew increasingly bad and the limited means available to fight the pain was the ever present whiskey - and Laudanum when it became unbearable. He had said good-bye to his Norwegian friend John Sivertsen during the summer of 1878. Sivertsen was discharged June 19th – and just six days later he reenlisted at Fort McHenry in Baltimore, Maryland. He had seen enough of Dakota.

Just like the winter of 1876, the winter of 1879 was brutally cold. Heavy snowfalls and temperatures thirty below zero brought everything to a standstill. Army life in Dakota was rough. Soldiers working on the new post at Bear Butte tried to dam

Bear Butte Creek to secure ice for next summer, but the dam did not hold and ice was obtained from the frozen Belle Fourche River instead. On May 22nd Major Marcus Reno arrived at the fort and took command. He was back after two years suspension from rank and pay following a court martial. Upon arrival he learned that one of his previous subordinates from the battle of the Little Bighorn – Captain Thomas French of Company M – had just started to serve a court martial sentence of his own. He had been charged with drunkenness and after a guilty verdict he was suspended from rank with half pay for one year, effective April 15th. French would continue his downward spiral due to alcohol and after being put on the retired list February 5th, 1880 - the reason given as "incapacitated due to intemperance" – he would die at Fort Leavenworth, Kansas on March 27th, 1882.

In May of 1879, 1st Lieutenant George D. Wallace – commander of Company G – was away from Fort Abraham Lincoln on several occasions. On May 9th he left on a trip overseeing the movement of military convicts to Fort Snelling, Minnesota. He returned later that month to prepare the move to the new post at Fort Meade. During the week end of May 25th Olaus started drinking heavily. It was the last week at Fort Abraham Lincoln before making the move to Fort Meade. His joints had been bothering him all winter and he drank more and more to counteract the pain, although he had recognized a long time ago the chronic effect of drinking and the dependency it created. He had watched the decline of officers like Weir and French close up – not to mention Lieutenant Edwin P. Eckerson, a hopeless alcoholic who had been court martialed and kicked out of the 7th Cavalry twice, the last time on May 15th 1878. Olaus was in no doubt as to where he was heading. However, disease, boredom and an environment generally conducive to drinking kept him from dwelling on consequences.

Enlisted men rarely had cash, and normally paid the post trader on payday. Olaus ran out of cash on Monday the 26th. Not knowing Lieutenant Wallace's whereabouts on Tuesday May 27th he simply wrote a receipt in his own name to post trader William Harmon, filled in the names of Wallace and 1st Sergeant Edward Garlick and purchased more whiskey on credit. The receipt read:

I, O.H. Northeg, hereby authorize the Commanding officer of my company to retain from my first pay the sum of twelve dollars, and pay the same to William Harmon, Post Trader for value received.
(Signed) O.H. Northeg.
Approved (Signed) Geo. D. Wallace, Comd'g Company.
Attest (Signed) Ed. Garlick, 1st Sergeant.

After two more days he did not feel like sobering up. The pain would return, both in his joints and in his head. On May 29th he wrote another two receipts for nine dollars, on the 30th another two receipts for ten dollars and on June 1st a last one for six dollars. That day the 7th Cavalry departed for Fort Meade, and Olaus was not feeling good.

Upon discovery of the receipts on payday Olaus was called to Lieutenant Wallace's office.

"Northeg." Wallace, known as an easygoing officer, seemed like he found the confrontation uncomfortable. He was eight years Olaus' junior, had not served in the Civil War and did not join the Army before 1872.

"Sir." Olaus waited for Wallace to proceed.

"This time you went too far."

"Sorry, Sir?"

"You went too far. I have read your service file. There is very little you have not seen and done in the sense of military service since you came to the United States, and you certainly have vast political capital invested in your long and honorable service, making you somewhat immune to missteps. However, this capital cannot prevent prosecution for blatant criminal behavior. What you committed by signing two officers' names on the receipts was fraud."

"Fraud, sir?" Olaus was taken aback. "How can it be fraud when my name is at the top of the receipt, clearly stating that I am the one making the purchase, and I will pay on payday?"

"Never the less it's fraud", Wallace continued. "You cannot sign two commanding officers' names on an official document and present the document as genuine when it is a forgery."

Olaus found further arguments futile. He felt there might be ulterior motives behind the upcoming prosecution. His 1st sergeant, Edward Garlick, was a young English career officer who – like Wallace - did not fight in the Civil War. Neither had he been at the Little Bighorn. He was on a four months' furlough in England when the battle raged. He came back to assume the position as 1st sergeant of a battle scarred company baptized by fire. He may have found it difficult to be respected by his surviving non-commissioned officers, the toughest layer of line officers in the army, as he had not been sharing in the dangers when almost half his regiment was wiped out by Indians. Sergeant Botzer was dead, Sergeant Considine was dead and Sergeant Lloyd had transferred to Washington, D.C. That left only two sergeants in Company G from the battle – Alexander Brown and Olaus Hansen. If Olaus' reasoning was correct - by signing Garlick's name he had played himself right into the hands of the 1st sergeant - and out of the 7th Cavalry. He saluted Wallace, made about face and left the room.

Olaus was placed under arrest and charged in violation of the 62nd Article of War – "Conduct prejudicial to good order and military discipline". A general court martial was scheduled for August 25th.

Monday August 25th, 1879 was a hot, dusty day at Fort Meade, Dakota Territory. Olaus Hansen came from the guard house where he had been in detention, waiting to appear in front of the general court martial. He entered the room in his parade uniform – a room which gave the impression of a dark dungeon after the bright light outside. When his eyes got used to the dim light he looked at the panel of officers present. Several interesting facts did not escape his attention. His first observation was that almost half the court was a virtual "who-is-who" from the battle of the Little Bighorn. Major Reno was president of the court, and there was Captain Frederick Benteen, Captain Myles Moylan – Aparejo Mickie from Reno Hill, who had been hiding behind a mule pack – and 1st Lieutenant George Wallace.

The appearance of 1st Lieutenant Wallace was Olaus' second observation. In a civil court of law the offended party was never a member of the court deciding the verdict and the length of the sentence – the conflict of interest was obvious.

There were four 2nd lieutenants on a court of nine members. From his knowledge about the slow advancement system in the U.S. Army, Olaus knew none of the lieutenants would go against the sentiment of the senior officers. They were yes-men.

He found it almost amusing that Major Reno was President of the Court. He had recently returned from a two-year suspension from rank and pay following a court martial. When he arrived at Fort Meade his problems continued. On August 3rd - according to witnesses - he had been "disgustingly drunk" at the residence of the post trader. On August 8th, about two weeks before Olaus' trial, he had been involved in an altercation in a public billiard saloon where he smashed out a window. Other incidents would follow, which were still in the future when Olaus stood trial on August 25th. On October 25th, just two months later, Reno would be involved in a drunken bar brawl, striking 2nd Lieutenant William Nicholson with a billiard cue – the very same William Nicholson present as one of the members of the court in the trial against Olaus Hansen. Olaus was certainly being judged by one of his peers.

If he had been in doubt about the outcome of the proceedings, the doubt vanished when he saw the prosecuting judge advocate: 1st Lieutenant David M. Scott, 1st Infantry. David M. Scott was serious about his prosecutions - he had goals, and he wanted convictions to attain them. By 1882 he would be provost marshal at the military penitentiary at Fort Leavenworth, Kansas.

Olaus was asked if he had objections to any member of the court, to which he answered in the negative. He knew the battle was already lost, and had hastily prepared a letter asking for leniency in exchange for a plea of guilty. It was denied. He was found guilty on all accounts and Reno read the sentence: - "to be dishonorably discharged from the service of the United States, forfeiting all allowances due or that may become due, except the just dues of the laundress and to be confined at such military prison as the reviewing authority may elect for the term of three years."

Olaus was stunned. Dishonorable discharge and three years!? That was a sentence for deserters. Soldiers who had committed what he considered serious criminal offences got discharge and prison, and he was sentenced for openly attaching his name to a credit receipt for buying drinks – even explaining the circumstances and committing to pay on payday? He had shown poor judgment in using his commanding officers' names to purchase whiskey, but three years in prison……..he did not think the sentence fit the crime.

On September 10th the sentence was reviewed by Commander of the Department of Dakota, Brigadier General Alfred H. Terry, who had been in charge of the Dakota Column at the Little Bighorn. Terry reduced the prison term to one year. Olaus was in the guard house at Fort Meade where he would stay until midsummer of 1880. In October Olaus had unexpected news - Captain Frederick Benteen was under arrest. He never found out why, but it was certainly clear that the enlisted men were not the only ones stepping out of line in the 7th Cavalry.

In early November Olaus heard that Major Reno had gotten himself deeper into trouble at the post by "- conduct unbecoming an officer and a gentleman". Eventually all the incidences compounded into a general court martial on November 28th, and Reno was dismissed from the service. The sentence was confirmed by President Hayes on March 16th and took effect April 1st, 1880. The irony was not lost on Olaus.

Olaus Hansen's letter to the general court martial on August 25th, 1879. The National Archives.

THE END

The months in detention dragged and the guard house was cold. Olaus continued to suffer from his rheumatism and was given "medicinal whiskey" and Laudanum for the pain. Because of the complete inactivity he started to have flashbacks to the Civil War and the Indian campaigns. Dreams – or nightmares, to be more exact. Shells bursting, comrades being blown up, heads split open by musket balls, blood everywhere. He had tackled the lingering impressions from the horrific battles during the Civil War for many years after the war ended – it had not bothered him too much. But the Indian Wars had brought it all back. He had ignored the gruesome mutilations he saw on the battlefield at the time it happened, because it was part of a harsh and busy campaign. But during the long, dark and cold nights in the guard house, when he had nothing to do and could not sleep, the images were vivid in his mind. Torsos sliced open, arms, legs and hands cut off and scattered around, bodies bristling with arrows, decapitated heads placed on the ground, facing each other in empty stares - or stuck on poles. He could not free himself from the image of his corporal's head under the overturned camp kettle.

He realized that his need for Laudanum was not only for his pain, but also for his haunting memories. 400 000 soldiers discharged after the Civil War had been opium addicts. He was not one of them, and he always thought it was because he was never wounded. Wounded men were liberally injected with morphine for their pains and opium was sprinkled on their wounds or taken orally as pills or tincture. Luckily he had escaped injuries – and treatment with opiates.

During the Indian campaigns – that became a different story altogether. Opiates were more accessible and highly recommended for any kind of ailment – just like whiskey. He never used it, however, before his rheumatism became unbearable. Escape from intense physical pain was an incredible feeling, and hard to fathom for those who had not experienced it. Laudanum had provided that feeling for Olaus, but now it had also started to relieve him from his psychological pains – helping him escape inner torment.

The day of his release arrived – to what kind of life he was not quite sure. It was reasonably easy for an ex-veteran soldier to be hired as a civilian laborer at the fort, and by late summer of 1880 he was a teamster driving a mule team. It could be hard work, but it was well paid - and he did need money to survive.

The Dakota weather continued to make a severe impact on Olaus' health. The temperature difference between the seasons was extreme – from more than 110 degrees during the summer to 45 below in the winter. Droughts, dust storms, hail storms and the occasional cyclone swept across the plains, but more than anything else - there was an incessant, unrelenting wind virtually all year round, almost to the point of taking a mental toll on his senses.

The winter of 1880 – 1881 was exceptionally frigid and the weather debilitating for somebody with Olaus' condition. The seven months between October and April saw record low temperatures across the region and severe blizzards struck – a three day storm already between October 15th and 18th, another between December 2nd and 4th and a third on Christmas Eve. The snow fall from the blizzards was so heavy the Chicago and Northwestern Railroad could not keep their trains running. After Christmas the temperature fell to 30 below. The next winter was milder, but with the autumn of 1882 came the onset of a period which would later be known as "The Little Ice Age of the 1880s".The winters between 1882 and 1887 became a series of seasons locking the Midwest in a frozen grip killing hundreds of people and causing thousands of cattle to starve to death

By the fall of 1882, driving the mule team was about all Olaus managed to do. His joints were stiff and aching, and walking, lifting, riding – all physical activity created more and more pain. He was forty one years old, but his body was much older. In June of 1882 he had a letter from Anne Marie. His mother, Kari had died on May 21st. His father died a few years before – now they were both gone. Even if he had not seen his mother for years – just to know that she was no longer alive made him feel very lonely. He was so much younger than his siblings and felt that he had enjoyed a special relationship with her. If he had any regrets about his lifelong stay in the United States, it was that he had not been able to see her.

He knew his family was disappointed in his decision to become a professional soldier. To volunteer for service in the glorious Civil War together with hundreds of thousands of young men fighting for a noble cause – that had been the right thing to do. However, to become a soldier in the post war army having a reputation of retaining vagrants, semi-criminals and immigrants shying away from the responsibilities of civilized society and spending their lives playing cards and drinking whiskey – that was a completely different matter.

His siblings had done exceedingly well. Anne Marie, through her marriage to Ingel Pedersen, had become one of the wealthiest women in Nannestad. Ole had done what he had set out to do – establish a prosperous farm in America and raised a large family. Hans had been the pioneer blacksmith of Lake Park, and later a successful farmer. Nils – who stayed behind when Olaus and Hans went to America - had bought a farm just last year. Olaus, on the other hand, roamed the American Frontier with no family, no money, no prospects for a future in civilian life – and a court martial and dishonorable discharge from the Army to add to his record.

On September 19th Olaus had some very bad news. His friend and fellow teamster David McWilliams was found dead in his bed, apparently from an overdose of Laudanum. McWilliams was the Scot who managed to shoot himself in the calf during the Little Bighorn campaign. Olaus suspected he was a heavy user, and probably had been for a long time, but he refused to believe it was suicide. The coroner was indiscriminate when he wrote death certificates – he did not distinguish between accidental and premeditated suicides. To him they were all suicides, and nobody was going to invest the time to distinguish between the two.

In late October Olaus was hauling wood with his mule team in Bear Butte Valley, staying in a cabin in the foothills of Bear Butte at night. On October 25th the cabin was very cold when he woke up, and the windows were covered with frost. Winter was approaching. A few days later a blizzard hit, dumping two feet of snow. At the beginning of November – after a few days of sunshine - a second storm struck. The violence of the blizzards surprised Olaus - the snowdrifts piled up against the cabin walls and the temperature dropped to twenty below. The wind howled and the windows were frozen over, and he was happy he had a large pile of firewood right outside the door. The pain kept bothering him - he could barely move around inside the cabin, and only with great effort did he manage to get wood from the outside to feed the crackling fire in the cast iron stove. He had enough provisions, several bottles of whiskey - and he had also secured a large vial of Laudanum.

On the night of November 4th it was cold – very cold – even when he filled the stove with wood and kept it full, the cabin did not warm up. He had to sit close to the stove to keep warm. On the bed over by the wall it was freezing cold, but still - he had to try to get some sleep. He expected several teamsters to arrive the following day, to haul the wood to the fort. He lay down and pulled the four blankets up to his chin. He had drunk the better part of a bottle of whiskey, but his joints were still aching. He took a sip of the Laudanum. That would soon make him feel better. About three hours later the fire was almost out. He knew he should get up and put more wood in the stove, but he felt comfortable under the blankets. The whiskey and the Laudanum kept him virtually pain free, and gave him a false sense of warmth. He started to fall asleep – a painless sleep free from mutilated bodies and severed heads. The fire went out and the temperature started to fall. He drifted off and was almost asleep when he noticed it was very cold, even under the blankets. He took another sip of the Laudanum – that would warm him up in a moment. As he drifted off again he heard a loud "thud!" He turned his head and looked at his hand. It was empty. The bottle of Laudanum had fallen to the floor. He closed his eyes.

The mail man plodded through deep snow in Norwegian December darkness up to the front door at Nordeeg. He knocked, and as the door opened the roaring flames from the fireplace threw a flickering light on his smiling face. "Letter from America!" he said. Anne Marie Hansen Wiig smiled and looked at the envelope - from Hans Hanson-Eger, Lake Park, Minnesota. She shut the door, sat down by the table and pulled the candle closer.

Olaus Hansen's headstone at the Old Post Cemetery, Fort Meade, South Dakota. Photo: Scott Nelson.

Name changes and name confusion

Norwegian immigrants used assumed names in America – and understandably so. The main language was English, and Norwegian names were exceedingly difficult to pronounce for the already established, English speaking population. Male names like Amund became Amon, Karl became Charles and female names like Kari became Carry. Sometimes the immigrants would simply take a completely different name altogether – and several different ones over a period of time.

In Norway it was common to take the father's first name as a last name (hence the expression: Patronymic last name). If your father was Hans, and your name was Ole, you would become Ole Hansen (Hans –sen, i.e. Ole, son of Hans). If you had a son and called him Hans, he would become Hans Olesen, or Olsen.

If your sister's name was Kari, she could become Kari Hansdatter (Hansdaughter), or also Hansen, like you. In America, because of the English pronunciation, almost all Hansen names became Hanson.

Sometimes it is extremely difficult to track ancestors from America to Norway. The name changes and the different ways the names were written almost force you to speak both languages fluently to be able to jump from one name to the next, as they change.

In the case of Olaus Hansen, he used only two different names when he signed official documents: Olans Hanson, and Olans H. Northeg. Olans was probably derived from the way he wrote his first name (see his signature in the book) and the fact that Olaus was a much more difficult name to pronounce than Olans.

However, his name was interpreted in at least eleven different ways by others, which obviously can make the confusion total. Below are all the variations I have come across - the two used by Olaus himself in the United States are written in bold letters.

Olaus Hansen, **Olans Hanson,** Owen Hanson, Owens Hanson, Claus Hanson, Claus Honson, **Olans H. Northeg**, Olans Northeg, Olaus H. Northeg, Orlaus Northeg, Olaus Northey, Orland H. Northey, Alans Nortech and Alans Nathey.

The Hansen children were very proud of their heritage, as indicated by their persistence in keeping the patronymic name Hansen. After marrying Lars Wiig while living at Nordeeg, Anne Marie gave her last name as Hansen Wiig. Ole changed his name to Ole H. Aarnæs, but he kept the middle initial H, and Bobbie Hoy says that he always signed documents as Ole Hanson. Hans Hansen changed his last name to Eger – the name of his local community in Nannestad - but he still wrote his name Hans Hanson-Eger. Nils, who stayed in Norway and bought two farms in 1881 and 1883, wrote his name as Nils Hansen Logna. Olaus, as we know, called himself Olans H. Northeg.

Sources consulted

Primary Sources

Microfilm

Brief History of U.S. Army Commands (Army Posts) and Description of their Records. *Record of U.S. Army Continental Commands, 1821 – 1920.*
Returns from Regular Army Cavalry Regiments – 7th Cavalry September 1866 – December 1873. *Record of Army Continental Commands, 1821 – 1920.*
Returns from Regular Army Cavalry Regiments – 7th Cavalry 1874 – 1881.*Record of Army Continental Commands, 1821 – 1920.*
Returns from Regular Army Cavalry Regiments – 7th Cavalry 1881 – 1888. *Records of U.S. Army Continental Commands, 1821 – 1920.*

Documents

National Archives and Records Administration (NARA). Records of the Adjutant General's Office 1780s – 1917:
Compiled military service records, RG 92.12.2.
Cards containing medical records and vital statistics – "carded records", RG 94.12.3.
Regular Army enlistment papers 1798 – 1912, RG 94.91.
Records of the Department of Veterans Affairs:
Pensions applications files based on the Civil War and the Spanish-American War, RG 15.3.
Records of the office of the Judge Advocate General (Army) 1809 – 1894. *RG 153.15.*
Register of Deeds, Sturgis, Meade County, South Dakota. *Coroner's report, Olans H. Northeg.*

Manuscripts

The Nathaniel C. Kenyon Diary. Rare books and special collections, W.S. Hoole Special Collections Library, the University of Alabama. 36 pp.

Digital Collections

Ancestry.com
Arkivverket – Digitalarkivet (The Digitized Norwegian State Archives).
Scanned Church Books:
Nannestad Ministerial Book 1815 – 1840, 1840 – 1850, 1850 – 1859, 1860 – 1872.
Nannestad – Holter Ministerial Book 1881 – 1890, 1891 – 1905, 1901 – 1917.
Nannestad – Nannestad Ministerial Book 1881 – 1890, 1891 – 1905, 1901 – 1913.
Nittedal Ministerial Book 1850 -1862.
Digital Collections Iowa State University Library. *The Civil War Diary of James Robertson 1862*, pg. 39 – 44.

Books and Pamphlets

Aalholm, O.A. 1955.*The Ancestry of the Holter family within the Engelsrud relatives in Nannestad 1600 – 1950.* (In Norwegian). Mariendals boktrykkeri, Gjøvik.119 pp.

Abrahamson, E.M., M.D. and A.W. Pezet. 1965. *Body, Mind and Sugar.* Holt, Rinehart and Winston, New York, Chicago and San Francisco. 206 pp.

Adams, Kevin. 2009. *Class and Race in the Frontier Army. Military Life in the West, 1870 - 1890.* University of Oklahoma Press, Norman. 276 pp.

Agnew, Jeremy. 2008. *Life of a Soldier on the Western Frontier.* Mountain Press Publishing Company, Missoula, Montana. 266 pp.

Agricultural Extension Service, The. 1940. *Fur Bearers and Game Mammals of Iowa.* Iowa State College, Ames, Iowa. 33 pp.

Alexander, W.E. 1882. *History of Winneshiek and Allamakee Counties, Iowa. Vol I and II.* Western Publishing Co., Sioux City. 739 pp.

Alexander, William. 1886. *List over Ex-Soldiers, Sailors and Marines living in Iowa.* Geo. E. Roberts, State Printer, Des Moines. 772 pp.

Allen, James. 1963. *Reconstruction: The Battle for Democracy 1865 – 1876.* International Publishers, New York. 256 pp.

Alnæs, Karsten. 1996 – 2000. *The History of Norway, Vol. II and III* (in Norwegian). Gyldendal Norsk Forlag, Oslo. 548 + 646 pp.

Ambrose, Stephen. 1996. *Crazy Horse and Custer. The parallel lives of two American warriors.* Anchor Books Doubleday, New York, London, Toronto, Sydney, Auckland. 528 pp.

Anderson, Marilyn and Gerry Schleuter. 1981. *The History of Lake Park.* Journal Publishing Co., Lake Park, Minnesota. 339 pp.

Anderson, Rasmus B. 1906. *The first chapter of Norwegian immigration (1821 – 1840), its causes and results.* Privately published, Madison, Wisconsin. 578 pp.

Anon. No year, a. *Historic Carlisle Barracks.* 38 pp.

Anon. No year, b. *The 1873 "Trapdoor" Springfield Rifle and Carbine & .45 Revolvers: Colt's M 1873, S&W "Schofield.* Manual, 47 pp.

Anon. No year, c. *Custer's Last Battle. By E.S. Godfrey (one of Custer's Troop Commanders) with comments by General James B. Fry.* 44 pp.

Anon. 1880. *First Reunion of the 12th Iowa V. V. Infantry.* The Printing House, Dubuque, Iowa. 63 pp.

Anon. 1884. *Second Reunion of the 12th Iowa V. V. Infantry.* C.B. Dorr Press, Dubuque, Iowa. 77 pp.

Anon. 1887. *History of the 15th Regiment Iowa Veteran Volunteer Infantry.* R.B. Ogden & Son Print, Keokuk. 720 pp.

Anon. 1888, a. *Third Reunion of the Twelfth Iowa Veteran Volunteer Infantry.* Manchester Press Steam Job Print. 46 pp.

Anon. 1888, b. *First Reunion of the Hornets' Nest Brigade.* Globe Printing, Oskaloosa, Iowa.

Anon. 1890. Caddo Parish and Shreveport City in: *Biographical and Historical Memoirs of Northwest Louisiana, 9 – 82.* The Southern Publishing Company, Nashville and Chicago.

Anon. 1892. *Fourth Reunion of the 12th Iowa Veteran Volunteer Infantry.* Press of the Daily News, Norfolk, Nebraska. 60 pp.

Anon. 1894. *Fifth Reunion of the Twelfth Iowa Veteran Volunteer Infantry.* Press of the Daily News, Norfolk, Nebraska. 65 pp.

Anon. 1896. *Sixth Reunion of the Twelfth Iowa Veteran Volunteer Infantry.* 7 pp.

Anon. 1901. *Seventh Reunion of the Twelfth Iowa Veteran Volunteer Infantry.* 4 pp.

Anon. 1903. *Eight Reunion of the Twelfth Iowa Vet. Vol. Inft.* Reporter Publishing House, Fayette, Iowa. 114 pp.

Anon. 1908. *Civil War Regiments from Iowa.* eBooksOnDisk, Pensacola, Florida. 118 p.

Anon. 1925. *Colt's Revolvers and Automatic Pistols.* Colt's Patent Fire Arms Manufacturing Co., Hartford, Connecticut. 40 pp.

Anon. 2003. *Caddo Parish Sheriff's Office.* Turner Publishing Company, Paducah, Kentucky. 136 pp.

Association of Graduates, U.S.M.A. 1980. *Register of Graduates and former Cadets, United States Military Academy, 1802 – 1980.* 827 pp.

Atkinson, Matt (ed). 2009. *Lieutenant Brennan's Letter: A Confederate Officer's Account of the Battle of Champion Hill and the Siege of Vicksburg.* Thomas Publications, Gettysburg, PA. 64 pp.

Bailey, Edwin C. and Charles Philip Hexom. 1913. *Past and present of Winneshiek County, Iowa; a record of settlement, organization, progress and achievement. Volume I.* S.J. Clarke Publishing Co., Chicago, Illinois. 354 pp.

Bailey, Victor. 1998. *"This rash Act". Suicide across the Life Cycle in the Victorian City.* Stanford University Press, Stanford, California. 350 pp.

Baker, Harold Douglas, Jr. 2002. *Misguided by Experience: A defense of Custer's actions at the Little Bighorn.* A thesis submitted to the Graduate Faculty of Louisiana State University and Agricultural and Mechanical College in partial fulfillment for a degree of Master of Arts in Liberal Arts. 90 pp.

Barnard, Sandy. 2000. *Digging into Custer's last stand.* Ventana Graphics, Huntington Beach, California. 164 pp.

Barnard, Sandy (ed). 2001. *Ten years with Custer. A 7th Cavalryman's Memoirs (John Ryan).* AST Press, Terre Haute, Indiana. 343 pp.

Barnett, Louise. 1996. *Touched by fire. The life, death and mythic afterlife of George Armstrong Custer.* Henry Holt & Co., New York. 540 pp.

Bearss, Edwin C. 1962. *Unconditional Surrender. The Fall of Fort Donelson.* Reprinted from Tennessee Historical Quarterly Vol. XXI, # 1 and 2. 47 pp.

Bedford, Stewart. 2002. *War and PTSD (Post Traumatic Stress Disorder).* AmErica House Book Publishers, Baltimore, Maryland. 106 pp.

Bergeron, Leandre. 1972. *The History of Quebec. A Patriot's Handbook.* NC Press, Toronto. 245 pp.

Berry, Charles R. Jr., Mark Wildhaber and David L. Galat. 2004. Fish Distribution and Abundance. *Population Structure and Habitat Use of Benthic Fishes along the Missouri and Lower Yellowstone Rivers, Vol. 3.* 282 pp.

Billings, John D. 1887. *Hardtack and Coffee, or the Unwritten Story of Army Life.* George M. Smith Co., Boston, Mass. 408 pp.

Blegen, Theodore C.1931. *Norwegian Migration to America 1825 – 1860.* The Norwegian-American Historical Association, Northfield, Minnesota. 413 pp.

Blegen, Theodore C. 1969. *Norwegian Migration to America. The American Transition.* Haskell House Publishers, LTD., New York. 655 pp.

290

Blehm, John L. Sr. and Karen. 2008. *Angel of Death. A Story of a Viet Nam Vet's War Experience and his Battle to overcome PTSD, the Cancer of the Soul.* IUniverse, Inc., New York, Lincoln, Shanghai. 135 pp.

Bore, Ragnhild Rein and Tor Skoglund (ed). 2008. *From Hand Power to High Technology – Norwegian Industry since 1829* (in Norwegian). Statistical Central Bureau, Oslo and Kongsvinger. 120 pp.

Boyd, Gregory A. 2010. *Family Maps of Allamakee County, Iowa.* Arphax Publishing Co., Norman, Oklahoma. 298 pp.

Boyd, Gregory A. 2010. *Family Maps of Clayton County, Iowa.* Arphax Publishing Co., Norman, Oklahoma. 292 pp.

Boyd, Gregory A. 2010. *Family Maps of Winneshiek County, Iowa.* Arphax Publishing Co., Norman, Oklahoma. 254 pp.

Bourke, John. 1971. *On the Border with Crook.* University of Nebraska Press, Lincoln and London. 491 pp.

Brady, Cyrus Townsend. 1971. *Indian Fights and Fighters.* University of Nebraska Press, Lincoln. 423 pp.

Brady, Cyrus Townsend. 1974. *Northwestern Fights and Fighters.* Corner House Publishers, Williamstown, Massachusetts. 373 pp.

Bray, Kingsley M. 1956. *Crazy Horse. A Lakota Life.* University of Oklahoma Press, Norman. 510 pp.

Brininstool, E.A. 1933. *The Custer Fight. Captain Benteen's Story of the Battle of the Little Big Horn June 25 – 26, 1876.* Reprint, Arrow and Trooper, Brooklyn, New York. 14 pp.

Brininstool, E.A. *1952. Troopers with Custer. Historic Incidents of the Battle of the Little Bighorn.* University of Nebraska Press, Lincoln and London. 343 pp.

Brininstool, E.A. 1995. *Fighting Indian Warriors. True Tales of the Wild Frontier.* Indian Head Books, New York. 353 pp.

Brown, Daniel Patrick. 2003. *The Tragedy of Libby and Andersonville Prison Camps.* Golden West Historical Publications, Ventura, California. 75 pp.

Brust, James S., Brian C. Pohanka and Sandy Barnard. 2005. *Where Custer Fell. Photographs of the Little Bighorn Battlefield Then and Now.* University of Oklahoma Press, Norman. 226 pp.

Budiansky, Stephen. 2008. *The Bloody Shirt.* Viking/Penguin, New York. 322 pp.

Carnahan, J. Worth. 1897. *Manual of the Civil War and Key to the Grand Army of the Republic and Kindred Societies.* The Easel Monument Association, Chicago, Illinois. 255 pp.

Carroll, John M. (ed). No year, a. *A Seventh Cavalry Scrapbook 1 – 13.* Arrow and Trooper, Brooklyn, New York. 371 pp.

Carroll, John M. (ed). No year, b. *The Gibson and Edgerly Narratives*. Privately printed. Bryan, Texas. 16 pp.

Carroll, John M. (ed). No year, c. *The Sunshine Magazine Articles*. Privately printed, Bryan, Texas. 27 pp

Carroll, John M. (ed). 1974. *The Benteen - Goldin letters on Custer and his last battle*. University of Nebraska Press, Lincoln and London. 312 pp.

Carroll, John M. and Byron Price. 1974. *Roll Call on the Little Bighorn, 28.June 1876*. John M. Carrol & Co., Mattituck, New York. 168 pp.

Carroll, John M. 1979. *The Court Martial of Captain Thomas Henry French. Justice or cover up?* Private Publication, Bryan, Texas. Reprint 1995 by Arrow and Trooper, Brooklyn, New York. 33 pp.

Carroll, John M. (ed).1982. *Custer's Chief of Scouts. The reminiscences of Charles A. Varnum*. University of Nebraska Press, Lincoln and London. 192 pp.

Carroll, John M. 1987. *A bit of Seventh Cavalry history with all its warts*. Arrow and Trooper, Brooklyn, New York. 25 pp.

Carroll, John M. 1993. *They Rode with Custer*. John M. Carroll & Co., Mattituck, New York. 290 pp.

Carroll, John M. 1994. *The Trials and Tribulations of Lieutenant Edwin P. Eckerson, 7th Cavalry*. Arrow and Trooper, Brooklyn, New York. 58 pp.

Chambers, Lee. 2008. *Fort Abraham Lincoln, Dakota Territory*. Schiffer Publishing Ltd., Atglen, Pennsylvania. 172 pp.

Chittenden, Hiram M. 1915. *The Yellowstone National Park*. Stewart, Kidd & Co., Cincinnati, Ohio. 397 pp.

Clark, Robert A. (ed). 1988. *The Killing of Chief Crazy Horse*. University of Nebraska Press, Lincoln and London. 152 pp.

Clark, Olynthus B. (ed). 1916. *Downing's Civil War Diary*. The Historical Department of Iowa, Des Moines. 358 pp.

Cloyd, Benjamin Gregory. 2005. *Civil War Prisons in American Memory*. A Dissertation submitted to the Graduate Faculty of the Louisiana State University and Agricultural and Mechanical College in partial fulfillment of the requirements for the degree of Doctor of Philosophy in the Department of History. 286 pp.

Cohan, Katie. 2011. *"The Bitter, Freezing Hours of Night". An investigation of Cold Injury Susceptibility in the Post-Civil War 7th Cavalry*. A Thesis for the Degree of Master of Art in Anthropology at the California State University, Chico. 155 pp.

Collier, Sam. 2007. *North Caddo Parish* (Images of America). Charleston SC, Chicago IL, Portsmouth NH, San Francisco Ca. 127 pp.

Collins, Henry Hill, Jr. (ed). 1981. *Harper and Row's Complete Field Guide to North American Wildlife*. Harper and Row Publishers, New York, Hagerstown,

Philadelphia, San Francisco, Cambridge, London, Mexico City, Sao Paulo, Sidney. 714 pp.

Colt, George Howe. 2006. *November of the Soul. The Enigma of Suicide.* Scribner, New York, London, Toronto, Sydney. 628 pp.

Conant, Roger (ed). 1975. *A Field Guide to the Reptiles and Amphibians of Eastern and Central North America.* The Peterson Field Guide Series. Houghton Mifflin Company, Boston. 429 pp.

Connery, Donald S. 1966. *The Scandinavians. A perceptive and intriguing Investigation of Nations whose People are – or perhaps are not – the best off in the World.* Simon and Schuster, New York. 590 pp.

Courtwright, David T. 1982. *Dark Paradise. Opiate addiction in America before 1940.* Harvard University Press, Cambridge, Massachusetts and London, England. 270 pp.

Cowles, Calvin D. 1891 – 95. *Atlas to accompany the Official Records of the Union and Confederate Armies.* Government Printing Office, Washington. 216 pp.

Crane, J.T. 1871. *Arts of Intoxication. The Aim, and the Result.* Carlton & Lanham, New York, E. Thomas, San Francisco and Hitchcock & Walden, Cincinnati. 268 pp.

Cross, Walt. 2010. *From Little Big Horn to the Potomac. The Story of Army Surgeon Dr. Robert Wilson Schufeldt.* Cross Publications, Stillwater, Oklahoma. 307 pp.

Current, Richard N. (ed). 1965. *Reconstruction (1865 – 1877).* Prentiss-Hall, Inc., Englewood Cliffs, New Jersey. 183 pp.

Custer, Elisabeth B. 1977. *Boots and Saddles or: Life in Dakota with General Custer.* Corner House Publishers, Williamstown, Massachusetts. 312 pp.

Custer, Elisabeth B. 1994. *Following the Guidon.* University of Nebraska Press, Lincoln. 341 pp.

Custer, Elisabeth B. 1994. *Tenting on the Plains or: General Custer in Kansas and Texas.* University of Oklahoma Press, Lincoln and London. 407 pp.

Daniel, Larry J. 1997. *Shiloh. The Battle That Changed the Civil War.* Simon and Schuster, New York. 430 pp.

Davies, Karen L. and E. Elden. 1992. *That fatal day. Eight more with Custer.* Powder River Press, Howell, Michigan. 30 pp.

Delo, David M. 1998. *Peddlers and post traders. The army sutler on the frontier.* Kingfisher Books, Helena, Montana. 278 pp.

DeTrobriand, Philippe Regis Denis de Keredern. 1941. *Army Life in Dakota.* The Lakeside Press, R.R. Donnelley & Sons Co., Chicago. 387 pp.

Dickinson, John A. and Brian Young. 1993. *A short History of Quebec.* Copp Clark Pitman Ltd., Toronto. 388 pp.

Donald, David. 1984. *The Politics of Reconstruction 1863 – 1867.* Harvard University Press, Cambridge, Massachusetts, London, England. 105 pp.

Donovan, James.2008. *A terrible glory. Custer and the Little Bighorn, the last great battle of the American West.* Little, Brown & Co., New York. 529 pp.

Donovan, Jim. 2001. *Custer and the Little Bighorn. The Man, the Mystery, the Myth.* Voyageur Press, Stillwater, Minnesota. 224 pp.

Donovan, Terrence J. 2011. *Brazen Trumpet. Frederick W. Benteen and the Battle of the Little Big Horn.* MojaveWest Publishing, Lancaster, California. 285 pp.

Doran, Robert. 2007. *Horsemanship at the Little Big Horn. A Horseman looks at the Custer Fight.* Infinity Publishing, West Conshohocken, Pennsylvania. 228 pp.

Dornbusch, C.E. (ed). 1962. *Regimental Publications & Personal Narratives of the Civil War. A Checklist. Vol. I, Northern States. Part IV – Iowa, Kansas, Michigan, Minnesota and Wisconsin.* The New York Public Library, New York. 93 pp.

Dowd, James Patrick. 1982. *Custer lives!* Ye Gallion Press, Fairfield, Washington. 264 pp.

Du Bois, Charles G. 1961. *Kick the dead Lion.* The Reporter Printing & Supply Co., Billings, Montana. 77 pp.

Du Chaillu, Paul B. 1903. *The Land of the Midnight Sun. Summer and Winter Journeys through Sweden, Norway, Lapland and Northern Finland. Vol II.* Harper & Brothers Publishers, New York and London. 474 pp.

Durham, Roger S. 2009. *Carlisle Barracks* (Images of America). Arcadia Publishing, Charleston, Chicago, Portsmouth, San Francisco. 128 pp.

Durkheim, Emile. 1951. *Suicide. A Study in Sociology.* Edited and introduced by George Simpson. The Free Press, Glencoe, Illinois. 393 pp.

Dustin, Fred. 1987. *The Custer Tragedy.* Upton & Sons, El Segundo, California. 275 pp.

Edwards, William B. 1962. *Civil War Guns.* The Stackpole Company, Harrisburg, Pennsylvania. 444 pp

Ege, Robert J. 1981. *Settling the Dust. The Custer Battle – June 25, 1876.* Werner Publications, Greeley, Colorado. 40 pp.

Egge, Phyllis Bridge. 1989. *Old Post Cemetery, 1873 – 1953. Fort Meade, South Dakota.* Old Fort Meade Museum and Historic Research Assn. 58 pp.

Elson, Henry W. 1912. *The Civil War through the Camera, together with Elson's New History.* Patriot Publishing Co., Springfield, Massachusetts. 592 pp.

Faldet, David S. 2009. *Oneota flow. The Upper Iowa River and its People.* University of Iowa Press, Iowa City. 240 pp.

Fapso, Richard J. 1990. *Norwegians in Wisconsin.* The State Historical Society of Wisconsin, Madison. 40 pp.

Fickert, Steve (ed). No year, a. *Indians at Greasy Grass.* Arrow and Trooper, Brooklyn, New York. 24 pp.

Fickert, Steve (ed). No year, b. *Eyewitness at the Little Bighorn. Feather earrings account, Red Horse's story, One Bull's version. Lt. Clarke's report and Sheridan's report to Sherman.* Arrow and Trooper, New York. 15 pp.

Ficklen, John Rose. 2009. *History of Reconstruction in Louisiana (through 1868).* Pranava Books, Dehli. 234 pp.

Flom, George Tobias. 1905-06. *Chapters on Scandinavian Immigration to Iowa.* Reprinted from The Iowa Journal of History and Politics. The State Historical Society of Iowa, Iowa City. 150 pp.

Foner, Eric. 2005. *Reconstruction. America's unfinished Revolution: 1863 – 1877.* Harper Collins Publishers, Inc./History Book Club, New York. 690 pp.

Foote, Shelby. 1986. *The Civil War. A Narrative. (1 – 3). Fort Sumter to Perryville, Fredericksburg to Meridian, Red River to Appomattox.* Vintage Books, New York. 843 + 989 + 1109 pp.

Force, M.F. 1881. *From Fort Henry to Corinth* (Campaigns of the Civil War). Reprint 2002 by Castle Books, Edison, New Jersey. 204 pp.

Foguera, Katherine Gibson. 1986. *With Custer's Cavalry.* University of Nebraska Press, Lincoln and London. 285 pp.

Fox, Richard Allan, Jr. 1993. *Archaeology, History and Custer's Last Battle. The Little Bighorn Reexamined.* University of Oklahoma Press, Norman and London. 411 pp.

Fox, Stephen. 2003. *Transatlantic. Samuel Cunard, Isambard Brunel and the great Atlantic Steamships.* Harper Collins Publishers, New York. 493 pp.

Frank, Joseph Allan and George A. Reaves. 2003. *"Seeing the Elephant". Raw Recruits at the Battle of Shiloh.* University of Illinois Press, Urbana and Chicago. 216 pp.

Franklin, John Hope.1961. *Reconstruction: After the Civil War.* The University of Chicago Press, Chicago and London. 259 pp.

Frost, Lawrence A. 1984. *The Custer Album. A Pictorial Biography of General George A. Custer.* Bonanza Books, New York. 191 pp.

Genoways, Ted & Hugh H. (eds). 2001. *A perfect Picture of Hell. Eyewitness Accounts by Civil War Prisoners from the 12th Iowa.* University of Iowa Press, Iowa City. 337 pp.

Gerteis, Louis S. 2001. *Civil War in St. Louis.* University Press of Kansas, Lawrence. 410 pp.

Gesne, Ann Urness. 1993. *Between rocks and hard places. Traditions, customs and conditions in Norway during the 1800s, emigration from Norway, the immigrant community in America.* Caragana Press, Hastings, Minnesota. 190 pp.

Gindlesperger, James. 1996. *Escape from Libby Prison.* Burd Street Press, Shippensburg, Pennsylvania.

Glazier, William W. 1987. *The Capture, the Prison Pen and the Escape. An Account of Prison Life in the South 1863 – 1866.* Heritage Books Inc., Bowie, Maryland. 370 pp.

Goodwin, David. 2001. *Ghosts of Jefferson Barracks. History and Hauntings of Old St. Louis.* Whitechapel Productions Press Publications, Alton, Illinois. 115 pp.

Gott, Kendall D. 1998. *The Confederate Command during the Fort Henry – Fort Donelson Campaign, February 1862.* Thesis for the Degree of Master of Military Arts and Science, Fort Leavenworth, Kansas. 125 pp.

Gott, Kendall D. 2011. *Where the South lost the War. An analysis of the Fort Henry-Fort Donelson Campaign February 1862.* Stackpole Books, Mechanicsburg, PA. 346 pp.

Grassino, Sandie and Art. Schuermann. 2011. *Jefferson Barracks* (Images of America). Arcadia Publishing, Charleston, South Carolina. 128 pp.

Gray, John S. No year. *A Sutler on Custer's Last Campaign.* Arrow and Trooper, Brooklyn, New York. 19 pp.

Gray, John S. 1991. *Custer's Last Campaign. Mitch Boyer and the Little Bighorn reconstructed.* University of Nebraska Press, Lincoln and London. 446 pp.

Greene, Jerome A. 1986. *Evidence and the Custer Enigma.* Vistabooks, Silverthorne, Colorado. 71 pp.

Greene, Jerome A. 1993. *Battles and Skirmishes of the Great Sioux War, 1876 – 1877. The Military View.* University of Oklahoma Press, Norman. 228 pp.

Greene, Jerome A. 2000. *Nez Perce Summer, 1877. The U.S. Army and the Nee-Me-Poo crisis.* Montana Historical Society Press, Helena, Montana. 554 pp.

Greene, Jerome A. (ed). 2006. *Indian War Veterans. Memories of Army Life and Campaigns in the West, 1864 – 1898.* Savas Beatie, New York and California. 370 pp.

Greipsland, Thorbjørn. 2005. *Norwegians in the Death Camps* (in Norwegian). Emigrantforlaget, Askim. 222 pp.

Grinnell, George Bird. 1915. *The fighting Cheyennes.* University of Oklahoma Press, Norman and London. 387 pp.

Groom, Winston. 1995. *Shrouds of Glory. From Atlanta to Nashville: The Last Great Campaign of the Civil War.* The Atlantic Monthly Press, New York. 308 pp.

Groom, Winston. 2009. *Vicksburg 1863*. Vintage Books, Vintage Civil War Library, New York. 482 pp.

Groom, Winston. 2012. *Shiloh, 1862*. National Geographic, Washington, D.C. 446 pp.

Hallbing, Kjell. 1976. *The Sun stood still over Little Big Horn* (in Norwegian). Gyldendal Norsk Forlag. 146 pp.

Hammer, Kenneth. 1965. *Little Big Horn Biographies*. Custer Battlefield Historical and Museum Association. 55 pp.

Hammer, Kenneth M. 1970. *The Springfield Carbine on the Western Frontier*. The Custer Battlefield Historical and Museum Association, Crow Agency, Montana. 18 pp.

Hammer, Kenneth (ed). 1976. *Custer in '76*. Brigham Young University Press, Provo, Utah. 303 pp.

Hardorff, Richard. No year. *Shadows along the Little Bighorn. Custer's Route to the Medicine Trail Coulee*. Arrow and Trooper, Brooklyn, New York. 48 pp.

Hardorff, Richard G. 1985. *Markers, artifacts and Indian testimony: Preliminary findings on the Custer battle*. Don Horn Publications, Short Hills, New Jersey. 71 pp.

Hardorff, Richard G. 1991. *The Custer Battle Casualties. Burials, Exhumations and Reinternments*. Upton and Sons Publishers, El Segundo, California. 182 pp.

Hardorff, Richard. 1993. *Hokahey! A Good Day to Die! The Indian Casualties of the Custer Fight*. University of Nebraska Press, Lincoln and London. 174 pp.

Hardorff, Richard. 1995. *Cheyenne Memories of the Custer Fight*. University of Nebraska Press, Lincoln and London. 189 pp.

Hardorff, Richard G. 1997. *Lakota Recollections of the Custer Fight*. University of Nebraska Press, Lincoln and London. 211 pp.

Hardorff, Richard. 1999. *The Custer Battle Casualties, II. The Dead, the Missing and the few Survivors*. Upton and Sons Publishers, El Segundo, California. 223 pp.

Hardorff, Richard. 2002. *Walter M. Camp's Little Bighorn Rosters*. The Arthur H. Clark Co., Spokane, Washington. 231 pp.

Hatch, Alden. 1956. *Remington Arms. An American History*. Rinehart & Company, Inc., New York & Toronto. 359 pp.

Hayes-McCoy, G.A. 1965. *Captain Myles Walter Keough*. O'Donnel Lecture, National University of Ireland. Reprint by Arrow and Trooper, Brooklyn, New York. 34 pp.

Hawkins, Walter. 1913. *Old John Brown. The Man whose Soul is marching on*. Reprinted by Wayne and Judy Dasher, Nashville Georgia. 31 pp.

Hedren, Paul (ed). No year. *Custer's Last Battle, by Captain Charles King.* 11 pp.

Hedren, Paul. 1991. *The Great Sioux War, 1876 – 1877. The Best from Montana the Magazine of Western History.* Montana Historical Society Press, Helena. 293 pp.

Hedren, Paul. L. (ed). 2003. *We trailed the Sioux. Enlisted men speak on Custer, Crook and the great Sioux War.* Stackpole Books, Mechanicsburg, Pennsylvania. 98 pp.

Henry, Robert Selph. 1938. *The Story of Reconstruction.* Grosset & Dunlap Publishers, New York. 633 pp.

Hofling, Charles K. 1981. *Custer and the Little Big Horn. A Psycho-biographical Inquiry.* Wayne State University Press, Detroit, Michigan. 119 pp.

Holand, Hjalmar Rued. 2006. *History of the Norwegian Settlements: A translated and expanded version of the 1908 De Store Norske Settlementers Historie and the 1930 Den Siste Folkevandrings Sagastubber fra Nybyggerlivet i Amerika.* Astri my Astri Publishing, Waukon, Iowa. 468 pp.

Hook Richard, 2004. *Warriors at the Little Bighorn* (Men-at-Arms 408). Osprey Publishing, Oxford, United Kingdom. 50 pp.

Horn, Stanley F. 1991. *The Decisive Battle of Nashville.* Louisiana State University Press, Baton Rouge and London. 189 pp.

Hoverstad, Torger Andersen. 1915. *The Norwegian Farmers in the United States.* Hans Jervell Publishing Co., Fargo, North Dakota. 150 pp.

Hunt, Elvid and Walter E. Lorence. 1937. *History of Fort Leavenworth 1827 – 1937.* The Command and General Staff School Press, Fort Leavenworth, Kansas. 301 pp.

Hutchins, James S. 1976. *Boots and Saddles at the Little Bighorn.* The Old Army Press, Ft. Collins, Colorado. 81 pp.

Hutchins, James S. (ed). *The Army and Navy Journal on the Battle of the Little Bighorn and related Matters, 1876 – 1881.* Custer Trails Series, Volume Eight. Upron and Sons Publishers, El Segundo, California. 261 pp.

Hutton, Paul Andrew (ed). 1992. *The Custer Reader.* University of Nebraska Press. 585 pp.

Ingersoll, Lurton Dunham. 1867. *Iowa and the Rebellion.* J.B. Lippincott & Co., Philadelphia, Dubuque, Iowa City, Burlington. 756 pp.

Ingstad, Anne Stine. 1977. *The Discovery of a Norse Settlement in America.* Universitetsforlaget, Oslo, Bergen, Tromsø. 430 pp.

Ingstad, Helge. 1965. *Westwards to Vinland. The Discovery of Pre-Columbian Norse House Sites in North America* (in Norwegian). Gyldendal Forlag, Olso. 284 pp.

Ingstad, Helge. 1985. *The Norse Discovery of America. Volume 2*. Norwegian University Press, Oslo, Bergen, Stavanger, Tromsø. 573 pp.

Iowa Adjutant General's Office. 1908. *Roster and Record of Iowa Soldiers in the War of the Rebellion together with Historical Sketches of Volunteer Organizations 1861 – 1866. Vol. II, 9th – 16th Regiment of Infantry.* State Printer, Des Moines, Iowa. 1199 pp.

Iowa Association of Naturalists. No year. *Iowa Prairies* (The Iowa Biological Communities Series, IAN 302). Iowa State University, Ames. 24 pp.

Iowa Board of Immigration. 1870. *Iowa: The Home for Immigrants, being a Treatise of the Resources of Iowa.* Mill & Co. printers and publishers, Des Moines. 96 pp.

Jackson, Donald.1966. *Custer's gold. The United States cavalry expedition of 1874.* University of Nebraska Press, Lincoln and London. 152 pp.

Jones, Lieutenant S. C. 1907. *Reminiscences of the Twenty-Second Iowa Volunteer Infantry.* Iowa City, Iowa, 210 pp.

Jordan, General Thomas and J.P. Pryor. 1996. *The Campaigns of General Nathan Bedford Forrest and of Forrest's Cavalry.* Da Capo Press. 707 pp.

Judge-Advocate General's Office. 1902. *A Manual for General Court Martial, Courts of Inquiry and Retiring Boards, and of other Procedure under Military law.* Washington Government Printing Office. 210 pp

Kent, Thomas H. and James J. Dinsmore. 1996. *Birds in Iowa.* Published by the Authors, Iowa City and Ames. 391 pp.

Kiner, F.F. 1863. *One Year's Soldiering. Embracing the Battle of Fort Donelson and Shiloh.* E.H. Thomas Printer, Lancaster, Pennsylvania. Reprint by Morgan Avenue Press, 2000). 184 pp.

Kingsbury, George V. 1915. *History of Dakota Territory. South Dakota, its History and its People. Vol I – V.* The S.J. Clark Publishing Co., Chicago, Illinois. 5 494 pp.

Kinsley, D.A. 1992. *Custer. Favor the Bold. A Soldier's Story.* Promontory Press, New York. 557 pp.

Kirkeby, Birger. 1962 – 71. *Nannestad Bygdebok (History of Nannestad Community), Vol. I, II and III.* Published by Nannestad Municipality. 856 + 597 + 565 pp.

Knight, Oliver. 1960. *Following the Indian Wars. The Story of the Newspaper Correspondents among the Indian Campaigners.* University of Oklahoma Press, Norman and London. 349 pp.

Knox, Thomas W. 1865. *Camp-Fire and Cotton Field.* Reprinted by Wayne and Judy Dasher, Nashville, Georgia. 335 pp.

Kollbaum, Marc E. 2002. *Gateway to the West. The History of Jefferson Barracks from 1826-1894. Volume I.* Friends of the Jefferson Barracks, St. Louis, Missouri. 261 pp.

Koury, Capt. Michael J. 1969. *Diaries of the Little Bighorn.* Old Army Press, Papillion, Nebraska. 82 pp.

Koury, Michael J. 1970. *The Terry Diary. Yellowstone Expedition – 1876.* Bellevue, Nebraska. 37 pp.

Kuhlman, Charles. 1952. *Legend into History. The Custer Mystery. An analytical Study of the Battle of the Little Bighorn.* The Stackpole Company, Harrisburg, Pennsyulvania. 250 pp.

Laing, Samuel. 1837. *Journal of a Residence in Norway, during the Years 1834, 1835 and 1836, made with a View to enquire into the Moral and Political Economy of its Inhabitants.* Longman, London. 220 pp.

Langeland, Knut. 1889. *The Norwegians in America* (in Norwegian). John Anderson & Co. Publishers, Chicago. 224 pp.

Langone, John. 1986. *Dead End. A Book about Suicide.* Little, Brown and Company, Boston and Toronto. 176 pp.

Larson, Robert W. 2007. *Gall. Lakota war chief.* University of Oklahoma Press, Norman. 301 pp.

Lawrence County Historical Society. 1981.*Some History of Lawrence County.* The State Publishing Co., Pierre, South Dakota. 729 pp.

Lee, Robert H. 1987. *Fort Meade. The peace keeper post on the Dakota frontier 1878 – 1944.* Old Fort Meade Museum & Historic Research Assoc., Fort Meade, South Dakota. 83 pp.

Lee, Robert. 1991. *Fort Meade and the Black Hills.* University of Nebraska Press, Lincoln and London. 321 pp.

Leeke, Jim (ed). 1998. *Smoke, Sound and Fury. The Civil War Memoirs of Major General Lew Wallace, U.S. Volunteers.* Strawberry Hill Press, Portland, Oregon. 288 pp.

Lehman, Tim. 2010. *Bloodshed at the Little Bighorn.* The Johns Hopkins University Press, Baltimore, Maryland. 219 pp.

Libby, Orin (ed). 1998.*The Arikara Narrative of Custer's Campaign and the Battle of the Little Bighorn.* University of Oklahoma Press, Norman. 217 pp.

Logsdon, David R. (ed). 2011. *Eyewitnesses at the Battle of Shiloh.* Kettle Mills Press, Lyles, Tennessee. 136 pp.

Longstreet, Stephen. 1993. *Indian Wars of the Great Plains.* Indian head books, New York. 337 pp.

Lonn, Ella. 1976. *Reconstruction in Louisiana after 1868.* Peter Smith, Gloucester, Massachusetts. 538 pp.

Lovoll, Odd S. 1984. *The Promise of America. A History of the Norwegian-American People.* University of Minnesota Press/Norwegian-American Historical Association, Minneapolis. 239 pp.

Lovoll, Odd. 2006. *Norwegians on the Prairie.* Minnesota Historical Society Press/Norwegian-American Historical Association, St. Paul. 324 pp.

Lowry, Thomas P. 2011. *Irish & German Whiskey & Beer. Drinking Patterns in the Civil War.* Privately published. 102 pp.

Lubetkin, M. John. 2006. *Jay Cooke's Gamble: The Northern Pacific Railroad, The Sioux and the Panic of 1873.* University of Oklahoma Press, Norman. 370 pp.

Luce, Edward (ed).*The Diary and Letters of Dr. James M. DeWolf, acting Assistant Surgeon, U.S. Army.* Transcribed and reprinted from North Dakota History 25 (2&3), 1958. 52 pp.

MacLean, Colonel French L. 2011. *Custer's best. The Story of Company M, 7th Cavalry at the Little Bighorn.* Schiffer Publishing Co., Atglen, Pennsylvania. 239 pp.

Magnussen, Daniel O. 2007. *Thompson's narrative of the Little Bighorn, annotated by Walter Cross.* Cross Publications, Stillwater, Oklahoma.

Marcot, Roy. 2005. *The History of Remington Firearms.* The Lyons Press, Guilford, Connecticut. 128 pp.

Marcus, Eric. 1996. *Why Suicide?* Harper San Francisco. 240 pp.

Marshall, Joseph M. III. 2005. *The Journey of Crazy Horse. A Lakota History.* Penguin Group, New York. 310 pp.

Marshall, Joseph M. III. 2007. *The day the world ended at the Little Bighorn. A Lakota History.* Penguin Group (USA) Inc., New York. 262 pp.

Marquis, Thomas B. 1931. *Wooden Leg. A warrior who fought Custer.* University of Nebraska Press, Lincoln. 389 pp.

Marquis, Thomas B. 1933. Two days after the Custer Battle. 8 pp.

Marquis, Thomas B. 1967. *Custer on the Little Bighorn.* Reference Publications, Inc., Algonac, Michigan. 132 pp.

Marquis, Thomas B. 1987. *Keep the last bullet for yourself. The true story of Custer's last stand.* Reference Publications Inc., Algonac, Michigan. 205 pp.

Martin, Greg (ed). 1996. *With Custer on the Little Bighorn by William Taylor.* Viking, Penguin Books, New York. 207 pp.

McChristian, Douglas C. 1993. *Reno-Benteen Entrenchment Trail.* Custer Battlefield Historical Museum Association, Montana. 12 pp.

McChristian, Douglas C. 1995. *The Army in the West, 1870 – 1880. Uniforms, Weapons and Equipment.* University of Oklahoma Press, Norman. 313 pp.

McDonough, James Lee. 1977. *Shiloh – In Hell before Night.* The University of Tennessee Press, Knoxville. 260 pp.

McFeely, William S. 1994. *Yankee Stepfather. General O.O. Howard and the Freedmen.* W.W. Norton & Company, Inc., New York. 351 pp.

McGuire, Randy R. 2001. *St. Louis Arsenal. Armory of the West* (Images of America). Arcadia Publishing Charleston SC, Chicago IL, Portsmouth NH, San Francisco Ca. 128 pp.

Mcintosh, John. 2002. *Custer's Southern Officer. Captain George D. Wallace, 7th U.S. Cavalry.* Cloud Creek Press, Lexington, South Carolina. 188 pp.

McKenney, Tom Chase. 2012. *Jack Hinson's One-Man War. A Civil War Sniper.* Pelican Publishing Company, Gretna, Louisiana. 400 pp.

McWorther. Lucullus Virgil. 2008. *Yellow Wolf: His own Story.* Caxton Press, Caldwell, Idaho. 328 pp.

Mead, William R. (ed). 1993. *Pictorial Atlas of the World.* CLB Publishing, Godalming, Surrey. 223 pp.

Meyer, Steve. 1993. *Iowans called to valor. The story of Iowa's entry into the Civil War.* Meyer Publishing, Garrison, Indiana. 129 pp.

Meyer, Steve. 1994. *Iowa valor.* Meyer Publishing, Garrison, Indiana. 511 pp.

Michno, Gregory F. 2007. *Lakota Noon. The Indian Narrative of Custer's Defeat.* Mountain Press Publishing Co., Missoula, Montana. 336 pp.

Miller, Francis Trevelyan and Robert Lanier (ed). 1911. *Photographic History of the Civil War, Vol. 1 – 10.* The Review of Reviews Co., New York. 3 463 pp.

Mills, Charles K. 1983. *Charles DeRudio.* Reprint from J.M. Carroll Co. by Arrow and Trooper, New York, 2000. 49 pp.

Mills, Charles K. 2011. *Harvest of barren Regrets. The Army Career of Frederick William Benteen, 1834 - 1898.* University of Nebraska Press, Lincoln and London. 432 pp.

Moore, Donald. 2011. *Where the Custer Fight began. Undermanned and Overwhelmed. The Reno Valley Fight.* Upton and Sons Publishers, El Segundo, California. 205 pp.

Moore, Rex (ed) 1979. *Dakota Cowboy Soldier. A collection of documented letters written by Michael Vetter, U.S. Army – 7th Cavalry Regiment Dakota Territory and Little Bighorn, Montana.* Presented by The Lake Region Pioneer Daughters, Fort Totten. Devil's Lake Manufacturing Corp., Fort Totten, North Dakota. 25 pp.

Morsberger, Robert E. and Katharine M. 1980. *Lew Wallace: Militant Romantic.* McGraw-Hill Book Company, New York, St. Louis, San Francisco, Dusseldorf, Mexico, Toronto. 559 pp.

Mulford, Ami Frank. 2009. *Fighting Indians with the 7th Cavalry. The Recollections of a Bugler of the Campaign against the Nez Perce Indians 1876-77.* Leonaur. 159 pp.

Mullaney, Killian, Lars Svensson, Dan Zetterstrøm and Peter J. Grant. 1999. *Birds of Europe*. Princeton University Press, Princeton, New Jersey. 400 pp.

Murray, Robert A. 1981. *The Army Moves West. Supplying the Western Indian Wars Campaigns*. 19 pp.

Mørkhagen, Sverre. 2009. Goodbye, Norway. Emigration to America 1825 – 1975 (in Norwegian). Gyldendal Norsk Forlag, 663 pp.

Nelson, David T. (ed). 1955. *The Diary of Elisabeth Koren 1853 – 1855*. Norwegian-American Historical Association, Northfield, Minnesota. 381 pp.

Nelson, Oley and Anfin Apland. 1945. *A brief History of the first Norwegian Settlements in Story and Polk Counties, Iowa, 1855 – 1945*. Privately printed, Des Moines, Iowa. 40 pp.

Nelson, Olof N. (ed). 1969. *History of the Scandinavians and the successful Scandinavians in the United States. Vol. I and II*. Haskell House Publishers LTD., New York. 518 + 280 pp.

Nevin, David. 1983. *The Road to Shiloh* (The Civil War). Time-Life Books, Alexandria, Virginia. 175 pp.

Newhall, J.B. 1846. *A Glimpse of Iowa in 1846; or the Emigrant's Guide and State Directory with a Description of new Purchase*. W.D. Skillman, Publisher, Burlington. 114 pp.

Nichols, Ronald H. 1992. *Reno Court of Inquiry*. Custer Battlefield Historical & Museum Association, Inc. Crow Agency, Montana. 675 pp.

Nichols, Ronald H. 2000. *In Custer's Shadow. Major Marcus Reno*. University of Oklahoma Press, Norman. 407 pp.

Nichols, Ronald H. 2002. *Men with Custer*. Custer Battlefield Historical & Museum Association, Inc. Hardin, Montana. 407 pp.

Nightengale, Robert. 1996. *1876. Little Bighorn*. DocuPro Services, Inc., Edina, Minnesota. 274 pp.

Norlie, Olaf Morgan. 1973. *History of the Norwegian People in America*. Haskell House Publishers LTD., New York. 512 pp.

Norwegian University, The. 1855. *Almanac for the Years 1847 – 1855* (in Norwegian). D.T. Malling, Christiania. 288 pp.

Nosworthy, Brent. 2005. *The Bloody Crucible of Courage. Fighting Methods and Combat Experience of the Civil War*. Carroll and Graf Publishers, New York. 753 pp.

Nott, Charles C. 1911. *Sketches of the war. A Series of Letters to the North Moore Street School of New York*. William Abbatt, New York. 232 pp.

O'Gallagher, Marianna. 1984. *Grosse Isle. Gateway to Canada 1832 – 1937*. Livres Carraig Books, Quebec. 185 pp.

O'Neil, Tom (ed). No year, a. *Critical notes on the line of march. 7th Cavalry from Fort Lincoln across Dakota by Major Frank L. Anders, 1939.* Arrow and Trooper, Brooklyn, New York. 48 pp.

O'Neil, Tom (ed). No year, b. *Marcus A. Reno. What was said of him at the Little Bighorn.* Arrow and Trooper, Brooklyn, New York. 14 pp.

O'Neil, Tom. 1990 - 1993. *Garry Owen Tid Bits I, II, III, V, VI and VII.* Arrow and Trooper, Brooklyn, New York. 233 pp.

O'Neil, Tom (ed). 1991. *Little Big Horn Scenarios.* Arrow and Trooper, Brooklyn, New York. 25 pp.

O'Neil, Tom (ed) 1992. *Sagas of Greasy Grass.* Arrow and Trooper, Brooklyn, New York. 22 pp.

O'Neil, Tom. 1992. *The Official Reports of Major Reno and Captain Benteen, Little Big Horn 25 June 1876 and Fields of Fire - The Reno Benteen Defense Perimeter by William Rector.* Arrow and Trooper, Brooklyn, New York. 16 pp.

O'Neil, Tom (ed). 1994. *Lieutenant Godfrey's Diary – Little Big Horn Campaign.* Arrow and Trooper, Brooklyn, New York. 21 pp.

O'Neil, Tom (ed). 1995. *Captain Louis Hamilton, United States Seventh Cavalry.* Arrow and Trooper, Brooklyn, New York. 14 pp.

O'Neil, Tom (ed). 1995. *Custer's last Command by Captain Francis M. Gibson, 7th Cavalry.* Arrow and Trooper, Brooklyn, New York. 7 pp.

O'Neil, Tom (ed). 1996. *Fort Abraham Lincoln. A short History. Building Diagrams. House Plans. Map.* Private publication, Brooklyn, New York. 14 pp.

O'Neil, Tom (ed). 1997. *Notebook of Lieutenant McIntosh.* Arrow and Trooper, Brooklyn, New York. 13 pp.

O'Neil, Tom (ed). 1997.*Reminiscences of General Custer's last Battle, by Richard Roberts, who was Custer's secretary in 1876 and on the last Campaign.* Arrow and Trooper, Brooklyn, New York. 38 pp.

Overfield, Loyd J. II. 1971. *The Little Big Horn, 1876. The official communication, Documents and Reports with Rosters of the Officers and Troops of the Campaign.* University of Nebraska Press.

Panzieri, Peter. 1998. *Little Bighorn1876* (The Campaign Series 39). Osprey Publishing Ltd., Oxford, United Kingdom. 96 pp.

Parker, George F. 1940. *Iowa. Pioneer Foundations.* The State Historical Society of Iowa, Iowa City. Vol. I and II. 532 + 579 pp.

Parker, N. Howe. 1855. *Iowa as it is. A Gazetteer for Citizens and a Hand Book for Emmigrants* Keen and Lee, Chicago, Illinois. 264 pp.

Parsons, John E. and John S. du Mont. 1953. *Firearms in the Custer Battle.* The Stackpole Company, Harrisburg, Pennsylvania. 59 pp.

Paulson, Ole. 1907. *Reminiscences* (in Norwegian). The Free Church Book Concern, Minneapolis, Minnesota. 245 pp.

Pennington, Jack. 2001. *The Battle of the Little Bighorn. A Comprehensive Study*. Upton & Sons Publishers, El Segundo, California. 373 pp.

Peterson, Roger Tory. 1980. *Eastern Birds. A Field Guide to the Birds of the Eastern and Central North America*. Houghton Mifflin Company, Boston, Massachusetts. 384 pp.

Peterson, William J. (ed). 1964. *The Annals of Iowa. Volume One – 1863*. Reprint, The Economy Advertising Co., Iowa City. 209 pp.

Philbrick, Nathaniel. 2010. *The Last Stand. Custer, Sitting Bull and the Battle of the Little Bighorn*. Viking/Penguin Group, New York. 446 pp.

Price, S. Goodale. 1952. *Ghosts of Golconda. Black Hills Historical Guide Book*. Western Publishers, Deadwood, South Dakota. 208 pp.

Prucha, Francis Paul. 1964. *A Guide to the Military Posts of the United States 1789 – 1895*. The State Historical Society of Wisconsin, Madison. 179 pp.

Prytz, Kåre. 1992. *Westwards before Columbus* (in Norwegian). H. Aschehoug & Co. (W. Nygaard), Oslo. 239 pp

Qualey, Carlton C. 1938. *Norwegian Settlements in the United States*. Doctoral thesis in political science at Columbia University. Norwegian-American Historical Association, Northfield, Minnesota. 287 pp.

Quinnett, Paul G. 2002. *Suicide. The Forever Decision*. Crossroads, New York. 156 pp.

Rae, William Frazer. 1993. *Westward by Rail. The New Route to the East*. Indian Head books, New York. 391 pp.

Rapid City Society for Genealogical Research, The. 1987. *Cemeteries, Meade County, South Dakota*. 100 pp.

Rebok, Barbara and Doug (ed). 2007. *Louisiana – History of Bossier Parish*. Reprinted from earlier historical writings. Plus Printing Co., Tucson, Arizona.

Reddick, Andy. 2007. *Squelching the Sesech. Iowa's Role in the Civil War*. Publish America, Baltimore. 174 pp.

Reed, David W. 1902. *The Battle of Shiloh and the Organizations Engaged*. The Government Printing Office, Washington, D.C. 121 pp.

Reed, David W. 1903. *Campaigns and battles of the twelfth regiment Iowa veteran volunteer infantry*. Evanston, Illinois. 348 pp.

Reedstrom, Ernest L. 1986. *Bugles, Banners and War Bonnets*. Bonanza Books, New York. 362 pp.

Reedstrom, E. Lisle. 1992. *Custer's 7th Cavalry. From Fort Riley to the Little Bighorn*. Sterling Publishing Co., Inc., New York. 156 pp.

Rich, Joseph W. 1911. *The Battle of Shiloh*. The State Historical Society of Iowa, Iowa City. 134 pp.

Richardson, William Thomas. 1913. *Historic Pulaski. Birthplace of the Ku Klux Klan, Scene of Execution of Sam Davis*. Privately Published. 108 pp.

Rickey, Don Jr. 1963. *Forty miles a day on beans and hay.* University of Oklahoma Press, Norman. 382 pp.

Rosen, Peter. 1895. *PA-HA-SA-PA or the Black Hills of South Dakota. A Complete History.* Reprint by HardPress Publishing, Miami, Florida. 645 pp.

Rosenberg, Morton M. 1972. *Iowa on the Eve of the Civil War. A Decade of Frontier Politics.* University of Oklahoma Press, Norman. 262 pp.

Rosholt, Jerry. 2003. *Ole goes to War. Men from Norway Who Fought in America's Civil War.* Vesterheim Norwegian-American Museum, Decorah, Iowa. 96 pp.

Ross, Allen. 2000. *Crazy Horse and the Real Reason for the Battle of the Little Big Horn.* Wiconi Waste, Denver, Colorado. 110 pp.

Sandoz, Mari. 1966. *The Battle of the Little Bighorn.* University of Nebraska Press, Lincoln and London. 191 pp.

Schneider, George A. (ed). 1977. *The Freeman Journal.* Presidio Press, San Rafael, California. 104 pp.

Scott, Douglas B. and Richard A. Fox, Jr. 1987. *Archaeological insight into the Custer battle. An assessment of the 1984 season.* University of Oklahoma Press, Norman and London. 137 pp.

Scott, Douglas B. and Richard A. Fox, Jr., Melissa A. Connor and Dick Harmon. 1989. *Archaeological perspectives on the battle of the Little Bighorn.* University of Oklahoma Press, Norman. 309 pp.

Scott, Douglas B. (ed). 1991. *Papers on Little Bighorn battlefield archaeology: The equipment dump, Marker 7 and the Reno crossing.* Reprints in anthropology volume 42. J&L Reprint Company, Lincoln, Nebraska. 236 pp.

Scott, Douglas B., P. Willey and Melissa A. Connor. 1998. *They died with Custer. Soldiers' bones from the Little Bighorn.* University of Oklahoma Press, Norman. 389 pp.

Sefton, James E. 1967. *The United States Army and Reconstruction 1865 – 1877.* Louisiana State University Press, Baton Rouge. 284 pp.

Semmingsen, Ingrid. 1980. *Norway to America.* University of Minnesota Press, Minneapolis. 213 pp.

Shell, Herbert S. 1975. *History of South Dakota.* University of Nebraska Press, Lincoln. 445 pp.

Sheridan, P.H. 1882. *Record of Engagements with Hostile Indians within the Military Division of the Missouri, from 1868 to 1882.* Headquarters Military Division of the Missouri, Chicago, Illinois. 48 pp.

Shugg, Robert W. 1966. *Origins of Class Struggle in Louisiana. A Social History of White Farmers and Laborers during Slavery and After, 1840 – 1875.* Louisiana State University Press. 372 pp.

Skarstein, Karl Jakob. 2005. *The War against the Sioux. Norwegians against Indians 1862 – 1863* (in Norwegian). Spartacus Forlag AS, Oslo, Norway. 272 pp.

Skarstein, Karl Jakob. 2011. *The Civil War. Norwegians fighting for America 1861 – 1865* (in Norwegian). Spartacus Forlag AS, Oslo, Norway. 368 pp.

Sklenar, Larry. 2000. *To Hell with Honor.* University of Oklahoma Press, Norman. 395 pp.

Smith, H.I. 1903. *History of the Seventh Iowa Veteran Volunteer Infantry during the Civil War.* E Hitchkok, Mason City, Iowa. 396 pp.

Smith Cherry L. 1989. *Sagebrush Soldier. Private William Earl Smith's View of the Sioux War of 1876.* University of Oklahoma Press, Norman. 158 pp.

Smith, Timothy B. 2006. *The Untold Story of Shiloh. The Battle and the Battle Field.* The University of Tennessee Press, Knoxville. 206 pp.

Snay, Mitchell. 2007. *Fenians, Freedmen, and Southern Whites.* Louisiana State University Press. 218 pp.

Speer, Lonnie R. 2005. *Portals to Hell. Military Prisons of the Civil War.* University of Nebraska Press, Lincoln and London.410 pp.

Stevenson, Joan Nabset. 2012. *Deliverance from the Little Big Horn. Doctor Henry Porter and Custer's Seventh Cavalry.* University of Oklahoma Press, Norman. 213 pp.

Stilwell Leander. 1920. *The Story of a Common Soldier of Army Life in the Civil War 1861 – 1865.* Franklin Hudson Publishing Co. 278 pp.

Sundt, Eilert,. 1855. *Marriage in Norway (in Norwegian).* D.S. Malling Boktrykkeri, Christiania. 155 pp.

Sundt, Eilert. 1855. *Mortality in Norway* (in Norwegian). D.S. Malling Boktrykkeri, Christiania. 171 pp.

Sundt, Eilert. 1857. *Morality in Norway, Vol. 1* (in Norwegian). Reprint 1968 Pax Forlag, Oslo. 371 pp.

Sundt, Eilert. 1859. *The Sobriety Conditions in Norway* (in Norwegian). J.Chr. Abelstedt, Christiania. 210 pp.

Sundt, Eilert. 1864. *Morality in Norway, Vol. 2* (in Norwegian). Reprint 1968, Pax Forlag, Oslo. 181 pp.

Sundt, Eilert. 1866. *Morality in Norway, Vol. 3* (in Norwegian). Reprint 1968, Pax Forlag, Oslo. 151 pp.

Sundt, Eilert. 1873. *Domestic Life in Norway* (in Norwegian). J. Chr. Abelstedt, Christiania. 215 pp.

Swanson, Glenwood J. 2004. *G.A. Custer. His Life and Times.* Glen Swanson Productions, Inc., Agua Dulce, California. 333 pp.

Swayne, Wager.1867. *Bureau of Refugees and Freedmen. Report of the Assistant Commissioner of Alabama, September 30th, 1867.* Barrett & Brown Printers and Binders, Montgomery, Alabama. 22 pp.

Swieder, Dorothy, Thomas Morain and Lynn Nielsen (ed).1991. *Iowa Past to Present. The People and the Prairie.* Iowa State University Press/Ames. 306 pp.

Swisher, Jacob A. 1943. *Iowa in times of War.* The State Historical Society of Iowa, Iowa City. 393 pp.

Sword, Wiley. 1988. *Shiloh: Bloody April.* Morningside Bookshop, Dayton, Ohio. 519 pp.

Taunton, Francis B. and Brian C. Pohanka. No year. *Custer's Field: "A Scene of Ghastly, Sickening Horror".* 46 pp.

Taunton, Francis B. 1977. *"Sufficient Reason?" An examination of Terry's Celebrated Order to Custer.* The English Westerners' Society, London. 100 pp.

Taylor, Joe Gray. 1974. *Louisiana reconstructed, 1863 – 1877.* Louisiana State University Press, Baton Rouge. 552 pp.

Thompson, Bailey and Patricia L. Meador. 1987. *Shreveport. A Photographic Remembrance 1873 – 1949.* Louisiana State University Press, Baton Rouge. 250 pp.

Thompson, Bill. 2004. *Iowa Bird Watching. A Year-Round Guide.* Cool Springs Press, Nashville Tennessee. 176 pp.

Throne, Mildred (ed). 1998. *The Civil War Diary of Cyrus F. Boyd, 15th Iowa Infantry, 1861 – 1863.* Louisiana State University Press, Baton Rouge. 138 pp.

Thwaites, Reuben Gold. 1908. *Wisconsin. The Americanization of a French Settlement.* Houghton Mifflin Company, Boston and New York. 475 pp.

Title Atlas Company. 1992. *Atlas of Becker County, Minnesota. Containing Maps, Plats of the Townships, Rural Directory, Pictures of Farms and Families, Articles about History etc. Vol. 1 & 2.* Minneapolis and Battle Lake. 250 + 236 pp.

Tousey, Thomas G. 1939. *Military History of Carlisle and Carlisle Barracks.* The Dietz Press, Richmond, Virginia. 447 pp.

Trofimenkoff, Susan Mann. 1983. *The Dream of a Nation. A Social and Intellectual History of Quebec.* Gage Publishing Ltd., Toronto, Ontario 344 pp.

Tunnell, Ted. 1984. *Crucible of Reconstruction. War, Radicalism and Race in Louisiana 1862 – 1877.* Louisiana State University Press, Baton Rouge and London. 257 pp.

Twombley, Voltaire P. 1901. *The Second Iowa Infantry at Fort Donelson February 15, 1862.* 27 pp.

Ulvestad, Martin. 1907. *The Norwegians in America. Their History and Record (in Norwegian).* History Book Company's Forlag, Minneapolis, Minnesota. 871 pp.

Utley, Robert. 1967. *Frontiersmen in Blue. The United States Army and the Indian, 1848 – 1965.* University of Nebraska Press, Lincoln and London. 348 pp.

Utley, Robert. 1973. *Frontier Regulars.* Macmillan Publishing Co., New York, London. 466 pp.

Utley, Robert. 1983. *The Indian Frontier of the American West 1846 – 1890.* University of New Mexico Press, Albuquerque. 325 pp.

Utley, Robert. 1988. *Cavalier in Buckskin.* University of Oklahoma Press, Norman and London. 226 pp.

Van de Water, Frederick. 1988. *Glory Hunter. A Life of General Custer.* University of Nebraska Press, Lincoln and London. 394 pp.

Waldman, Charley W. 1964. *Early day history of Sturgis and Fort Meade in the beautiful Black Hills of South Dakota. Volume 1.* Privately printed. 176 pp.

Walton, George. 1973. *Sentinel of the Plains: Fort Leavenworth and the American West.* Prentiss – Hall, Inc., Englewood Cliffs, New Jersey. 210 pp.

Ware, Eugene F. 1907. *The Lyons Campaign in Missouri, being a History of the First Iowa Infantry.* Crane and Company, Topeka, Kansas. 410 pp.

Warmoth, Henry Clay. 1930. *War, Politics and Reconstruction. Stormy Days in Louisiana.* The Macmillan Company, New York. 285 pp.

Weibert, Don. 1989. *Custer, Cases and Cartridges. The Weibert Collection Analyzed.* Private Publication, Billings, Montana. 328 pp.

Weibert, Henry and Don.1985. *Sixty-six years in Custer's shadow.* Falcon Press Publishing Co., Inc, Billings, Montana. 174 pp.

Welch, James and Paul Stekler. 1995. *Killing Custer: The Battle of Little Bighorn and the fate of the Plains Indians.* Penguin Books USA, New York. 320 pp.

Wert, Jeffrey D. 1996. *Custer. The controversial Life of George Armstrong Custer.* Touchstone, New York. 462 pp.

Westfall, Douglas Paul. 1997. *Letters from the Field. Wallace at the Little Big Horn.* The Paragon Agency Publishers, Orange, California. 86 pp.

White, Howard Ashley.1970. *The Freedmen's Bureau in Louisiana.* Louisiana State University Press, Baton Rouge. 227 pp.

Whittaker, William (ed). 2009. *Frontier Forts of Iowa. Indians, Traders and Soldiers, 1682 – 1862.* University of Iowa Press, Iowa City. 267 pp.

Whyte, Robert. 1848. *The Ocean Plague: Or, A Voyage to Quebec in an Irish Emigrant Vessel: Embracing a Quarantine at Grosse Isle in 1847.* Coolige and Wiley, Boston. 127 pp.

Wilcox, Alvin H. 1907. *A Pioneer History of Becker County, Minnesota.* Pioneer Press Co., St. Paul. 757 pp.

Wilder, Laura Ingalls. 1971. *The Long Winter* (Dakota 1880 – 1881). Harper & Row, New York. 337 pp.

Williams, Roger L. 2009. *Military Register of Custer's last Command.* The Arthur H. Clark Co., Norman, Oklahoma. 429 pp.

Wilson, R.L. 1985. *Colt. An American Legend.* Artabras, New York, London, Paris. 406 pp.

Wilson, R.L. 1991. *Winchester. An American Legend.* Chartwell Books, Inc. 404 pp.

Windolph, Charles. 1947. *I fought with Custer. As told to Frazier and Robert Hunt.* University of Nebraska Press, Lincoln and London. 236 pp.

Winters, John D. 1963. *The Civil War in Louisiana.* Louisiana State University Press, Baton Rouge and London. 534 pp.

Winthrop, William. 2010. *Military Law and Precedents, Vol. 1.* General Books, Memphis Tennessee. 588 pp.

Winthrop, William. 1920. *Military Law and Precedents, Vol. 2.* Government Printing Office, Washington. 338 pp.

Wish, Harvey (ed). 1966. *Reconstruction in the South 1865 – 1877. First Hand Accounts of the American Southland after the Civil War, by Northerners and Southerners.* The Noonday Press. 318 pp.

Woodworth, Steven E. 2005. *Nothing but Victory. The Army of the Tennessee, 1861 – 1865.* Alfred A Knopf, New York. 760 pp.

Woodworth, Steven E. 2009. *The SHILOH Campaign.* Southern Illinois Press, Carbondale. 168 pp.

Articles in Periodicals

Anon. A. 1862. A flying trip through Norway. *Harper's New Monthly Magazine Vol. 25 (147)*, 289 – 306.

Anon. 1964. Alone. Suicide. Alcoholism, Homosexuals, Old People – and other aspects of Loneliness. *20th Century*, 1 – 160.

Barnard, Sandy. 2004. Mark Kellogg – The 7th Cavalry's First Embedded Reporter. *The Crow's Nest 4 (1)*, 10 – 17.

Bray, Robert T. 1996. Archaeological Investigations at the Reno-Benteen battle site, Little Bighorn battlefield, Montana. *The Missouri Archaeologist 57*, 58 – 95.

Brown, Richard Maxwell. 1985. The Enduring Frontier: The Impact of Weather on South Dakota History and Literature. *South Dakota State Historical Society*, 27 – 57.

Carroll, John M. (ed). 1974. Custer Battle. *The Teepee Book 1916 Vol. 2 (6)*, 541 – 652.

Churchill, James O. 1969. Wounded at Fort Donelson. A First Person Account. *Civil War Times Illustrated 8 (4)*, 18 – 26.

Cox, John E. 1931. Soldiering in Dakota Territory in the Seventies: A Communication. *North Dakota Historical Quarterly VI (1)*, 63 – 81.

Eastman, Dr. Charles Alexander. 1968. Custer was not massacred. *Pioneer West 2 (2)*, 27 – 29 & 62 – 65.

Dundee, John W., Martin Isaac and Richard J. Clarke. 1969. Use of Alcohol in Anesthesia. *Anesthesia and Analgesia 48 (4)*, 665 – 669.

Ernst, Leif Rudi. 2004. A Dane who survived the Little Big Horn Fight. Jens Mathiasen Møller aka Jan Moller. *The Crow's Nest 4 (1)*, 18 – 21.

Glover, Alison J. 1946. Acute Rheumatism. *Annals of the Rheumatic Diseases 5 (4)*, 126 – 130.

Gray, John S. 1976. The Pack Train on George Custer's last Campaign. *Nebraska History 57 (1)*, 53 – 68.

Hauge, Ragnar. 1996. The History of Alcohol in Norway (in Norwegian). *Norsk Epidemiologi 6 (1)*, 13 – 21.

Hinman, Eleanor H. 1976. Oglala sources on the life of Crazy Horse. *Nebraska History 57 (1)*, 1 – 52.

Hubbard, Elbert. 1915. The Custer Battle. *The Teepee Book Vol. 1 (6)*, 106 – 122.

Jordan, Robert Paul. 1986. Ghosts on the Little Bighorn. *National Geographic Vol. 170 (6)*, 786 – 813.

Leff, S. 1955. Modern Trends in Acute Rheumatism. *Annals of the Rheumatic Diseases 15 (1)*, 33 – 39.

McGinnis, Anthony. 1981. A contest of wits and daring: Plains Indians at war with the U.S. Army. *North Dakota History, Journal of the Northern Plains 48 (2)*, 24 – 32.

Messner, William F. 1975. Black Violence and White Response: Louisiana 1862. *The Journal of Southern History 41*, 19 – 38.

Michno, Greg. 1994. SPACE WARP: The Effects of Combat Stress at the Little Big Horn. *Research Review: The Journal of the Little Big Horn Associates 8 (1)*, 22 – 30.

Oke, W.S. 1857. Acute Rheumatism. *The British Medical Journal 1 (21)*, 428 – 430.

Parmelee, Mary Manley. 1915. A child's recollection of the summer of -76. *The Teepee Book Vol. 1 (6)*, 123 – 130.

Peterson, William J. 1959. Iowans in the Civil War. *The Palimpset 40 (9)*, 369 – 450.

Powell, Peter J. 1975. High Bull's Victory Roster. *Montana the Magazine of Western History Vol. 25 (1)*, 14 – 21.

Rich, J.W. 1908. Color Bearer of the Twelfth Iowa Volunteer Infantry. *The Iowa Journal of History and Politics 7 (4)*, 503 – 581.

Russell, Peter. 2008. No Ordinary Trooper. The Extraordinary Story of James Pym, Company B. *The Crow's nest 8 (2)*, 6 – 15.

Smith, Solomon K. 2000. The Freedmen's Bureau in Shreveport: The Struggle for Control of the Red River District. *Louisiana History 41 (4)*, 435 – 465.

Stands in Timber, John. 1966. Last Ghastly Moments at the Little Bighorn. Edited and introduced by Margot Liberty. *American Heritage XVII (3)*, 14 – 21.

Stinson, Byron. 1972. Hot Work in Mississippi: The Battle of Tupelo. *Civil War Times Illustrated Vol. XI (4)*, 4 – 9 and 46 – 48.

Sword, Wiley. 1978. The battle of Shiloh. *Civil War Times Illustrated XVII (2)*, 2 – 50.

Throne, Mildred. 1954. Letters from Shiloh. *Iowa Journal of History 52 (3)*, 235 – 280.

Throne, Mildred (ed).1956. Iowans in Southern Prisons, 1862. *Iowa Journal of History 54 (1)*, 67 – 88.

Throne, Mildred (ed). 1957. Comments on the Hornet's Nest – 1862 and 1887. *Iowa Journal of History 55 (3)*, 249 – 274.

Throne, Mildred. 1957. Iowa and the Battle of Shiloh. *Iowa Journal of History 55 (3)*, 209 – 248.

Trenticosta, Cecelia and William C. Collins. 2012. Death and Dixie: How the Courthouse Flag Influences Capital Cases in Louisiana. *Harvard Journal of Racial and Ethnic Justice 27*, 125 – 165.

Van Duzee, E.M. 1868. Incidents of prison life in 1862.*The Annals of Iowa 6 (1)*, 54 – 64.

Vandal, Gilles. 1991. Bloody Caddo: White Violence against Blacks in a Louisiana Parish 1865 – 1876. *Journal of Social History 25 (2)*, 373 – 389.

Vandal, Gilles. 1991. The Policy of Violence in Caddo Parish, 1865 – 1884. *Louisiana Journal of History 32 (2)*, 159 – 182.

White, Kenneth. 1981. The Alabama Freedmen's Bureau and Black Education: The Myth of Opportunity. *The Alabama Review, a Quarterly Journal of Alabama History Vol. XXXIV (2)*, 107 – 124.

White, Kenneth. 1981. Black Lives, Red Tape. The Alabama Freedmen's Bureau. *The Alabama Review, a Quarterly Journal of Alabama History Vol. XXXIV (2)*, 241 – 258.

Selected Internet Sources

Eggspuehler, Jack. N.Y. *The Diary of Jacob S. Ripley, 12th Iowa Infantry Company A, in Civil War 1862.* 33 p.

Iowa in the Civil War. A special project of the IAGenWeb. Biographies, letters and Diaries of Iowa soldiers.

Martin, Thomas St. 2009. *With a bang, not a whimper. The winter of 1887-1888.* University of Minnesota, Duluth.

Pickenpaugh, Roger. 2012. *Prisoner Exchange and Parole.* Essential War Curriculum, Virginia Center for Civil War Studies at Virginia Tech. 13 p.

Steckel, Richard H. 2005. A history of the standard of living in the United States. EH. *Net Encyclopedia.* 11 p.

Vergano, Dan. 2011. *Little House author right on 1880s winter.* USA Today.

Audiovisual Sources

American Experience, The. 1992. *Last Stand at Little Big Horn.* WGBH Educational Foundation/Thirteen WNET.

American Experience, The. 2004. *Reconstruction. The Second Civil War.* WGBH Educational Foundation.

American Experience, The. 2012. *Custer's Last Stand.* WGBH, Boston.

Bill Armstrong Productions. 1990. *Custer's Last Trooper.*

Biography Channel, The. 1997. *George Armstrong Custer, America's Golden Cavalier.* A&E Television Networks.

Burns, Ken. 1990. *The Civil War.* Florentine Films and WETA TV. 5 discs.

Feuerhead, Edward. 2008. *Terrible Swift Sword. Civil War – America Divided.* Creation Films, Mill Creek Entertainment.3 discs.

Feuerhead, Edward. 2011. *The Complete Civil War.* Image Madacy Entertainment. 2 discs.

History Channel, The. 2001. *The true Story of the 7th Cavalry.* A&E Television Networks.

History Channel, The. 2006. *Aftershock.Beyond the Civil War.* A&E Television Networks.

History Channel, The. 2009. *The Civil War.* A&E Television Networks. 7 discs.

New Explorers, The. 1997. *Betrayal at the Little Big Horn.* A&E Television Networks.

War File, The. 2007. *The Battle of the Little Bighorn* (History of Warfare). Allegro Corporation.

Made in the USA
Lexington, KY
12 February 2015